MW00441926

Praise for

THE LIFE CYCLE OF A CEO

"I have few regrets, but I wish I would have had a copy of *The Life Cycle of a CEO* before I onboarded as CEO in 2020. Now, starting my fifth year, I'm so glad I have a copy of this deeply researched book full of actionable and helpful tips. A must-read for incoming and current CEOs."
　　　　　　　　　　　　　　　　　　　　—Carol Tomé, CEO, UPS

"The most successful CEOs can absorb data and process it to adapt quickly in an always-changing, competitive landscape. In *The Life Cycle of a CEO*, Claudius A. Hildebrand and Robert J. Stark offer both new and established leaders insights into how some of the most formidable CEOs of this generation have built and grown businesses, faced challenges, and managed crises—all of which are critical to master during a CEO's tenure."
　　　　　　　　　　　　　—Stephen A. Schwarzman, chairman, CEO and
　　　　　　　　　　　　　　　　　　　　　　　cofounder, Blackstone

"An essential read for anyone aspiring to understand the profound and evolving challenges of top corporate leadership. Hildebrand and Stark masterfully dissect the myths surrounding CEOs, presenting a rich analysis based on comprehensive research and interviews. This book offers invaluable insights into the stages of a CEO's tenure, providing a groundbreaking roadmap for success and resilience in the highest echelons of business. It's a definitive guide for leaders seeking to navigate the complexities of their role with wisdom and adaptability."
　　　　　　　　　　　　—Dr. Marshall Goldsmith, author of *What Got You
　　　　　　　　　　　　　　　　　　　　　Here Won't Get You There*

"*The Life Cycle of a CEO* offers both inspirational flag-planting and road-building lessons toward excellence in all phases of a CEO's journey. Hildebrand and Stark bring unparalleled analysis to a wealth of qualitative and quantitative data, weaving stories and examples into a compelling narrative that has provided me with key insights I wish I had when I stepped into the role. A critical addition to the CEO leadership literature." —Shantanu Narayen, chair and CEO, Adobe

"Hildebrand and Stark have masterfully captured the essence of the CEO journey and provide a map through the terrain of leadership. It's an essential read for any leader committed to navigating their journey with insight and foresight."
—Roger Ferguson, former president and CEO, TIAA

"*The Life Cycle of a CEO* offers a compelling framework that mirrors many of the pivotal moments I've experienced. Every chapter brims with actionable strategies to overcome the inherent obstacles to leadership." —Darren Walker, president, Ford Foundation

"We talk about the first hundred days, but what happens next? In their essential book, Hildebrand and Stark masterfully combine the art of storytelling and science of data to illuminate the challenges and triumphs of a CEO's journey from novice to elder. A must-read for current and aspiring leaders alike."
—Herminia Ibarra, Charles Handy Professor of
Organizational Behavior, London Business School

"A groundbreaking exploration of corporate leadership that challenges conventional wisdom with rigorous analysis and compelling narratives. Hildebrand and Stark dismantle myths surrounding the 'omnipotent' CEO, instead offering a human-centered perspective on the challenges executives truly face, as well as the pivotal moments that can create career-changing growth. An essential read for anyone interested in understanding the realities of leadership at the highest levels."
—Hubert Joly, former CEO, Best Buy; senior lecturer,
Harvard Business School; and author of *The Heart of Business*

"Effective leadership requires adaptability, vision, and regular reflection—lessons I've learned in my own career leading large organizations. *The Life Cycle of a CEO* leverages thorough research and rich storytelling to bring to life the different stages of a CEO's journey, making clear that the throughline for success is growth and transformation."
—Chris Nassetta, president and CEO, Hilton Worldwide

"*The Life Cycle of a CEO* revolutionizes our understanding of what it takes to lead and changes the conversation around CEO success. It is a compelling call to action for leaders at all levels to rethink their approach to leadership and personal growth in service of their organizations."
—Ram Charan, global advisor to CEOs and corporate boards, and coauthor of *Execution*

"In our work with the world's top CEOs, we've seen firsthand the complex challenges leaders face at each stage of their tenure. *The Life Cycle of a CEO* provides an invaluable roadmap, backed by robust data and rich insights from an impressive array of chief executives. This is a must-read for any CEO looking to beat the odds and achieve sustained success."
—Scott Osman and Jacquelyn Lane, 100 Coaches Agency

"In this groundbreaking book, Hildebrand and Stark have brilliantly described the stages of the CEO journey. Critically, they have highlighted an essential skill for success through this cycle—the ability to keep learning and adapting. Their insights and concrete advice will have a profound impact on CEO performance, and the book will become required reading for executives in any role thinking about how to maximize the impact of their leadership."
—Tim Welsh, vice chair, Consumer and Business Banking, US Bancorp

"This an important work for the many executives, CEOs, and board members who are involved in the development, selection, and coaching of CEOs. Every situation is different, but the book provides an invaluable framework and perspective to guide you. An essential read."
—Nigel Travis, former CEO, Dunkin' Brands

"A terrific study of attributes needed in a successful CEO, especially over time. I really like the concept of personal evolution. It's essential for CEO success, and the book provides a great roadmap."

—David Cote, former CEO, Honeywell

"A must-read for C-suite executives, CEOs, and corporate board directors. Based on profound research, including a captivating collection of stories from luminaries like Ajay Banga, Indra Nooyi, and Chris Nassetta, the book offers a treasure trove of insights into the intricacies of the CEO journey. Hildebrand and Stark explore the dynamic stages of leadership—from the initial boom in performance to the art of leaving a legacy—while highlighting the crucial importance of forging powerful board relationships and debunking common myths. I've learned the critical importance of identifying the early signs of stagnation, implementing strategic pivots, and the unique pressures faced by leaders in different organizational contexts, such as private equity versus public companies."

—Sheena Iyengar, S.T. Lee Professor, Columbia Business School, and author of *The Art of Choosing*

"By drawing on systematic data on the careers and performance of over 2,000 CEOs and framing the challenges and opportunities of the CEO role in terms of a life cycle, Hildebrand and Stark have laid out a powerful roadmap to guide CEOs and aspiring CEOs in realizing their goals and objectives. The book is an effective antidote to the all-too-common mythologizing of the CEO role based on extreme, outlier cases. As such, the authors have performed a real service not only for those who occupy the position at the top of the organization chart, but also for all those individuals who have the good fortune to work for corporate leaders who take to heart the insight and inspiration that this work provides."

—Joel Podolny, CEO, Honor Education, and former dean, Yale School of Management

The Myths & Truths
of How Leaders Succeed

THE
LIFE
CYCLE
OF A
CEO

Claudius A. Hildebrand
& Robert J. Stark

PUBLICAFFAIRS

New York

PublicAffairs
Hachette Book Group
1290 Avenue of the Americas, New York, NY 10104
www.publicaffairsbooks.com
@Public_Affairs

Printed in the United States of America

First Edition: October 2024

Published by PublicAffairs, an imprint of Hachette Book Group, Inc. The PublicAffairs name and logo is a registered trademark of the Hachette Book Group.

The Hachette Speakers Bureau provides a wide range of authors for speaking events. To find out more, go to hachettespeakersbureau.com or email HachetteSpeakers@hbgusa.com.

PublicAffairs books may be purchased in bulk for business, educational, or promotional use. For more information, please contact your local bookseller or the Hachette Book Group Special Markets Department at special.markets@hbgusa.com.

The publisher is not responsible for websites (or their content) that are not owned by the publisher.

Print book interior design by Amy Quinn.

Library of Congress Cataloging-in-Publication Data
Names: Hildebrand, Claudius A., author. | Stark, Robert J., author.
Title: The life cycle of a CEO : the myths and truths of how leaders succeed / Claudius A. Hildebrand and Robert J. Stark.
Description: First edition. | New York : PublicAffairs, 2024. | Includes bibliographical references and index.
Identifiers: LCCN 2024404141 | ISBN 9781541702820 (hardcover) | ISBN 9781541702844 (ebook)
Subjects: LCSH: Chief executive officers. | Success in business.
Classification: LCC HD38.2 .H63 2024 | DDC 658.4/092—dc23/eng/20240802
LC record available at https://lccn.loc.gov/2024404141

ISBNs: 9781541702820 (hardcover), 9781541702844 (ebook)

LSC-C

Printing 1, 2024

CONTENTS

INTRODUCTION
DISCOVERING THE
LIFE CYCLE

"This guy isn't going to cut it."

We are engulfed in the cult of the charismatic leader lionized for displays of confidence, who single-handedly propels a company to phenomenal success. This idolatry obscures the truth of what it takes to be a great CEO. Consider the case of one leader who took the helm of a major conglomerate that was in dire straits.

On a sweltering May evening a few months after his appointment to the job, Dave, drenched in sweat, showed up for dinner at a ritzy industry conference in Florida. He was wearing a wool suit, while the crowd of elite Wall Street analysts and high-powered corporate leaders, in stark contrast, were decked out in lightweight summer pants and golf shirts. Dave hadn't gotten the memo. But how fitting, given the widespread skepticism about him. The leading business media was reporting that he wasn't up to the job. One analyst at the dinner, Scott Davis, overheard another guest sneer about Dave: "This guy isn't going to cut it."[1]

In fact, Dave hadn't been the first choice for the CEO position, or even the second or third choice. Word was five others had been offered the job before him. What's more, a couple of years earlier he'd been unceremoniously fired from his position as divisional president at a leading competitor. No one would have suggested from his educational background, either, that he was CEO material. Not only did he not have a degree from an elite school, but it also took him six years to graduate. He hated college and he'd dropped out for a time.[2]

As Dave's first year in the CEO seat progressed, the sneering assessments of that Florida night prevailed on the Street; the company's stock slid 40 percent. Dave didn't make any of the bold moves analysts and media pundits said were needed: no big acquisition, no strategic pivot, no major layoffs. Not only that, when he called a gathering of overseas division leaders, almost half didn't show up, and they explained later that they thought meeting with him would have been a waste of time.[3]

Scott Davis was the only analyst of all those covering the company who wrote positively about Dave and his plans for a turnaround.[4] When Scott issued a buy rating for Dave's company's stock that October, his boss warned him the decision might be the end of his Wall Street career. He received a flood of criticism from investors, which he describes as "bordering on harassment."

Why was he bullish on Dave? Because he'd looked beyond the simplistic notions about what Dave lacked. He focused, instead, on the fact that in the divisional leadership role Dave had previously occupied, he'd methodically made smart investments in new products and operational transformation, which laid the groundwork for great improvements in results. Those moves weren't flashy, and they didn't supercharge performance in a quarter or two. But they were just what Dave should now enact at the ailing conglomerate, Scott thought.

Sure enough, anyone who followed his buy advice made a fantastic bet.

Dave is Dave Cote, who at the helm of Honeywell achieved one of the most impressive company turnarounds of any CEO in the twenty-first century. In his sixteen years in the job, from 2002 to 2017, he took the company—deemed "unfixable" by one leading analyst—from the brink of disaster to a share price rise of 245 percent. That's compared to 115 percent for the S&P 500 during the same period. As for the company he was booted from, that was General Electric. Cote was fired by legendary GE CEO Jack Welch after Welch appointed Jeffrey Immelt as his successor. Welch later said he did not see Cote as "really in contention."[5] Oh, the twists of fate. In the years of Cote's stellar tenure at Honeywell, GE's stock slid by 25 percent, and in what Bill Gates has described as "one of the greatest downfalls in business history," in 2021, GE announced it would split itself into three firms, each a shadow of its former self.

Perhaps no story demonstrates more clearly how flawed are prevailing notions of what CEO success requires. CEOs have been the subject of so much mythologizing. As Jeffrey Sonnenfeld, founder of the Chief Executive Leadership Institute and an expert on corporate leadership, laments, "CEOs are worshipped as rock stars, if not nearly deified." So often they are depicted as highly charismatic corporate saviors who parachute in with superhuman strategic vision and unshakable confidence and work immediate wonders.[6] Alternatively, they're demonized as greedy villains, heartlessly sacrificing workers' livelihoods in order to secure their grossly exorbitant pay, if not scheming to destroy the planet. Perhaps no CEO storyline is as popular as that of the hero undone. As Sonnenfeld puts it, the same leaders are profiled as saviors, "dragon slayers one moment and the next moment vilified as the very dragons they presumably conquered."[7] It's high time—well past time—to take CEOs off their pedestals *and* call off the firing squads.

All the mythologizing is so unfortunate. It has popularized badly misguided notions about how a CEO can succeed in a job that's not only crucial to the economic foundations of our society but also so cognitively, emotionally, and physically challenging that nearly a third of those appointed last fewer than three years in the role. The mythmaking has obscured so many important lessons we can learn from observing how CEOs struggle mightily with the changing challenges of the role, and overcome them, not only in the early going but also throughout their tenures. Central to the flawed depictions is the notion that CEOs succeed because they are the rare leaders who "have what it takes." "The myth of the omnipotent CEO," writes Peter Senge, another leading expert on corporate management, depicts them as "the few special people blessed with the capability for command and influence. They have become leaders precisely because of their unique mix of skill, ambition, vision, charisma, and no small amount of hubris."[8] In our own work helping CEOs build their skills and engage in personal development, we have seen just how flawed that perception of omnipotence is. Even the highest performers, who've achieved successful, long tenures, didn't start the job as the fully formed forces of nature described in the prevailing mythology. Many had serious deficits they had to work hard to correct once in the role. Then, even after successfully navigating the intense challenges of the first couple of years, they had to continue to put themselves through difficult processes of growth.

Understanding how CEOs succeed requires understanding how the challenges of the role evolve over time and how CEOs who thrive adapt to meet those changing challenges. Chris Nassetta, who took the helm of Hilton Hotels in 2007 and has led the company to strong growth, highlighted this in speaking with us about his success. "I'm a very different leader than I was twenty years ago, or even ten years ago. I've adapted."

The Life Cycle of a CEO was born from an analytical breakthrough that clears the fog of the mythmaking. We began investigating whether there was a systematic way to understand superior CEO performance over time, a common thread in how CEOs succeed that would have significant value not only for those in the CEO role but also for boards of directors, analysts assessing company prospects, and aspirants to the CEO job.

We conducted an unprecedented study. Using novel techniques, we rigorously analyzed the performance of every twenty-first-century CEO of the S&P 500 throughout the years of their tenure. We then conducted over a hundred interviews with CEOs and board directors about the demands of the job and how they changed over time. We wanted to understand not only the leadership decisions CEOs made but also how they played the inner game to develop the mental fortitude, emotional resilience, and self-awareness required. We also wanted to learn why those who stumbled in the job failed. This research led to the discovery of the CEO Life Cycle—a series of five distinct stages of tenure, which each present a unique set of headwinds and tailwinds that demand CEOs grow in new ways.

The CEO Life Cycle, and the rich stories and insights CEOs shared about how they met the challenges of each stage, provide a groundbreaking road map for CEOs to anticipate and successfully navigate the profound demands of the job. What's more, understanding how the successful CEOs we're profiling challenged themselves to overcome their deficits and build new skills in each stage of the Life Cycle will prove enormously useful for leaders at all levels. Because the CEO job is especially taxing, the leadership and personal growth lessons shared in the pages that follow are rich in insights about the requirements for success for anyone in business. They will also provide crucial guidance to directors seeking to support CEOs and to all those with a stake in evaluating a CEO's leadership.

In the rest of this chapter, we describe the nature of our CEO Life Cycle study and why it allowed us to develop a unique understanding of CEO success. We then introduce each of the phases of the CEO Life Cycle, which we portray more fully in the following chapters.

◀◀◀◀◀ ▶▶▶▶▶

One reason the hero mythology has rooted so firmly is that coverage of CEOs focuses intensively on particular dramatic moments in their tenure. A CEO may make a splash when they're appointed, as was true for Mary Barra when she was named General Motors chief and became the first woman at the helm of a major US automaker. Most other coverage focuses on moments of either great success or great failure, with particularly voluminous attention paid to scandalous failures. Coverage is also intensively concentrated on a handful of CEOs who achieve virtual celebrity status. One study of newspaper coverage of CEOs found that, for example, 48 percent of all articles that mentioned CEOs by name were about just five people.[9] Yet, even for these most heavily covered leaders, we hear so little about the many other challenges they faced during so much of their tenures.

We hear about the highest of highs and the lowest of lows, and precious little about the more challenging steady grind of executing a long-term strategy. Or the years of in-depth analysis and testing done before a big achievement hits the market; big wins are often depicted as springing out of a CEO's mind in a flash of insight. What we're left with are disjointed snapshots, akin to a set of photos marking particular moments throughout one's lifetime with no story of what happened in the intervening years.

When it comes to the fuller stories told in CEO biographies and memoirs, they focus largely on the specific company challenges the leader dealt with rather than on the general nature of the CEO job and the common challenges it presents as one's tenure progresses. Much of a technology company CEO's story will be about contending with emerging technologies, such as cloud computing and artificial intelligence. A CEO of a consumer-goods company will recount challenges with launching new brands and adapting to changing consumer preferences. The leader of an industrial manufacturer might focus on how they turned the company around by implementing a more efficient production process. The rich specificity of these CEOs' experiences is both highly informative and fascinating. Yet, the differences in those industry and company specifics can make understanding the general nature of the CEO job difficult because the job seems so different in so many ways for different CEOs. Which is true, of course. But our research, and volumes of research by others, reveals the important underlying commonalities. Learning to expect the challenges common across all CEO positions is an important complement to knowledge about the specifics of the company and industry one is taking charge of.

Researchers have made efforts to discover commonalities across industries, but very little analysis has focused on how a CEO's challenges in the job change over time. Little attention has been paid to how CEOs grow in the role, how they compensate for weaknesses in their skills and experience, or how they rekindle their energy and passion as years proceed.

Much has been written about the four or six or eight characteristics of high performers that account for their success, be it extroversion, confidence, or a large appetite for risk-taking. These studies give the impression that the people who most closely fit the mold are the most likely to succeed. Yet, Stanford economist Nicholas Bloom, who has tried for twenty years to determine the characteristics of the most effective corporate leaders, cautions, "You look at the data, there's ten different recipes for success. Sure, there are some people who are better than others, but it's damn hard to tell what it is."[10]

The focus on traits and the skewed media coverage perpetuate the myth of the fully formed leader. We don't often hear how those who eventually succeeded struggled in their early years and then again later in their tenure, even with great success behind them. The features of the CEO job that people wrestle with most in their early years, past the first ninety to a hundred days, aren't highlighted. The particular challenges of the middle and later years, which require them to reignite their passion or engage in personal reinvention, get relatively little attention. George Paz led a substantial transformation of the pharmacy business Express Scripts over the course of eleven years, and he shared with us that at some point in every CEO's tenure, "You've got to admit that what you've been doing that made you successful is no longer what's going to make the company a success." The longer a CEO's tenure, the more times this will be true.

The study of CEO success has been a lot like the craft of athletic scouting before the advent of the Moneyball era—too focused on star players and on a select set of innate abilities and not focused enough on how all leaders can enhance their odds of success. To uncover those insights, a scientific, data-driven approach is required. That was key to the success of Oakland A's front-office executive Billy Beane, as famously portrayed by Michael Lewis in his book *Moneyball*. Beane embraced *sabermetrics*, the use of statistics to "search for objective knowledge about baseball." Leading baseball analyst Bill James coined the term in recognition of the work of the Society for American Baseball Research, or SABR, the acronym on which the term is based.[11] The society pioneered the application of statistics to the analysis of player performance, and Beane applied sabermetrics to massive troves of player performance data over time. His striking discoveries enabled him to spot lower-cost recruits who had potential instead of paying the high costs of hiring players deemed to have the best odds of succeeding. Beane found, for example, that better than some player traits long thought to be the best indicators of future success, such as hitting power and running speed, two performance statistics predicted whether a player would help a team score more runs: on-base percentage (OBP) and slugging percentage, the latter being a measure of a batter's productivity.[12]

In light of his findings, Beane changed his recruiting for the 2002 season and looked for players with strong numbers in those two statistics rather than for higher-ticket sluggers. That he thereby fielded a strong team, which made it to the playoffs, at lower cost has been emphasized. But the more significant influence has been on the increased use of data analytics to change how baseball and other sports are being played and how players are being trained and coached. In baseball, for example, starting pitchers now pitch fewer innings because statistics revealed that relief pitchers are more likely to get batters out after their third time at bat. Detailed maps of where players have hit the ball are used for "shifting," repositioning fielders often dramatically to the left or to the right, closer up or farther out, when a particular batter steps up to the plate.

In basketball, analytics showed that taking more three-point shots leads to higher scoring. Teams have adapted to prioritize three-point shooting, changing the dynamics of offense in the NBA. The result has been record-breaking numbers of three-point attempts per game across the league, with the percentage of total shots taken that are three-pointers increasing from 17 percent in 2000 to 39 percent in 2020. Some individual players have dramatically upped their game. For example, before Channing Frye moved from the Phoenix Suns to the Portland Trail Blazers, just 3 percent of his shots were three-point attempts. His new coaches told him to work on making the longer-range shots, and that year he increased his percentage of three-point attempts to 43.4 percent, which significantly boosted his total points scored.[13]

These discoveries were made possible because so much data had been compiled for so many players for so many years of performance. After we created our massive database of CEO performance, analysis allowed us to identify many ways that leaders can work on their abilities, just as Channing Frye did, first to enhance their chances of being selected for a CEO job and then to up their game while in the role.

THE CEO LIFE CYCLE PROJECT

The five stages of the Life Cycle are delineated by ups and downs of CEO performance that are associated with years of tenure rather than with the particular issues the company faced or economic headwinds and tailwinds. The Life Cycle pattern is as follows: a sharp rise in performance the first year followed by a significant downturn in the next year, with performance then rising again for several years of strong growth (generally years three to five) but giving way to another several-year period (generally years six through nine) characterized by stagnating performance. The last stage, starting with year ten, is a period of stronger performance that is more stable year to year than in any other period. After discovering the pattern, we conducted further quantitative analysis and interviewed CEOs to delve deeply into what could explain those ups and downs. This research produced a wealth of findings about the distinctive challenges of each Life Cycle stage and how a CEO can navigate them.

The database we compiled to conduct our analyses included leaders who started before 2000 and were still in leadership positions during our study's time frame and ones who started in that period and are still leading. This totaled 2,077 CEOs. (More details on the sample can be found in Appendix 2.) The data comprised a range of financial metrics for each CEO, including revenue growth, return on invested capital (ROIC), operating income, operating expenses, capital expenditure, mergers and acquisitions (M&A) activity, and total shareholder return (TSR), which is the total amount an investor earns from a stock, including capital gains, dividends, stock splits, and special distributions.

We tracked the CEOs' performance from their exact start dates; for example, Dave Cote started at Honeywell on February 19, 2002. For CEOs who left the role, we tracked up to their departure date; for Cote, March 31, 2017. This allowed us to chart their performance from anniversary to anniversary rather than by calendar years, which gave us precise data for exactly the duration of each CEO's tenure. Otherwise, if we'd used calendar years, some performance data of their predecessor and their successor would have been included and skewed our findings. If a CEO started in June, say, we excluded the company's performance data from January through May of that year.

This method of capturing CEOs' individual performance data allowed us to look for patterns over time across tenures that spanned very different years. So, for example, we could compare performance during a tenure from 2001 to 2015 to performance during a tenure from 2006 to 2020. This allowed us to see whether any pattern appeared in years one through two or in years three through five and on throughout the years of tenure. The first analysis we did was to chart changes in total shareholder return for each CEO. Although a CEO's performance can be evaluated on many other bases, such as revenue growth or ROIC, TSR is the best measure for our purposes. It offers a more comprehensive view of performance than share price alone, and it's not subject to accounting manipulations. What's more, it is based on the collective views of a vast number of market players, and it's the statistic best suited to represent overall performance.

Next, to discern whether any pattern of performance was associated with the amount of time a CEO occupied the role, we had to neutralize the effects on TSR of the booms and busts in business and industry cycles. So, we included performance data for the overall market, using the S&P 500, which enabled us to examine how changes in a given company's TSR compared to changes in the market. For example, during the Great Recession of 2008, most companies experienced a steep decline in TSR, but some outperformed the market, and others realized even steeper declines than average. The S&P 500 company data also allowed us to capture swings in performance by industry, so we could neutralize those effects as well.

The key to neutralizing overall market and industry swings in shareholder returns was aggregating performance data for so many CEOs who started on so many different dates. Take the case of the Great Recession. For CEOs who started in 2008, the recession's effects showed up for two to three years, starting in their first year in the job. For CEOs who started in 2007, the effects started showing up in their second year. And for those who started in 2006, the impact began in their third year. In this way, for the full sample of CEOs who started in those years, the effects are spread over years one, two, and three. By aggregating so many CEO tenures over such a long range of time—the first twenty years of this century—we spread out the effects of all the other booms and busts that happened during those years in the larger economy and in the relevant industries. What we were left with was the CEO Life Cycle of ups and downs in performance that were associated with the years of CEO tenure rather than with the larger macroeconomic and industry headwinds and tailwinds.

Our next step was to dig into the details of CEOs' experiences as they progressed through the Life Cycle stages. We wanted to discover aspects of the job, changes in the job over time, and, crucially, requirements for success in each stage that could account for the Life Cycle pattern. This part of the study involved both analyzing more of the quantitative data through the course of CEOs' tenures and interviewing CEOs and directors. As the practitioners of sports analytics know, data analysis can get you only so far; it must be combined with qualitative wisdom. After sabermetrics caught on, even as sports teams ramped up their data gathering, installing extensive and more sophisticated camera systems to capture more and more detail, such as speed and force of swings and the angle at which a ball left a hand, they began to see diminishing returns. They needed to combine the quantitative findings with the observations and learning scouts, coaches, trainers, and players had gleaned from years in the game.

Similarly, we needed to learn from CEOs what might account for the Life Cycle pattern. As we dug into how their experiences evolved as their tenures progressed, they explained the distinctive challenges they faced in these different periods. We also learned how those who were successful in meeting the challenges did so and what pitfalls others fell into that impaired their performance. Finally, we probed their earlier career experiences to learn how they had equipped themselves for being selected for the job. That has allowed us to offer important advice on how prospects can best build up their experience and skills to rise into and then thrive in the role.

We conducted these interviews over the course of five years, speaking with CEOs and directors from a wide range of sectors and industries, including industrial machinery, consumer packaged goods, banking, fast-food and quick-service restaurant chains, health care, hospitality, and energy. We interviewed CEOs widely lauded as the most successful over the past two decades, as well as many others who have achieved spectacular results but with less media coverage. We also spoke with leaders who had quite difficult tenures and who left the role earlier than they had hoped due to problems such as loss of board support, poor results, and personal issues, including health problems and burnout.

These leaders shared a great wealth of stories and reflections about issues they confronted, from organizational management problems to strategy challenges and crises in their industry or the larger economy. They opened up about the intensity of pressure they felt, frustrations they'd wrestled with, and personal growth they had pushed themselves through. As remarkably accomplished as they were when they stepped into the role, even the most successful CEOs shared that they were not anticipating, and were not prepared for, many of the new challenges. They opened up about the fear and self-doubt they felt as they took charge. They described hard inner work done to admit to themselves areas of weakness and seek input in order to develop new skills. They were wonderfully generous in admitting the errors they made and the self-doubt they struggled with. We heard about the methods they employed to stretch themselves so that they were always learning and adapting to the ever more rapid changes all businesses must contend with. They discussed ways to combat the sway of cognitive biases that can lead to missed opportunities and horrible misjudgments. They described how they inspired their teams and employees to collaborate and seize opportunities to be strong leaders themselves.

To further flesh out our understanding of the challenges these CEOs faced, we delved deeply into the media coverage of them and their companies, both in the mainstream business media and the specialty periodicals. We also pored through earnings calls and analyst reports to gain more detail about how the moves made by CEOs were being perceived and challenges they were being asked to explain.

These combined research avenues allowed us to uncover many commonalities in the CEO journey over the course of the five Life Cycle stages. They've been hard to see because every CEO journey is unique in so many other ways. Every person steps into the CEO role contending with a particular set of challenges. Some are brought in to lead turnarounds, others to accelerate growth according to a predecessor's strategy. Key competitors may be struggling or may be eating voraciously into market share. Global expansion or selling off underperforming businesses may be a priority. Shocks to the macroeconomy may pose an existential threat or present a golden opportunity. The industry may be riding powerful tailwinds or fighting long-term prevailing headwinds. The executive team may be highly effective or in need of a shakeup. The organization may be comparatively efficient, with a strong and motivating culture, or mired in outmoded systems and plagued by managerial infighting.

Indeed, all these differences mean that every CEO journey, in all its detail, is in fact unique. Yet we found that within that wide-ranging variability commonalities abound regarding facing new challenges and seizing opportunities in the different stages of tenure. So, too, are there commonalities about the inner experience of being in the role, from feelings of self-doubt to mounting confidence and fatigue from the extraordinary demands of the job, as well as commonalities in the kinds of ongoing learning and personal growth that must be done in order to succeed in each phase.

The discovery of these common challenges of the CEO Life Cycle and how successful CEOs have managed them allows us to offer a distinctive guide to bending the curve for success.

BENDING THE CURVE

Think of the CEO Life Cycle as a framework like other tools that have emerged from quantitative study used for anticipating challenges in business. One such is the Innovation Adoption Curve, originally developed by Everett Rogers, which charts the rate of diffusion of a new technology throughout a society. Rogers compiled voluminous data about farmers' adoption of new, scientifically enhanced crop seeds, famously delineating four phases of diffusion, which form a bell curve. It begins with a small group of early adopters, progresses to a larger group of early majority adopters, then a comparably sized group of late majority, and finally, a smaller group of laggards.[14] The curve has helped legions of product managers and entrepreneurs better anticipate when they should ramp up production and promotion of a new product and better time innovation of next-generation products.

Similarly, the CEO Life Cycle will help leaders play a better game by anticipating the evolving challenges of the CEO job and preparing for them. It will help CEOs recognize when they are heading into a new stage of their tenure and stay vigilant about avoiding common pitfalls made in that stage. Additionally, it will help them stay on offense, proactively engaging in new learning and personal growth, ahead of the curve, as they progress through the stages. The findings can also help boards anticipate issues CEOs may face and engage with CEOs more vigorously to provide support at critical junctures.

Before we offer an initial description of each of the Life Cycle stages, we should highlight that the Life Cycle is a model and any given CEO may progress to a next stage according to different timing. The stages are not rigidly delineated by the years of a CEO's tenure. Many CEOs experience only two or three stages because they leave the role before progressing further. And, again, individuals have widely varying experiences of their stages because of the specific factors they face and their skill set and approach to challenges.

We'll explore the nature of the stages, and variations in how CEOs experienced their challenges, more fully in the chapters devoted to each of them. Here, now, is a concise overview of the five stages.

LAUNCH

The first twelve months in the job of CEO are a critical period of getting your sea legs while navigating a torrent of new demands. Even the most experienced executives, who have performed well in a series of highly demanding leadership positions, for example, chief operating officer (COO) or business unit leader, find the intensity of learning about the job and coping with the rush of challenges daunting.

Especially challenging is what we call the *hourglass effect*. As with the grains of sand in an hourglass, all components of the company's business, inside and out, ultimately run through the CEO. Not only is this a massive weight of responsibility, but CEOs are in a tug-of-war for their time, between dealing with inside matters and dealing with external affairs. They are generally shocked by how much time the external responsibilities, such as investor relations and meeting with key customers or regulators, require. Nothing has prepared them for this.

In this and a number of other ways, mastering the challenges of the Launch stage requires great agility with *both/and* thinking. CEOs must, for example, attend to both near-term and longer-term matters. Otherwise, they will suffer a terrible jolt in later years when the failure to attend to the longer term catches up with them.

Exacerbating the difficulty of this stage is the disconcerting experience of suddenly having all eyes on you. Not only are the executives who report to you watching you closely, but so too are all employees as well as the board and the panoply of external stakeholders. Pepsi CEO Indra Nooyi beautifully captures the disorienting nature of stepping into the role in her memoir *My Life in Full*: "When I walked into the building as CEO . . . I had that strange feeling that many top leaders have tried to explain: I was 'it,' like a game of tag. I felt like everyone was watching me and waiting for me to tell them what to do next."[15] Many leaders are unsure of whom to turn to for advice and are concerned—often rightfully so—that people might not be telling them the full story of the massive ocean liner they've just taken charge of.

There is great irony in assuming the top position. As Randy Hogan, who steered Pentair for seventeen years, told us, "CEOs are positioned to be the least well-informed people about the company of any employee in the company." In this early phase of tenure, the reason often is that direct reports and leaders around the organization are reluctant to speak up about issues before they have a good sense of how a leader will receive that information and respond. This may be true even if they've been colleagues or have collaborated on projects previously. The problem is exacerbated when a new CEO believes they must project an image of utter self-assurance and is reluctant to ask questions and admit a lack of knowledge in some areas. For CEOs in the Launch stage, practicing the arts of observation and listening is crucial.

The prevailing advice is that CEOs should make bold moves early on, but whether to do so and which moves to make are matters for rigorous scrutiny. Joe Hogan, former CEO of ABB, a manufacturer of electrical components and equipment, recounted that Wall Street's prevailing wisdom about quick bold moves would have suggested he sell off one of ABB's businesses right away because it wasn't core to the company's current business focus. But he visited that business as part of an extensive discovery process in his first six months and realized that it was actually a great asset.

Crucial in the Launch stage is to rigorously scrutinize whether any playbooks you may have found effective in the past should be applied in making first moves or cast aside. Joe Hogan advised, "Throw out the playbook filled with actions and instead bring one full of questions." Leaning hard on past experiences may be setting yourself up for failure.

CEOs often get swept up in a powerful "honeymoon" tailwind of optimism during this phase. Not only is the board of directors flush with confidence in their choice, but so are the markets. New leaders also commonly inherit an array of low-hanging-fruit problems to solve that their predecessor, no matter how successful, neglected dealing with or expressly put off; the market generally anticipates these quick solutions and their existence can drive up the share price. Yet the intensity of the daily demands and the huge learning curve tend to make a new CEO doubt that they're getting this vote of confidence. That can make the experience of the next stage all the more complicated.

CALIBRATION

In the Calibration stage, which generally starts in the second year, boards, markets, and other stakeholders reassess a CEO's performance. For their part, CEOs may also perceive the need to reassess and perhaps adjust strategy or otherwise alter their plans.

If exuberance about the CEO's appointment led to an initial lift in share price, that is now reversed. Our data shows a stark "sophomore slump" downturn in TSR for many CEOs in the second year. This is sometimes due to an excessive honeymoon lift or early moves not yet producing significant results—or, at least, results that market arbiters deem sufficient.

With the blush off the rose, CEOs face tougher questioning about moves they're making or not making. Market analysts might still be undecided about how effectively the leader is leading. Analysts tend to scrutinize decisions and explanations of results more closely. With so much less knowledge of what's happening inside the business than the CEO has, and lacking the hands-on experience of making improvements, their views may well be misguided. Strong management of board and shareholder expectations and perceptions is critical. Indeed, often the core problem is the *perception* of performance, which makes powerful and highly persuasive communication with the board, shareholders, and analysts a CEO's priority. One director told us, "Even when you think you're communicating too much, you're probably not communicating enough."

Making matters more difficult, if the CEO hasn't encountered a crisis before this, one is likely to kick up in this period. As Enbridge CEO Greg Ebel said, "Somewhere in the first twelve to eighteen months you are going to run into a buzzsaw. You won't know what it is."

Riding through the storm requires considerable self-management, such as containing frustration with your team and other players because the pace of change is slower than anticipated. The pressure and uncertainty about whether to stay the course or make a correction can also trigger a host of biases. Confirmation bias may lead to seeing current difficulties in the guise of past experience, which can encourage a CEO to dig in on a flawed course of action. Our research shows that a higher proportion of repeat CEOs compared with first-timers were ousted in this stage, by almost double, possibly demonstrating their overreliance on past experience.

The good news is, what doesn't kill you makes you stronger. Former Yum! CEO David Novak stressed this point about the downturn of the sophomore slump: "Going through the U forces the CEO to mature and learn from data and experience. You get more knowledge and at the end it pays off. The U is where you really prove yourself."

REINVENTION

Reinvention, starting around year three, is when the early moves CEOs have made begin to show stronger results. If such results are kicking in, trust builds, both inside and outside the firm. The most successful CEOs leverage that confidence in them to launch large-scale initiatives during this period, generally from years three to five. These moves might include pursuing M&A opportunities, stepping up R&D, launching important new products, or pursuing ambitious global growth.

One CEO who pulled off a major feat in this period is John Lundgren. He took the helm of toolmaker Stanley in 2004 and, during his first few years, did a great job integrating the company's three largest acquisitions in its history—despite being a complete novice to the tools business. He was recruited from his position as president of European Consumer Products at Georgia-Pacific to cast a set of fresh eyes on the tool business. Stanley's performance had stagnated, and the board decided getting outside perspective was important.

During Lundgren's early years, while Stanley's earnings rose from $2 billion to $4 billion, those of the other leading toolmaker, Black & Decker, stagnated. When the housing crisis of 2009 hit, the share price of both companies took a hit, but that hit was much greater for Black & Decker, with its share price dropping twice as much as Stanley's did. That opened the door to merger talks, and Lundgren deftly seized the day, orchestrating an agreement with Black & Decker that the *New York Times* DealBook described as "the perfect deal."[16] So perfect was the fit—with virtually no overlap in their product offerings—that the two firms had discussed merging on and off for twenty-eight years, yet talks had always broken down. Stanley's share price soared 64 percent that year.

With the tailwinds of success buoying them, leaders may also have more latitude to take actions that might not be positively perceived by the market and for which the board may need more convincing. Deft management of those reactions is imperative.

Another striking feature of the Reinvention stage is that the leader must begin to grapple with the question of how long to stay in the role. Some CEOs step into the role intent on pursuing longer-term missions. Larry Merlo, for example, took the helm of CVS to execute a long-term strategy of transforming the company from a pharmacy chain into a health services provider.

Yet for others, whether to stay or perhaps seek a new challenge becomes an increasingly fraught question in these years. Serious grappling with the issue is required, not only to ensure that you do not overlook exciting opportunities to chase but also to discern whether you can sustain the drive and dexterity to succeed in the years to come.

COMPLACENCY TRAP

In years six to ten, maintaining the drive to keep improving performance and evolving as a leader becomes particularly challenging for many CEOs, and they fall into complacency. Although performance may not slide dramatically, it often stagnates. This is the leadership equivalent of sailing into the Doldrums.

A band of territory that circles Earth from 5 degrees north of the equator to 5 degrees south, the Doldrums are characterized by little to no wind. Although the result is calm seas, sailors dreaded entering the Doldrums because it slowed their progress to a near halt. So, too, can CEOs enter a doldrums period, when they become too comfortable with the calm seas of this stage.

A pernicious cause of this misplaced comfort is the status quo bias, a cognitive quirk that leads us to be overly satisfied with the way things are rather than driving for improvements. The complacency the status quo bias encourages often leads to a prolonged period of mediocre results. For two out of three CEOs in our database, performance was lower in their years six to ten than it was in years one to five. Some gave up their gains of the first five years altogether. Results may not actually dive into negative territory, but if they do, they vacillate up and down around a mean, which only reinforces the sense that one can let up on the gas.

The danger is exacerbated when boards also become less energetic in pushing for vigorous changes in strategy or operations. As director Ann Hackett shared, "It's easy to get into incremental mode." A CEO's internal team may resist a continuous quick pace of change.

The sense of security in the Complacency Trap may lead a CEO to take their eyes off of problems brewing on the horizon or under the calm surface they're gliding on. A great irony of the Doldrums that caught many a seaman off guard is that the region is also plagued with sudden, severe storms. Similarly, CEOs who fall into complacency may be blindsided.

In contrast, leaders who thrive during these years stay vigilant and keep pushing change and growth while also watching out for storms brewing. They are highly cognizant of the danger of complacency, and they continue to find ways to push themselves and their companies.

One CEO who pushed his company to great feats in this stage is Piyush Gupta. In roughly years six through ten, with great passion he embraced the challenge of transforming DBS Bank into a digital innovator. He drove the bank in adopting artificial intelligence

(AI), "opening the wallet" of the bank's capital to hire a phalanx of data scientists, and setting a standard of conducting one thousand experiments a year.[17] No AI expert, Gupta had to pour himself into learning about the technology, and he even took part in a competition run by Amazon, not only to learn more about the ins and outs of AI development but also to inspire employees throughout the organization to embrace the reinvention.

For those who lead their companies well through the Complacency Trap, the final stage of their tenure is a distinctive period of pressing full speed ahead while preparing to hand off the job to a successor.

LEGACY

The Legacy years, a CEO's culminating stage from year ten on, are characterized by a tricky and often psychologically challenging dual mandate to keep pushing hard to drive performance while also shifting focus to prepare for departure from the role, which is inevitable. Only a fraction of CEOs stay in the job longer than fifteen years.

This stage is bittersweet. Common in these years is the gratification of seeing earlier transformations and investments come to fruition. The likelihood that a good year will be followed by another steadily increases. Our data shows that CEOs who stayed in the role past year ten beat the S&P 500 through the overall course of their tenure, more than those in any other length of tenure.

Yet, a CEO's longevity in the role can pose difficulties in achieving that strong performance. For one thing, CEOs may find it increasingly difficult to get hard-hitting feedback, a revenge effect of having been successful. With such a long run of notching impressive gains, many potential critics of a CEO's decisions, including the board, are reluctant to second-guess them. Our data shows that only about 3 percent of CEOs in their Legacy years are forced out, which demonstrates the deference boards show to these long servers. They're free to determine the timing of their departure themselves. This is true even in cases when it's clear that new leadership would catalyze a needed new cycle of innovation.

CEOs, similar to great athletes, may be tempted to stay past the optimal time of their departure. Stepping down from the role is always a difficult decision. The status of the role, not to mention the many perks it affords, is hard to walk away from. For these longest-serving leaders, their whole identity may become tightly intertwined with the role. But those who stay on too long may damage their legacy, especially if they don't attend well to grooming a successor and smoothing the transition.

To shore up their legacy and ensure a successful transition of power, CEOs must manage the feat of continuing to vigorously drive the company's growth while preparing for departure. Successfully navigating this challenge requires a mindset of focused concern on ensuring the good fortune of the company. Former CVS CEO Larry Merlo beautifully expressed this orientation. He told us he felt good about stepping down because he could say to his successor, "The seeds of transformation are planted. I left you a strategy you can finish out. That gives you enough time to write the next chapter."

As these summaries of the evolving challenges of the CEO role showcase, the journey of a CEO is one of intensive learning. They need all the support they can get, and we hope this book plays a meaningful role. Enabling CEO success is important not only for CEOs but also for all stakeholders in a company. CEOs play an enormously important role in society. The quality of their leadership has a powerful impact on the nature of work life at their firms and the economic fortunes of employees, including return on investment in 401(k)s and IRAs. CEOs can be the driving force spurring innovation that leads to enormous improvements in our lives. They can also help build momentum for tackling pressing social and political issues. The flip side, of course, is that CEO failure can have disastrous results, causing large-scale job loss, evaporating vast quantities of shareholder returns, and even derailing important progress in innovation.

In the chapters ahead, we more fully explore the distinctive challenges of the five stages of the CEO Life Cycle and, through a wealth of stories, share nitty-gritty ins and outs of succeeding in the job, as well as cautionary tales of failing. We begin with a chapter about best routes for ascending to the CEO role that highlights the necessity of building your leadership muscles through wide-ranging stretch moves. Chapters 2 through 6 cover the experiences of the five stages, focusing on the most important aspects of leadership in each phase and the primary pitfalls.

In Chapter 7, we address the dramatically different CEO Life Cycle of CEOs who work for companies owned by private equity (PE) firms. A rapidly increasing share of companies in the United States and around the world are under PE management, and PE firms continue to snap up companies, so becoming a PE CEO is an option any aspirant to the role can consider. The financial expertise, operations expertise, and resources that many PE firms have developed can be great supports for a CEO. Yet, there are also trade-offs, particularly less autonomy in decision-making. We interviewed PE CEOs and leading PE firm executives and provide key insights so that you can assess your interest in and fitness for working under PE management.

Chapter 8 delves into the challenges of CEO succession planning. Far too many companies do not have a robust succession-planning process, and this lack contributes to the difficulties new CEOs experience in their early years in the job. We explore the reasons successions are so often fraught, and we present an optimal process for succession planning. It makes identifying and developing CEO prospects an ongoing part of the company's leadership development process, which ensures that a good field of candidates is at hand whenever a CEO transition is set in motion. Any person in business who aspires to rise to the CEO job can pursue the development processes that should be part of succession planning, even if their company has no formal process for offering this training. Gaining the right kinds of experience will, in fact, make the difference in being selected for the job and in doing it well.

On that note, we'll move on to Chapter 1 and explore the best means of building the skills to step into the role of CEO.

1

ASCENT

"No one is prepared to become CEO,
no matter how much they think they are."

ommy Caldwell, widely considered the world's most accomplished rock climber, clings with every bit of his might to tiny
fingerholds 1,300 feet up the sheer granite face of the Dawn Wall.
His climbing partner, Kevin Jorgeson, shouts words of encour-
agement from below. The Dawn Wall is the southeast portion of
Yosemite's massive rock formation El Capitan, which rises three
thousand vertical feet. No climber has attempted to scale the
wall before because climbing it has been considered impossible.
But Caldwell thinks he has found a way, a circuitous route involv-
ing daring lateral traverses and moves over and around repeated
expanses of utterly unscalable rock.

The Dawn Wall is so called because as dawn breaks it's bathed
in golden sunlight. But right now Caldwell is enveloped in darkness, the sun having set long ago. The cliff face is illuminated only
by a small sphere of light from his headlamp. He has never practiced the moves he is attempting; he's improvising a route around

an 8.5-foot horizontal stretch of wall called the Dyno—the climbing term for a bold leap—across which there are no foot- or handholds at all. Until tonight, he thought the only way across would be to jump and grip onto a sliver of rock that protrudes a mere inch from the cliff face. He practiced that jump many hundreds of times and has never been able to stick it. Then suddenly this night, as he prepared for yet another attempt, he studied a photo of the cliff face and perceived another way to bridge the gap: a perilous climb down 40 feet, then over and up in a sweeping 200-foot circular loop around the Dyno. Moving tentatively inch by inch, feeling his way through the darkness, he completes what has been described as "the world's hardest down climb."

Ten days later, after nineteen days on the wall sleeping in a portaledge tent affixed to the cliff face at night, Caldwell attains the summit. Having charted the way, he is followed shortly by Kevin Jorgeson.[1]

A CAREER AS A CLIMBING WALL

The Dawn Wall ascent stands as a fitting metaphor for preparing for and then succeeding in the CEO role. Although becoming CEO is often regarded as achieving the summit in a career, getting the job is better seen as the equivalent of Tommy Caldwell making his way past that especially challenging Dyno stretch of the ascent. He still had the steepest part of the climb to go, which is also true for CEOs once they've landed the job. When they step into the role, they're only partly up the wall, with the toughest part of the ascent yet to come. Summiting should be seen as achieving success throughout the course of your tenure as CEO and, crucially, leaving the company in a strong position to face future challenges. In our experience, far too many aspirants to the role focus too narrowly on *getting* the job and do not consider seriously enough what will be required to succeed in the role. This lack of preparation makes the first years, which are always extremely challenging, even more difficult.

The best preparation for success is putting yourself through a rigorous and highly intentional process of personal evolution, which begins many years before you are in contention for the job, ideally at the beginning of your career. The more leaders use their time before becoming CEO to broaden their experience and push themselves to learn how to learn very quickly and develop new leadership abilities, the more successful their transition into the CEO job will be. They'll also be better equipped for all the twists and turns of the stages throughout the Life Cycle.

In our interviews with CEOs, we probed not only into their experiences in the role but also into their earlier careers. We learned a great deal about the kinds of opportunities they pursued and the work they did to develop their understanding of organizations and how to lead them. They also made clear how that learning and personal growth were crucial for contending well with the intense pressures and emotional and cognitive demands of the job.

Because we hope this book is valuable for people who aspire to the role as well as those in it, including those quite early on in their working lives, we devote this chapter to best preparations in the climb up.

Optimally, preparation for the way up involves seeking out wide-ranging roles that will stretch you, roles that often extend well outside your comfort zone but that provide broad experience and allow you to develop a whole-enterprise systems perspective of how companies operate. Preparation also entails hard inner work, pushing yourself to address any weaknesses in your leadership skills. Particularly challenging is the transitioning from a leader who relies mostly on the directive, command-and-control style of leadership, which may have produced great results in prior positions, to a collaborative influencer who delegates authority and understands how to lead through inspiration and empowerment. Companies have become too complex for CEOs to lead with the traditional command-and-control style. Leaders who are most successful in harnessing their firm's talents and organizational capabilities understand that companies are complex, adaptive systems, which they cannot fully control. They realize they must lead their company's growth using the force and clarity of the vision and strategy they articulate and their abilities to energize, galvanize, and enable people.

Few, if any, leaders have fully developed all these capabilities by the time they take over as CEO. But those with the best chance of succeeding have done concerted work to develop their leadership skills, and they continue to do so once they've stepped into the role and all throughout their tenures.

Caldwell and Jorgeson summitted the Dawn Wall because they had vigorously devoted themselves to understanding what the ascent required of them. They then strenuously prepared their bodies and minds to meet those challenges. Over the course of six years, the two put themselves through a series of preparatory climbs on particularly difficult stretches of the wall, discovering increment by increment how to piece together their winding route to the top. Both pushed themselves well beyond what they thought were the limits of their strength and tried bold new moves along the way. Jorgeson even learned a whole new area of climbing: he excelled at bouldering, climbing relatively small rock formations, but he had not yet tried climbing a "big wall," in climber parlance. His first attempt was on the most difficult big wall in the world. Caldwell accepted Jorgeson as his partner because he appreciated Jorgeson's bouldering expertise, knowing it was a great complement to his own skills in charting their route. In turn, Caldwell shared his hard-won expertise with Jorgeson. This is another core competency for CEO success: developing the ability to spot the talented individuals whose skills and experience you'll need and devoting yourself to helping them strengthen and round out their abilities.

Also crucial to the Dawn Wall ascent was the climbers' bold ambition and dedication, which inspired a small army of supporters, including several of the other most talented climbers in the world, who climbed up or rappelled down the wall to bring Caldwell and Jorgeson provisions. Similarly, no CEO can perform well without inspiring followership at all levels of the organization. The popular myth of the "hero" leader who alone has the vision to chart a brilliant course for the future and the sheer power of will to make change happen is not only utterly flawed but also dangerous. As CEO adviser Damien Faughnan cautions, "The heroic model of leadership is a terrible way to be a CEO. It's disempowering and slows an organization down because the CEO is overly involved in too many issues. The minute the CEO gets involved, everybody is tools down, we've got to wait and see what the CEO thinks. They also second-guess themselves, and decision-making that should be happening at lower levels gets escalated to the CEO." CEOs must instead inspire leaders throughout the company to take initiative and give them the leeway to perform, reserving for themselves the work that only the CEO can do.

CHARTING A WINDING ROUTE

As with the Dawn Wall ascent, the surest path to success is not a linear ladder climb but a winding route that involves bold and often risky "investment moves" to gain breadth as well as depth of experience. These moves pay off in spades when you face all the new challenges of the CEO job. The more you get comfortable with discomfort and learn how to seek the advice and support you need to succeed with a daunting set of new responsibilities, the stronger those muscles will be when you run into vexing challenges. Examine the career trajectories of successful CEOs and you will find that most have made daring choices about which opportunities to pursue that mightily challenged them and forced them to grow. Traversing laterally into different functions, divisions, regions, and industries helps you develop valuable complementary skills that will pay great dividends in continuing your climb. Not only do boards prefer candidates with a great breadth of experience, but gaining that breadth will develop your whole-system understanding of how companies operate and can be steered. Sometimes even being willing to take steps down to pursue a promising pathway to the top spot, as Tommy Caldwell did, is advised. Former Macy's CEO Terry Lundgren stepped down as CEO of Neiman Marcus to take the position of divisional CEO of the merchandising group at the much larger Federated Department Stores, which was later renamed Macy's. Lundgren put in three years in that role and then four as chief marketing officer before being appointed CEO. That "down climb" was an investment Lundgren was willing to make because he was so compelled by the vision and challenge of taking a larger company to great new heights.

Speed to the top is not always of the essence. More important is making sufficient career moves so that you proactively develop greater operational, strategic, and leadership prowess. Particularly valuable is at least one role as a general manager of a large unit or division. Few boards are willing to put a leader in the CEO role who doesn't have that experience.

Some of the most successful CEOs, constantly challenging themselves to keep learning, have made truly staggering career leaps in order to develop new skills. Ajay Banga is a great case in point. He led Mastercard through a transformation that resulted in a cumulative total shareholder return of 1,581 percent through the course of his twelve-year tenure, besting the S&P 500 by almost fivefold. On the way to that role, he pushed himself to gain ever-broadening experience.

Banga grew up in India, and as he came of age, American and European corporations were establishing operations there. He was intent on making his way into a large global corporation, and after graduating from the prestigious Indian Institute of Management, he set his sights on a first job at Nestlé's India division specifically because the company was known for moving people quickly into positions across functions. Nabbing a job in marketing, within eight years he'd moved into roles in sales and product management. Then, at age twenty-nine he was vaulted into the role of head of Nestlé's Eastern Region, with hundreds of people across a wide geography under his management. He thrived in the job, and further ascent at Nestlé seemed assured.[2] But Banga decided to make a bold move.

Though he loved Nestlé, when he saw a better opportunity to reach higher career levels at PepsiCo, which was growing in India, he "jumped off the deep end" to take a position in an entirely new industry: fast food.[3] Pepsi had acquired the Kentucky Fried Chicken and Pizza Hut chains, and Banga's job was assisting in establishing their first restaurants in India. Yet, just two years later, Pepsi sold off its restaurant business to the newly formed Tricon Global Restaurants (later renamed Yum! Brands), which would run the businesses with a franchise model. That was not of interest to Banga; he wanted to continue learning the ropes of how major American corporations are run. So, he decided to make a second bold leap into another entirely new industry: banking.

He joined Citigroup as head of marketing and sales in India, and over the course of fourteen years, he stretched himself with a great diversity of roles. "I never said no to a transfer," he recalled.[4] He gained international experience as head of sales, marketing, and business development for Central Europe, the Middle East, and Africa. Moving to New York, he took over running retail banking for North America and then the global consumer business, during which time he was also head of marketing for the whole company. In 2008, he was promoted to chief executive officer of Citigroup Asia, and he was one of a small number of executives in leading contention to succeed Citi CEO Vikram Pandit. Yet, he once again decided to make a major leap.

"I defied the logic," Banga told us about taking the position of president and COO at Mastercard in 2009 at age forty-nine, with the expectation that he would succeed CEO Robert W. Selander, who planned to step down the following year. The move was widely seen as a big step down for Banga. Mastercard was a David compared to the Goliath of Citibank, with four thousand employees versus Citi's three hundred thousand. What's more, as Banga highlighted, "for all of the good work Mastercard did in electronic payments, it was often mistakenly seen as a vulture at the heart of global payments." Several lawsuits accused Mastercard of charging excessive fees on transactions. So, why did he want the job? "I didn't see the next ten years of my life being adequately interesting if I stayed in banking," he shared. By contrast, he thought Mastercard was ripe for exciting innovation. For one thing, the mobile payments revolution had kicked off, led by start-ups like Square and PayPal, and was inspiring legions of entrepreneurs all around the world to jump into the game. "Every day there was somebody sitting in a house in Vladivostok or San Francisco trying to tell the world that they were the kings of the future." They were furiously innovating payment applications and launching start-ups. "You've got to embrace innovation and run toward these disruptors," he shared. "The last thing they expect is for you to come running toward them." Which is exactly what Banga made sure Mastercard did. He saw great opportunity for Mastercard to become a leader not only in mobile payments but also in other hot areas of financial technology where the entrepreneurial upstarts were aiming to gain dominance, such as cybersecurity and cryptocurrencies.

While COO, he applied his experience in organizational development to quickly build up the company's technological talent by creating Mastercard Labs. He stepped into the CEO role eight months after his start and proceeded to transform the company into a highly agile technology innovator—despite Mastercard lacking a tradition of innovation: in an employee survey at the time he took over in 2010, employees ranked "innovation" twenty-sixth out of twenty-seven characteristics of the company.[5] Banga had no direct expertise in technology, but he'd learned to lead as an influencer, not as a command-and-control manager. He appointed talented tech start-up founder Garry Lyons to the new role of chief technology officer and gave him a long leash. "I told him, 'Knock yourselves out. I don't want to control your work by asking to see spreadsheets justifying your investments. Try things out. But give me a couple of things to commercialize every couple of years. If you don't, I will replace all of Labs,'" Banga recalled.[6] Such autonomy is a tech innovator's dream. New offerings poured forth, in data analytics, artificial intelligence services, cybersecurity, and instant payments with blockchain, among others.

During Banga's twelve-year tenure, from 2010 to 2022, the innovation he spearheaded drove a rise in market capitalization from $30 billion to $300 billion and catapulted Mastercard from 256 on the list of the world's most valuable companies to 21.[7]

Leaping into new industries, as Banga did, isn't the only way to make great stretch moves. Many successful CEOs have benefited in the role from being with the company they take charge of for many years. And boards generally prefer internal hires. In fact, our data shows over the past two decades 76 percent of CEO appointments have been of internal candidates. While for smaller companies under $10 billion in market cap, the share of insider appointments is slightly lower at 66 percent, it grows consistently with the size of company. In the biggest companies, those with $50 billion or more in market cap, the share of insider appointments reaches 87 percent. Company insiders hold an important advantage because they understand the inner workings of the company and its culture.

Many of the most successful CEOs we studied, such as Microsoft's Satya Nadella, worked their whole career in one industry. Many also worked at one company for most of their career, as was also true for Nadella: he joined Microsoft after two years in his first job as an engineer for Sun Microsystems. GM CEO Mary Barra, who achieved the breakthrough feat of becoming the first woman appointed to lead one of the Big Three US car manufacturers, worked only at General Motors over the course of thirty-three years before her leap to CEO in 2013. She started working for GM, inspecting hoods and fenders at a Pontiac factory, even before she graduated from college. And she earned her undergraduate degree in electrical engineering from General Motors Institute (which later became Kettering University).

Key, though, in staying within one industry or one company is moving rapidly into many different functions and taking on particularly challenging roles. Mary Barra is exemplary in this regard. She held a strikingly broad range of positions. Her first job after graduation was senior engineer at Pontiac. After then winning a GM fellowship to get her MBA, which she earned from Stanford, she held roles as executive assistant to the CEO and general director of communications, and then she took on the daunting challenge of managing the company's badly ailing flagship, the

Detroit-Hamtramck assembly plant. The job would have been tough for anyone, but as a woman in an extremely male-dominated environment, she had to also contend with sexist skepticism. She did so artfully, and kept stretching, including into the corporate role of executive director of Vehicle Manufacturing Engineering, where she oversaw a large staff of engineers.[8]

From there, she made the highly unconventional sideways move to VP of Global Human Resources, which helped her learn valuable people development skills. She instituted a new process of regular performance reviews, requiring managers to devote quality time to employee development, and did away with hidebound bureaucracy, such as by trimming down a ridiculously detailed ten-page dress code to two words: "Dress appropriately."[9] Two years later, in 2011, having impressed CEO Dan Akerson, who'd been appointed the year before, she took on the high-profile position of senior VP of Global Product Development, which put her in charge of design and quality control for all new vehicles.[10] She made transformational changes. The Obama administration chose Akerson to take charge of bringing GM out of bankruptcy following the 2008 financial crisis and the company's bailout. Akerson was determined to do away with the horribly inefficient product development processes of the "Old GM," which were dominated by a long-serving group of senior executives. Barra was tasked with a reorganization of engineering, and she performed so well in streamlining operations and driving down costs that Akerson also put purchasing and supply chain for the whole firm under her management. This was taking charge of a nest of vipers, according to Akerson, who recalls that "engineering and parts buyers just hated each other."[11]

Succeeding in such a diversity of roles—and such tough ones— proved instrumental in Barra's selection as a rare "leapfrog" CEO. She was appointed to CEO from a position below the C-suite, from which, as we'll see shortly, an overwhelming majority of CEO appointments are made.

Particularly notable about the stretch moves of the most successful CEOs is not only how wide-ranging they were but also how rapidly they were made. Most stayed in one role no longer than three years. They relentlessly pushed themselves to learn how to quickly learn, which often involved great risk. Satya Nadella at Microsoft, for example, agreed to take charge of developing a search engine, a whole new terrain of engineering for him. It was also an extremely high-stakes mission, vying with the totally dominant Google search engine. What's more, he had to lead a group of engineers with expertise he himself didn't have. The CEO at the time, Steve Ballmer, asked him if he'd like the job but also cautioned, "You should think about it, though. This might be your last job at Microsoft because, if you fail, there is no parachute."[12]

By moving across functions and divisions, the high performers we studied also forced themselves to adapt to the different cultures that prevailed in different functions and units, and those who took posts overseas also had to adapt to different national cultures. Even within one company, silos tend to develop highly differentiated cultures. For Mary Barra, working in GM's human resources group was many worlds away from managing the factory floor, and managing factory workers was worlds away from leading designers and engineers.

Many also defied traditional silos. They helped bridge gaps between divisions that plague so many companies by breaking out of the bounds of their function or specific job mandate and spearheading cross-functional initiatives or initiatives entirely beyond the confines of their job description.

Adobe CEO Shantanu Narayen, who has led the company through repeated successful transformations, exemplifies this boundary busting. He shared, "I've never believed in swim lanes," meaning he didn't want to be confined to narrow silo-specific responsibilities. He made many unconventional moves, starting with his choice of a first job. After receiving his degree in computer engineering, he decided to join a small automotive start-up in Silicon Valley rather than one of the big tech firms because, as he explained, he could get "more rapid-fire learning" there.[13] Hopping to Apple next, he worked in product engineering for six highly successful years but then decided to take the daunting leap to cofound a picture-sharing start-up, Pictra. Though the start-up failed within two years, the experience proved highly valuable to Narayen, not the least in that he was hired by Adobe because the company's CEO at the time, Bruce Chizen, was so impressed by Narayen when he pitched Chizen to buy Pictra. Chizen didn't want the start-up, but he perceived the great talent of the founder.[14]

A self-professed "product geek," Narayen nonetheless made an important mark on Adobe's sales operations when he recommended to Chizen that the structure of commissions be changed to incentivize stronger sales of newer business software products. Chizen went ahead with the change, and business software sales skyrocketed 42 percent the next year. Chizen recalls of Narayen, "He was always pushing me, but behind the scenes."[15] Narayen himself reflects, "I just kept volunteering for more." That included championing the $3.4 billion acquisition of Macromedia, the company's largest purchase at the time. It put the Flash media-playing software, which was installed on 98 percent of all personal computers, in Adobe's hands and drove enormous growth for Adobe.[16]

Larry Merlo, who led CVS Health through its transformation from pharmacy to health-care-services goliath, broke through the traditional wall between pharmacists and the business teams that run pharmacy companies. He started his career as a pharmacist, working behind the counter at a Peoples Drug store. In the pharmacy business, most pharmacists, except those who own their own stores, report to the store managers and manage only the small team working in the pharmacy itself. But the business side of operations fascinated Merlo, and he made the stretch move into corporate management, rising rapidly into a regional vice president role and then, when Peoples Drug was acquired by CVS in 1990, ascending quickly to the role of executive vice president for stores. That was despite not having an MBA.[17] He credits taking on leadership projects outside of his specific role as a key factor in his rise to CVS CEO. "My business school was being tapped on the shoulder for special projects," he said. Those included leading the integration of the Revco Drug Chain in 1997, even though he'd never been involved in an acquisition before, much less managed the ever-vexing job of making a merger work.[18] Merlo went on to lead several more integrations, including, as we'll explore more fully later, a particularly fraught and expensive acquisition that he made work despite widespread outcries on Wall Street that it never would.

Ajay Banga, drawing on a deep personal passion for uplifting the billions of impoverished people around the world, took the initiative at Citi to spearhead a microfinance business. He'd seen the crushing effects of poverty in his home country of India, and he learned that a lack of access to financial credit was a major impediment to people improving their fortunes. "We discovered as we went along," he recalled about the microfinancing initiative, "that what was holding back principally women from advancing along the socioeconomic ladder was the inability to access finance."[19] Developing a business at one of the world's leading banks that securitized small loans of $50 or $100 to entrepreneurs in the developing world not only set a new standard in the growth of microfinance but also, as we'll see in the next chapter, provided Banga with vital learning that he used to craft a vision statement of a new mission for Mastercard that drove the corporation's explosive growth.

At some companies, leadership development processes identify high-potential leaders as far as three or four levels below the C-suite and move them into stretch roles. As discussed in Chapter 8, some firms link this larger leadership development process with succession planning, focusing on a subset of developing leaders as the most likely candidates for the CEO role. Under Ajay Banga's leadership, this is what Mastercard did. He instituted a formal process that developed a strong and deep bench of leadership talent and led to the successful selection of his successor. In the absence of such a formal leader development process, those aspiring to the CEO spot should put themselves forward for consideration for whatever new roles will best contribute to rounding out their experience. Do so with delicacy, of course, and discuss your desire to move on with your current manager.

When it comes to one vital area of development—the people skills of leadership—the good news is that any leader at any level can put themselves through the paces of gaining the skills. This is a mission that anyone aspiring to the CEO role must take very seriously.

MASTERING INFLUENCING SKILLS

Research shows that social skills are increasingly prioritized in executive hiring, particularly so in selecting CEOs. In fact, a study of five thousand job descriptions for C-suite job openings between 2000 and 2017 found a great increase in emphasis on people skills. And the increase was greatest in announcements for CEOs.[20]

Why the stronger emphasis on people skills? Because research on business leadership in the past few decades shows that the highly directive, command-and-control style of leadership, which dominated in the twentieth century, is not adequate to the faster-paced, more volatile business challenges of the twenty-first century. It stifles innovation and problem-solving. It's also a huge turnoff, in particular, for Millennial and Generation Z workers, who are the majority of the workforce.

Prakash Melwani, global chief investment officer of private equity leader Blackstone, is constantly hiring CEOs for the portfolio companies under Blackstone's management. He told us in no uncertain terms, "What makes a great CEO is the softer skills. They empower and inspire people. That's essential, because no CEO is going to be able to drive the growth of a company without that." CEOs must learn to lead through influence rather than command and control. They must focus their time and energy on a core set of two or three main objectives that only they can take the lead on. Freeing themselves for this rigorous focus requires finding ways to empower and energize the leaders below them and employees at all levels to drive results and take the initiative on spotting opportunities for innovation and organizational growth.

We conducted a study that corroborated the importance of leading through influence. We examined individual assessments of the leadership capabilities of 235 candidates in 75 CEO succession processes that were conducted over the course of a decade. We then focused on the 47 CEOs selected out of that pool to lead public companies, which meant good data was available on company performance. Next, we examined correlations between leadership skills and company performance, as measured by shareholder return, operating margins, and revenue growth. This data was complemented by in-depth interviews with CEOs and candidates about their approach to leadership. Analysis of how different leadership styles matched with performance showed that the highest performers were the most accomplished in influencing through empowerment. This is not to say that the directive style of leadership is never appropriate. Some situations call for it, for example, crisis management. But, generally, the best results come from leading through empowering others.

Scott O'Neil, the CEO of Merlin Entertainments, shared that earlier in his career, when he was president of Madison Square Garden, an executive coach offered him advice that would change how he led from that point onward. That advice was, rather than being a warrior, which was his approach to leading, he had to become a sage. He recalled, "At Madison Square Garden, I put together three proposals that would have been completely transformational for the company. And I didn't get any of them done." He realized that he had a choice to either be effective as a leader *or* be right all the time. He's become much more adept by changing his leadership style to emphasize empowering, engaging, and inspiring workers. Commenting on how different are the expectations and desires of Millennial and younger workers regarding how they're managed, he reflected, "The social contract is different. Employees want to feel that you care about their whole self, that you're not just trying to squeeze the extra dollar out of them."

But what exactly are the people skills needed? Our study found that the most important people leadership skills to work on are thoughtful and active listening, expressing and demonstrating empathy, conveying humility, collaborating, fostering psychological safety, and communicating a clear and motivating vision. These are the skills that enable leading with influence. Some may doubt that skills like empathy and humility can be developed, thinking that they are simply innate traits or are fostered during childhood and can't be adopted by fully formed adults. In our work with executives, however, we've seen that substantial progress in developing the skill of expressing empathy and humility is absolutely achievable. It certainly isn't easy, though.

Doing it right involves putting yourself through a deeply challenging and often quite discomforting process of personal growth. You've got to look deeply into yourself, develop great self-awareness, and do hard work to change default behaviors that are undermining your leadership. These commonly include micromanaging, which results from wanting to be in control of all aspects of the business; asserting your views too forcefully, which shuts down others sharing valuable alternative views; and overemphasizing admonishment and failing to recognize contributions. As Damien Faughnan said, the most successful CEOs are "the people who really work to understand who they are" and who have a great "capacity for deep reflection about themselves." Failing to embrace this discipline of self-interrogation and relentless people skills development is a leading cause of executives stalling in their careers or failing in the early years of their CEO tenure.

Shantanu Narayen, CEO of Adobe, exemplifies the influencer style of leadership. He recalled that when he stepped into the CEO position at Adobe, "I quickly realized there was no direct control, it was all influence." He described how he worked intensively on developing his people leadership skills. For example, one target of growth he set for himself on his way into the CEO role was communicating his vision more clearly and persuasively to his executive team. He became aware of the need to develop this skill when he was promoted from team member to team leader in charge of Adobe's product innovation team. With such a broader scope under his watch, he could no longer rely on meeting frequently with his reports to direct them and monitor progress. He realized he needed to lean more on keeping them aligned with the strategy through his communication. As he put it, he had to learn to become skilled at flag planting in addition to road building. What he means by "flag planting" is articulating in a vivid and concise way the mission he wanted his team to advance. He shared, "When I first took the role of COO, I was a road builder. I knew what to do; I was very familiar with all of the technology. But I realized I couldn't mandate what everybody should come in and do every day." He also came to appreciate that "when you have an idea and somebody embraces it and it becomes theirs, they will improve it. What they produce will become ten times better than if they think they're doing it because you told them to."

He made a concerted effort to develop his flag-planting communication skills, pouring himself into crafting the wording of his communications. This involved really pushing himself to boil down his vision for the company's guiding mission into highly persuasive and memorable words, such as *creative collaboration* and *accelerating document productivity*. "I obsess over that," he said, stressing the importance of "learning the power of the written word, because if you get that right, your message will flow off the tongue. If it flows off the tongue, you'll use it with passion." Then, he emphasized, people will be inspired to rise to the occasion and interpret the guidance as best suits the products or services they're working on.

Demonstrating how effectively Narayen has inspired employees all around the corporation with his words is an account by Priyank Shrivastava, an Adobe business unit leader based in Bangalore.[21] He was inspired to lead his team to create a new product after hearing Narayen speak at the company's annual sales meeting in 2013. One of the visionary transformations Narayen led at Adobe was transitioning the company from selling software for installation—software in a box—to offering cloud-based services through a subscription model. Narayen launched the change process in 2012, making Adobe the first technology company to move to the cloud, with all the rest eventually following. The strategy led to explosive growth. But in 2013, the transformation was in its infancy, and Narayen was evangelizing the vision at the sales conference.

"As our CEO outlined Adobe's cloud vision," Shrivastava recalled, "I found myself thinking about how my business unit could contribute." When he got back to Bangalore, he pitched his team on the idea of building a cloud-based learning product. "At Adobe," he wrote, "we're always encouraged to innovate, and ideas are welcomed and valued. This culture of openness gave us the confidence to present our idea to Shantanu." So open to ideas is Narayen, in fact, that when Shrivastava and team members visited Adobe headquarters some months later and "decided to park ourselves in the pantry next to Shantanu's office," hoping to grab his unscheduled attention, Narayen allowed them to present a quick product demonstration. He greenlighted work on the project, and when they presented the finished version to Narayen at the next annual sales conference, he exclaimed, "What you guys have built has blown me away!" In 2015, the product, called Adobe Captivate Prime, was successfully launched.

The highly intentional work Shantanu Narayen described is the only way to make substantial progress in developing one's ability to lead through influence. Building on our study findings that CEOs who lead through influence were the most effective, we followed up by conducting interviews to learn about the development advice and training these leaders had received. We asked leaders to describe how they made the journey to becoming the highly effective leaders they were. What emerged is that a leader's evolution generally proceeds in iterative cycles, with steps forward often followed by backsliding into old habits and then a renewed effort at change. It's a process of trial and error, and often of fits and starts, as the daily grind of immediate demands diverts attention from one's inner work. Those who continue to progress in the journey typically go through a three-phase cycle.

First, they are confronted with a necessity for change either because they took on a new challenge that reveals the shortfalls in their leadership or through feedback from their higher-up, colleagues, or mentor. Recall that Narayen's aha realization was that he would not be able to lead the product team through his former directive style. The willingness—or, better, eagerness—of leaders to recognize areas in themselves for development and their receptiveness to feedback about areas of weakness are crucial to success. This initial self-awareness building is the foundation for all further evolution.

Once leaders realize the necessity of change, they can begin to explore the possibilities of change. This second phase involves considerable discomfort and a good deal of frustration because new skills take more work to build than anticipated. Falling back into old habits is common, especially when dealing with high-pressure situations. Backsliding should be expected and not taken as an indication of failure. Progress unfolds through an iterative process of steps forward, lapses backward, and then steps forward again.

With perseverance, positive reinforcement kicks in, which provides sustaining fuel for continued effort through the third phase of leader evolution. In the case of Shantanu Narayen, he has become one of the most inspiring and empowering corporate leaders of his generation. Adobe has kept ahead of the curve of innovation in its field through a steady stream of breakthrough innovations that are in exquisite alignment with the goals he has articulated.

Although continued growth and development while CEO is essential to success, we cannot emphasize enough the importance of taking advantage of the years before you become CEO to do as much work on your leadership skills as possible. Seek development support from your company and, if possible, from coaches and advisers or formal development programs. To have a good understanding of your development needs, you must examine how the roles you have occupied have shaped your profile of strengths and determine where you still have gaps.

THE LEADING LAUNCHPAD POSITIONS

Whatever winding route you take toward contention for a CEO appointment, you will gain a huge advantage in being considered for the job by stepping into one of three C-suite roles. Our research shows that from 2000 to 2020, approximately 77 percent of CEOs were appointed from one of these positions: chief operating officer (COO), which is frequently combined with the president's title, accounted for the lion's share of appointments, at 50 percent; divisional chief executive officer (DCEO) came in at 19 percent; and chief financial officer (CFO) accounted for 8 percent of appointments. Another 13 percent of appointments were of experienced CEOs. Leapfrog appointments accounted for only about 5 percent, with the remaining percentage including appointments from comparatively new C-suite roles, most commonly chief technology officer, which unsurprisingly were concentrated in technology firms.

We conducted research to evaluate how well these roles provide valuable "last mile" experience that contributes to CEO success. For all CEOs appointed from 2000 through 2020, we evaluated which CEOs, by role, performed in the top quintile, midrange, and bottom quintile, as measured by TSR over the full course of their tenure. Results show that the boards' priorities have been on target: DCEO appointments had 10 percent better odds than COOs of being among the top-quintile performers.

As for former CFOs, analysis shows that, although they often get off to a very strong start, their performance tends to lag beginning in their third year. For the full course of their tenure, they accounted for the smallest share of top performers, at just 8 percent. They also accounted for the highest percentage of bottom-quintile performers. In examining their performance according to measures in addition to TSR, including revenue growth, return on invested capital, and profitability, we found that their strong early performance is largely due to their experience with finding efficiencies. This often leads them to continue to focus heavily on driving growth in profitability by taking cost out of the business and shoring up the company's balance sheet. The market generally rewards them in the first two to three years for those achievements. But over time, the emphasis on holding down costs versus driving revenue growth through product, marketing, and sales innovation, and revenue performance, which few CFOs have experience in, impedes growth. Rod Little, CEO of consumer-brands company Edgewell, rose from the CFO role. He shared with us, "It's very easy to remain in the CFO lane as a new CEO instead of putting your energy disproportionally in other places."

Another striking finding in our analysis is that leapfrog CEOs have the highest odds of becoming top performers. Their odds were 17 percent higher than COOs', likely because those who have come to the notice of the board despite not having risen into the C-suite have demonstrated an ability to powerfully impact company performance. These leaders have developed a combination of expertise and leadership capabilities that enables them to lead transformational change, whether through organizational engineering, driving strategic development of new products, leading M&A, or even championing new lines of business or business models. This was true for Mary Barra. When her predecessor Dan Akerson was asked why she was selected for the job rather than one of the three C-suite executives who were seen as the most likely choices, Akerson described the enormous impact Barra had. He particularly emphasized her role in restructuring the product development and supply chain processes. "Mary went into an organization [the global engineering group] that quite frankly four years ago was in chaos and brought order and started to fundamentally transform how we do product development." In addition, she had transformed sourcing in the supply chain and how purchases and expenses were tracked, as well as greatly boosted capital expenditure efficiency and improved customer satisfaction. "She was central to that whole evolution," he said.[22]

This was true also for a leapfrog CEO whose early moves we'll consider in Chapter 2, Chuck Robbins. After seventeen years working at Cisco, he took over the helm from John Chambers, who had led the firm for twenty years. Robbins was senior vice president of worldwide sales operations when the Cisco board voted unanimously to elevate him, choosing him over two leading contenders from the C-suite, president Robert Lloyd and COO Gary Moore. Chambers said Robbins was "an execution machine" and the leading force behind "the reinvention of Cisco's sales organization." Robbins also exercised great influence outside his sales silo. He was a driving force in advancing a new strategy to transform Cisco from a company selling predominantly computing hardware into a cloud-based software services provider. As part of that push, he spearheaded the acquisition of Meraki, a cloud-based start-up that was a leader in cloud networking services, an essential component of building Cisco's cloud capabilities.[23]

For both Barra and Robbins, strong people skills are also cited as reasons for their selection. Dan Akerson said of Barra that "her managerial skills, her interpersonal skills, her ability with people" were important factors.[24] John Chambers pointed to Robbins' ability to "inspire, energize, and connect with Cisco employees and customers."[25]

A LAUNCH DEVELOPMENT PLAN

Even after leaders have reached these heights, they almost certainly still have significant gaps in their experience and leadership capabilities. If you aspire to move on to the CEO job, making the best possible use of your time in this prior position to further develop knowledge and skills in those areas is invaluable in meeting the unique challenges of being CEO. Take a highly deliberate approach to assessing your strengths and weaknesses relative to the demands of the CEO job, and ensure you have a plan and expert support to address important gaps or further sharpen strengths. The more work you can do at this stage, the better foundation you have not only for transitioning into the role but also for continued growth throughout the CEO Life Cycle.

Up until this point, you likely have benefited from stretch roles, along with periodic leadership development training to address capabilities needed below the CEO level. In fact, we find that leaders who make it to the C-suite get less development support than they did before reaching this level. If you haven't already established rigorous self-directed means to pursue development, do so now. Busy as you might be in your current role, know that the demands on your time will be even more intense when you're at the helm. This is a time to really dig in and be tough with yourself, focus on the additional demands of the CEO job, and create a plan for optimizing your time to pursue growth in those areas.

Some aspirants to the role have little or no experience in various aspects of the CEO job. For example, an executive who's worked primarily in operational roles for the last two or three positions before becoming COO likely has limited experience presenting to and building relationships with board directors. They may also need to work on gaining a deeper understanding of the corporate strategy and the strategic development process. Someone in the CFO role, by contrast, is getting regular board exposure and strategy-development experience but may need to work on developing a stronger understanding of product innovation and customer relations. A CEO of an overseas division may need to focus special attention on building stronger relationships with executives at headquarters and in other divisions and on gaining a better whole-enterprise perspective.

Each leader also has a unique set of people leadership strengths and weaknesses. Someone may have become exceptionally skilled in combating their inclination to take charge of discussions, learning instead to sit back and listen intently to encourage input, a hallmark of an influencer leader. But that same leader may still need to work a good deal on inspirational communication and relinquishing control in some areas in order to focus on the highest-level priorities.

We work with executives who are in contention for the CEO role and who are CEO-elects to help them take advantage of the time remaining before they step into the job to accelerate their learning. This involves crafting a rigorous development plan with them, to make a concerted effort to address their gaps. If your company doesn't provide assistance in leadership development, you can map out your strengths and weaknesses and create a game plan for working on them.

Crucial to the process is establishing ways of receiving feedback about the progress you're making. Most successful leaders not only are receptive to critiques of their abilities and management style but also proactively seek feedback. In fact, executive coaches Marshall Goldsmith and Howard Morgan found that was the distinguishing factor for success in a study of more than ten thousand managers' personal development tracks: sharing your growth goals with people you then ask to provide feedback on your progress was the only factor that differentiated successful self-development approaches from unsuccessful ones. In addition to formal evaluation processes, successful leaders seek informal input from both higher-ups and direct reports.[26] A number of CEOs we talked with shared their methods for getting regular and honest feedback. One asked a member of his executive team to periodically survey the rest of the team to provide their assessments of how he was doing on the various fronts he'd shared he was working on. The answers were made anonymous and compiled for him to study. Another asked a small group of trusted colleagues to let him know when he slipped back into old bad habits. They were hesitant at first, but whenever someone did share feedback, he expressed heartfelt gratitude, and over time, they all opened up with their thoughts.

This is like setting up a belaying system for your climb. In big-wall climbing, climbers are always harnessed to a system of ropes attended to by other experienced climbers. A belay device is a brake that's used to apply more tension to a rope or to slack it in order to assist the climber in staying on course. Think of those you ask for feedback as your belayers. They're providing you vital support to keep you from falling.

For your belayers to openly share with you, it's crucial to not be defensive about criticisms. Of course, that's much easier said than done. But if you really dig in and discipline yourself to be receptive, you can become highly skilled at making others feel comfortable providing criticism. Hubert Joly, who led a remarkable turnaround as CEO of Best Buy, shared his own journey in learning how to make productive use of feedback. Before joining Best Buy, while CEO at CWT (formerly Carlson Wagonlit Travel), Joly began working with the executive coach Marshall Goldsmith. "Up until then," he recalled, "I was a perfectionist and mightily struggled with feedback. Whenever a negative point was made in a '360,' I would ask, 'Who said that?' Marshall helped me change my perspective. The process he took me through was painful, because I had to stand in front of my team and say, 'Based on everything you've shared with Marshall, I have decided to work on these three things, and I'm going to follow up with you on how I can get better at them.' This was incredibly difficult at first, but now it's become super easy to say, 'I'm not perfect and I need help.'"

In stark contrast, one big mistake some aspiring CEOs make is focusing on getting the job rather than on actually doing the hard work to develop the extra skills needed to succeed in the position. Instead of genuinely engaging with development work, such as Joly did by learning how to productively harness criticism, they go through the motions, thinking they can make a show of doing the work that will impress the board. In one case, a COO was critiqued for not holding his team accountable for problems with execution on deliverables. But because he believed he already had what it took to do the CEO job, exhibiting an overly confident "I got this" view of himself, he put only half-hearted effort into the work he was assigned to more effectively manage his team. He didn't realize that progress candidates made on their development goals would be rigorously assessed, and by not making a serious commitment to the work, he undermined the board's confidence in his ability to devote himself to learning and personal growth, which they knew were crucial to success as CEO. So, he was taken out of contention.

When we create development plans with leaders in launchpad positions, we break down areas for development into four core categories: strategic vision, mobilizing team and organization, stakeholder engagement, and self-development. Your current position provides you with good development in some of these areas, but not in others. CFOs, for example, obtain good experience with strategy and with board relations, whereas COOs generally do not. Clearly, your plans should focus on the types of experience your current role is not helping you with.

For COOs, the most important things to focus on are as follows:

- Developing a longer-term strategic vision for the company versus intense focus on shorter-term operations
- Building the skill to powerfully communicate a compelling vision that resonates with different audiences
- Widening exposure to finance, marketing, and sales and markets in other geographies to develop a nuanced understanding of the distinctive subcultures in the organization and relationships with key personnel across the company
- Understanding the broader range of the company's external stakeholders, such as large investors, regulatory bodies in key geographic locations, business-to-business customers, and retail consumers

For divisional CEOs, who are often located away from headquarters and focused intensively on managing their own P&L, especially beneficial will be these capabilities:

- Developing stronger relationships with the entire executive leadership team
- Gaining a better understanding of the enterprise as a whole—especially those parts of the business they've had little exposure to—and learning about the interdependencies across the organization
- Volunteering for company-wide initiatives, such as the rollout of new technology platforms, sustainability initiatives, or business process reengineering to broaden their aperture
- Devoting time to deepening understanding of overall corporate strategy and the particular challenges of other divisions

- Seeking exposure to stakeholders they have had little, if any, engagement with, including industry groups, key investors, communities, and policymakers, to learn to manage stakeholder expectations

CFOs will particularly benefit from developing these skills:

- Broadening understanding of the entire stakeholder landscape. CFOs already have a strong understanding of the analyst community, such as by participating in earnings calls that address investor concerns. But they should learn about key suppliers, plant operations, and customers about whom they may know little.
- Devoting time to assessing opportunities and challenges concerning longer-term top-line growth beyond quarterly and annual results and taking tolerable risks to drive innovation for the future of the company
- Seeking ways to lead at scale and through others to broaden their background working with a smaller functional team
- Taking a structured and systematic approach to talent management and coaching to help team members address gaps and leverage strengths

People in leapfrog positions have less visibility into the workings of the enterprise as a whole than do those in the C-suite. They also have less experience with and knowledge of the executive team and little, if any, exposure to the board. They should focus on these development strategies:

- Seeking opportunities to gain the attention of the executive team and board by spearheading large initiatives in, for example, digital transformation, diversity, M&A integration, or product rollout, for which executive team and board approval is required

- Requesting opportunities to interact with the board during formal sessions or other activities, including making formal presentations in board meetings
- Finding ways to gain exposure to external perspectives through engaging with the company's many stakeholders, from investors and analysts to trade organizations and customers
- Deepening understanding of the business' full range of functions and investing in building relationships with functional leaders

These are, of course, general guidelines. Your plan should be more specifically tailored to the gaps in your experience and leadership skills. To illustrate how a detailed development plan can be crafted for a particular leader, we'll share about one we created for a CFO. Dan had ample experience in developing strategy, so we focused his plan on the three other areas.

For team and organization building, he went through a series of exercises for evaluating the strength of his leadership team, which included assessing their key capabilities and judging their potential to adapt and grow into higher positions. He also ranked team members in terms of their ability to create value and to enable those they lead to create value.

Next, Dan assessed how well the team was operating as a collective, grading them on a scale from the baseline performance level of a working group to a high-performance team and developing techniques to improve team chemistry and camaraderie. We also asked him to assess aspects of the organization's culture that were holding the company back. This involved examining procedures and routines that led to negative behaviors and identifying new procedures and routines to put in place to build a stronger culture. In addition, Dan identified employees across functions and layers in the organization who were forces in fostering positive aspects of culture, such as those who were most trusted by their reports and their colleagues and those who were most receptive to and willing to drive change. As CEO, he would be able to elicit their involvement in building support for changes.

For stakeholder engagement, because he was strong in relations with board directors and market analysts and investors, the focus was on engagement with stakeholders he'd had little or no experience with. These included media, regulators, community leaders, industry advocacy groups, and customers. He ranked them into primary and secondary groups and then further refined his understanding of which would be the most important to focus his time on if he became CEO. We then explored methods for engaging with these other stakeholders to build trust and vary his communication style as appropriate for each.

When it came to people skills, he needed to develop his self-awareness, particularly about his tendency to micromanage, as well as improve his emotional regulation. He often felt highly stressed, and that was leading to tension in his interactions with direct reports and other colleagues. Dan needed to show more of himself—he could come across as very much a "numbers person"—and he had to learn to build stronger bonds with people outside of his immediate reporting group.

We had him take a hard look at his tendency to micromanage, which led to working on his skills in delegating, coaching, and understanding how to remove obstacles for others, such as unnecessary approvals. Impressing upon him the positive effects of influencing rather than direct control, we had him experiment with different ways to be more inspirational and approachable in conversations and meetings. This included helping him build empathy skills, sharing ways of better reading the emotional states of others, and tailoring his ways of communicating to show people that they are understood, respected, and cared for.

Finally, to address the stress that plagued him, we helped him develop techniques to manage his energy. This involved having him rigorously assess high- versus medium- and low-priority demands and prioritize more effectively.

Dan worked hard on all these fronts, and he made a successful transition into the CEO position and has astutely navigated the early stages of his tenure.

To introduce how a plan focused on strategic vision might look, we'll share the work we suggested to an executive named Elizabeth. As the company's COO, she had achieved impressive results in implementing operational improvements, and she was the leading contender for the CEO role in part for that reason. But she needed to develop her vision for the company's future. She could pursue growth by focusing on overseas markets, which had good potential for grabbing market share. Another focus could be growing direct-to-consumer sales versus the current emphasis on higher-ticket business-to-business sales. She could also, more radically, build an entirely new services business. One exercise she engaged in was to determine which course she thought was best by considering three core strategic questions: Where do I want to win? What do I want to win? How do I intend to win?

Elizabeth concluded that going after market share overseas would be more straightforward, but growing the direct-to-consumer retail business was the option with the highest potential. She also came to understand that this would require a culture change in the organization to become more customer-centric. The company would additionally need to build up a great deal more retail expertise. Her strategy needed to include steps for implementing those changes, and she devoted time to road-mapping those.

Given that many employees were likely to push back about the changes because of anxiety about where the company was heading and their job security, her development also needed to address how she could communicate the strategy in an inspirational manner. Devoting time to learning how to become a compelling influencer and powerfully sell her vision was a key part of her self-development work.

This work paid off when she was asked to present her strategic vision to the board, and she was selected. As CEO, she has vigorously pursued the vision and has been making impressive strides.

As should be the case with all leaders once they've ascended to the role, Dan and Elizabeth are continuing to work on their leadership skills and learning more about their organizations, the challenges they are facing, and the horizons of further strategic evolution. Their devotion to the intentional preparation work greatly aided them in managing the intensity of the Launch stage. But they also quickly discovered how much ongoing growth they would need to do, and with more intensity. One incontrovertible truth of the Launch year is that no matter how well you are prepared, you must expect the unexpected.

2

LAUNCH

"Everybody wants you to say
something dramatic."

*E*xhilarated and *daunted* are the feelings expressed when we speak with people in their early days on the job as CEO. Most are thrilled to be in charge, finally the one who ultimately calls the shots. Many insider appointments have been eager for years to put the changes they're making in motion. Those from the outside are invigorated by diving into a new organization, if not a new industry, and the opportunity to start afresh with a new set of challenges. They're all reeling from the intensity of the firehose of information coming at them and the enormous pressure they feel to prove they have the right stuff. Many wrestle mightily with the magnitude of pressure they're under.

In late 2022, Kevin Parkes took the helm at Finning International, which sells heavy equipment for industries such as mining and construction. He'd been with the company for twenty-one years and rose through a series of senior leadership roles, including COO at the time of his appointment. He spoke with us near the end of his first year, in which he led impressive earnings per share growth of 24 percent, a substantial increase over prior years. Looking back on his first months, he reflected, "It was scary taking on the role, in part because I'd been with Finning for a long time. I was looking forward to the opportunity to put my stamp on the company, but I also felt a good deal of anxiety. There was the expectation that I knew everything and had a plan in my pocket ready to execute, which was a lot of pressure."

He's in good company: that crush of pressure has similarly been felt by CEOs who went on to achieve great success—and they felt it despite being exquisitely well suited for the role and having deep knowledge of the company and its key issues. When Indra Nooyi took charge at PepsiCo in 2006, she had been part of the team that championed the company's strategy for over a decade. She started in the position of chief strategist in 1994 and rose to CFO before her appointment as CEO. "By virtue of the fact that I was involved in all the key decisions going back to 1994 and I was CFO and president, and so close to Roger Enrico and then Steve [Reinemund], the two prior CEOs," she said, "I was fully aware of the issues." The two most pressing ones were that Pepsi's business in China "was just bleeding" and the bottling companies Pepsi worked with were putting a terrible squeeze on profits. She knew those would be her top issues to focus on right from the start and that taking them on was going to be a horribly heavy lift. Writing about her early days in her memoir, she recounts, "I felt the weight of the job. I was upbeat and confident on the outside, but, inside, reality was taking hold."[1]

David Novak, who led Yum! Brands for seventeen years, increasing its market capitalization by over 800 percent, acutely felt the need to show he was the right choice—despite the fact that he'd had a stellar career at Pepsi, where he supercharged sales of Mountain Dew and, among other triumphs, came up with the idea for Cool Ranch Doritos, one of the company's most successful new products ever.[2] He'd moved on to great success leading two of Yum!'s three restaurant chains while they were part of Pepsi. Yum!—initially called Tricon Global Restaurants—was formed in 1997 when Pepsi sold off Pizza Hut, Taco Bell, and Kentucky Fried Chicken. The chains were ripe for sale in no small part because of Novak's leadership. As head of marketing for Pizza Hut, he'd driven a doubling of the chain's sales and profits and then, having been promoted to lead both Pizza Hut and KFC, pulled off a turnaround of KFC, which had slumped badly, doubling its profits in his first three years. It was no surprise when Novak was appointed president of Tricon. Working in a close partnership with CEO Andrall Pearson, he was expected to step up when Pearson retired, and he did so two years later in a smooth handover, having led major operational improvements and launched a flurry of successful new products, like KFC's wildly popular Colonel's Crispy Strips, which won him the accolade of "Quick-Serve Artist" in *Adweek* magazine.[3]

Yet, he felt that in his early days in the CEO seat, "I was in prove-myself mode. I knew that I was young, I was forty-six. I had never been a CEO. In my own mind, I felt like I had to demonstrate to our people, and the world, that I should be the leader."

Compounding the pressure is that all eyes are on you, from the board that has just put its faith in you, to the senior leadership throughout the organization and employees on the front lines and factory floors. Tim Guertin, who led Varian Medical Systems, described this feeling of being in a fishbowl particularly vividly: "Everybody's watching you, and what you do and how you act and what you say, and just how you hold your head when you walk down the corridor." He'd been with Varian for thirty years when he stepped into the job of CEO, having started as an engineer in the trenches, so the engineering teams knew he had the chops. He'd also been general manager of customer support and two other divisions. He had a strong network that stretched all around and up and down the company, and his talent had been highly visible in his two prior jobs, as corporate executive VP and then president and COO. Nonetheless, he was strikingly forthright about the great deal of anxiety he felt in his early days. "Looking back now," he said, "the emotion I felt most vividly was fear. There is a lot of fear in the CEO job in the first three to six months." The good news, he added, is that "after that, you start to get comfortable."

Those coming from the outside may feel even more pressure to quickly impress insiders, including members of the senior leadership team who may have been passed over for the job. When Joe Hogan was appointed CEO of medical device maker Align Technologies in 2015, he had a successful track record as CEO of $40 billion power and automation technologies company ABB behind him. Not to mention a twenty-three-year career before that at GE, where he'd held a wide range of executive positions, notably CEO of GE Healthcare, where he led a doubling of revenue from $7 billion to $16 billion in eight years.[4] He shared that the intense feeling of all eyes being on you can trigger insecurity. That, he cautioned, can provoke a dangerous impulse to overcompensate and put on a show of supreme confidence. "Everybody wants you to say something dramatic. Your ego will tell you, 'Assert what you know, show everybody how smart you are.' That's a trap." This trap can ensnare even highly accomplished leaders because, as Hogan reflected, "We're all insecure. I don't care how successful you've been. I'd be lying if I said I didn't walk in and wonder, 'Can I really do this job?'"

The great pressure, and the anxiety and fear of failure that accompany it, results not only from the extra load of responsibility and the sudden sensation of being thrust into the spotlight as the bigwig, the sole leader of leaders. It also results from the jolt of surprise you feel about just how different the CEO job is from any other role you have held, including CEO of a major company division.

This is an inescapable difficulty of the Launch stage. Bill George, who helmed Medtronic to stellar results for ten years, said, "No one is prepared to become CEO, no matter how much they think they are. You have to grow into the job. You think you know how to run a business, but that's really more the COO role."[5] Indeed, in a recent global survey of 422 CEOs, 68 percent shared that they believed they hadn't been fully prepared for the role.[6] They believed they had the required strategy and operations skills, but the gap in their preparation lay in what they discovered is unique to the CEO role: how unexpectedly emotionally challenging it is and the great intellectual agility it requires. They had underestimated how different the job is from any other leadership role they'd had in ways that are profoundly disorienting in the early days.

THE HOURGLASS EFFECT

For CEOs of public companies, as with grains of sand through an hourglass, all components of the company's business, inside and out, ultimately run through them. CEOs are the one leader accountable for all internal affairs and all external affairs, the one person with whom all bucks stop, whether these are problems that arise within the company—no matter how far down the hierarchy—or outside issues.

This means that from day one, a new CEO must negotiate a highly demanding push and pull between affairs on the outside versus those within. We call this tension the *hourglass effect*. It can challenge you throughout your tenure, but it is especially disorienting in the early days, while you're getting your sea legs.

Our interviewees described being stunned by two key aspects of the hourglass effect. Piyush Gupta summed them up beautifully: "First, you're lucky if you get 50 percent of your time to run the company. That's a massive change. Second is working with a board. In all of the other leadership roles I was in, I had a boss. I worked for one person. Now, you work with a collective. That's quite tricky."

The majority of a CEO's time that is not spent running the company is taken up by relations with external stakeholders. Foremost among them is the board, and as discussed shortly, many CEOs find establishing a strong relationship with directors particularly difficult among their new challenges. Then there are large investors, including pension fund and hedge fund managers; activist investors; Wall Street analysts; key customers and suppliers; regulators; local government and community leaders; federal government players; lobbyists; union leaders; and the media, which may come calling with uncomfortable questions or seeking words of wisdom at any moment. Sometimes the most demanding, and potentially lacerating, external stakeholder is the court of public opinion, which can quickly morph into an Inquisition if a CEO addresses an issue that hits the news in a way others consider as unaware or callous. Former Disney CEO Bob Chapek, for example, fell under a hailstorm of criticism for not issuing a statement about Florida's passage of the so-called Don't Say Gay bill in 2022. The bill banned teachers from instructing children in kindergarten up to third grade on sexual orientation and gender identity and banned instruction for older children "that is not age-appropriate." This legislation provoked a massive public protest, and many CEOs issued statements criticizing it. Though Chapek did later issue a critical statement about the bill, his initial decision not to publicly address it has been credited with building momentum for his ouster later that year, which was championed not the least by Bob Iger.[7]

Even if you better understand the stakeholder landscape from your personal development work and have started building relationships with key stakeholders, your involvement with this wide array of important, influential people is likely still limited. Learning the ropes of interacting with them takes time, and the importance of doing so can't be underestimated. Missteps in managing stakeholders can sink a CEO at any point in their tenure, but a rocky start invites intense scrutiny of their fitness for the job.

The inside demands of the role tend to dominate discussions in succession planning and interviews for the job. But management guru Peter Drucker wrote, "To define the meaningful Outside of the organization is the CEO's first task," and cautioned that "the definition is anything but easy, let alone obvious."[8] Although it may be clear that regulators and government officials are key stakeholders, politics that demand the CEO's attention may bubble up unexpectedly from the full landscape of public issues. CEOs who took on the role prior to the Supreme Court's overturning of *Roe v. Wade*, for example, were expected to issue statements about the ruling and create policies to support employees who seek abortions. Navigating such volatile terrain can be enormously challenging, and especially so for a CEO who is new to the job.

Further complicating handling outside affairs is that CEOs have little, if any, control over when they'll have to address them and how much time they'll have to spend on them. This challenge contrasts with the handling of most internal issues, which can, of course, still be enormously difficult to prioritize. But with them, the CEO has the authority to set a strict agenda and delegate responsibilities to trusted team members. The CEO is ultimately accountable for internal issues but can assign much of the heavy lifting to trusted reports. That might include leading the integration of an acquired company or taking over primary leadership of a vital strategic initiative, as CEO Ajay Banga did when he delegated the development of new technology offerings at Mastercard to his chief technology officer, Garry Lyons. Outside demands may intrude entirely of their own will: regulators may require meetings at their convenience; Congress may summon a CEO to testify in hearings; shipping lanes may be disrupted at any moment. Leaders within the organization can be assigned roles in stakeholder management (and should be) and a good public relations team can take the lead with the media, but the CEO cannot escape being the ultimate voice of the company, the chief negotiator and chief public relations manager.

Attending to shareholder relations is a responsibility that many CEOs would prefer to do much less of. Yet, delegating too much of the task to an investor relations team is a perilous path. Making a strong case to major shareholders for the moves you are making is a public company CEO's absolute imperative; those investors will want access to you and to hear your views in your own words. Quarterly earnings calls are bellwether market assessments of the company's performance, particularly of the CEO's plans for addressing issues and stoking future growth. The first earnings call comes on fast and furiously, within the first to third month on the job. Preparing for and attending investor days and shareholder meetings require considerable time, and unpersuasive presentations can be terribly costly.

The amount of time Piyush Gupta had to devote to shareholder relations surprised him when he became CEO of DBS. He had to work hard for several years to win over the investment community, despite his stellar credentials for leading the bank and the remarkable results he achieved almost immediately. He had risen through the ranks at Citibank in a twenty-seven-year career, becoming

CEO for South East Asia Pacific and developing a wide and deep understanding of the leading edge of banking innovation, including digital transformation. He even briefly exited Citi to found his own tech start-up, the failure of which, he says, taught him invaluable lessons. But DBS had developed such a negative reputation as a laggard; the joke on the Street was that *DBS* stood for "Damn Bloody Slow." Investor skepticism ran deep. "It took me an extraordinarily long time to get shareholders to start thinking of us differently, and much, much longer than I anticipated," Gupta said.

Other outside time commitments, for which invitations flood in—to attend conferences, give speeches, join policy-planning committees, participate in charitable initiatives, and direct other company boards—may become dangerously distracting. Some, however, can be great occasions for gaining a wider perspective of the business and the political and social issues of the day, as well as networking with other CEOs and leaders of all kinds. Serving on a board is one of the more time-consuming commitments, and Nigel Travis, the long-serving CEO of Dunkin', shared that he learned a great deal from the time he devoted to being a director for home accessories retailer Bombay when it was going through bankruptcy and a director for Office Depot when it faced an onslaught by an activist investor. Prior board experience can also be a great accelerator for incoming CEOs in developing relationships with their directors.

But these pulls on time can be siren calls, treacherous in their allure and taking too much time away from core responsibilities. Richard Anderson, former Delta and Amtrak CEO, warned that leaders can "easily go spend 20 to 25 percent of time on extracurriculars," if they're not vigilant. The costs versus benefits of these commitments must be weighed carefully. In the Launch stage, with such a press of competing priorities, setting strict limits is vital.

THE LONELINESS AT THE TOP

We've never talked with a CEO who hasn't agreed that the job involves a disconcerting feeling of loneliness, at least in the beginning. Even though it's often been said, in books and the media, that the job is lonely, actually experiencing the loneliness is surprising and difficult. UPS CEO Carol Tomé told us she always thought, "How lonely can it be?" but quickly discovered that she did feel a degree of loneliness when she stepped into the role.

Loneliness results from certain distinctive features of the role. One is that, for the most part, people within the company, including former close colleagues who felt free to challenge you on issues, may become more deferential to you, electing to keep their perspectives close to the vest. That may be true even with your direct reports on the executive team. Leaders at lower levels of the company will likely be even more reluctant to voice concerns and surface issues to you. As Piyush Gupta reflected, "As CEO, you never get told the full truth. Everybody puts a spin on information by the time it comes to you."

Meanwhile, CEOs must not share too openly with those below them. CEOs are privy to issues and information that must not be disclosed, including sometimes even with direct reports. Perhaps there is a personnel issue regarding a senior executive or a move you're exploring, such as a divestiture or layoffs, that should not be widely disseminated.

Further contributing to this distinctive form of isolation is that CEOs don't have one boss to report to, as has always been true before. They instead report to the board, but as opposed to close, regular contact with an in-house manager, contact with board members is less frequent and requires building a relationship with ten, twelve, or more individuals. That relationship with the board is extraordinarily complex; board relations are another unique aspect of the CEO role.

One issue with boards, which contributes to CEO loneliness, is that they may become complacent. After the selection process, they sometimes shift into deference mode, encouraging the CEO to decisively take charge and ceding virtually all responsibility for strategy and company performance to the CEO instead of working in true partnership. One CEO we interviewed said, "The board goes from, well, you're one of management, and they'll seek your thoughts, to all eyes turn to you, and what are we doing now? That's quite stunning at first." What's more, in recent years fewer former or current CEOs are sitting on boards of other companies, which means many sitting CEOs lack that peer on the board who truly understands what they are dealing with. One CEO recounted how he was hoping to add another public company CEO to the board to address this issue: "Ideally, I would like someone who is older than me and a public company CEO with ten years or more experience. The board members are a bit deferential, and they need to have the spine to stand up to me, even if they are wrong."

Yet CEOs can't just demand that board members engage more closely with them. "You have to lead the board," Piyush Gupta said, "and persuade them of the direction you want to take the company, but at the same time, they are the bosses. It's not straightforward." Further complicating the relationship is that the CEO generally does not know who on the board supported them for the job and who did not. Some directors who had doubts about you may scrutinize you particularly closely as you take the reins. Cheryl Grisé served on five large company boards, including those of MetLife and Dollar Tree. She said, with boards "there's more and more pressure and less patience" from investors about acting to replace CEOs who are not performing well. So, you may find yourself with a highly deferential board or one that's challenging you. In either event, developing a strong relationship will take considerable time. CEOs told us this was another major chunk of time they were not prepared to have to carve out.

Developing good channels of communication and relationships of trust with your direct reports and with board members must be top priorities for CEOs in the Launch stage. Piyush Gupta noted that "whether you are lonely or not depends on how you work with the board and the senior management team." He developed a strong, highly collaborative relationship with his board. And as for his management team, he described them as a kitchen cabinet. "We have lunch together once a week. We know each other's families," he said, and that closeness means that he doesn't feel lonely.

CEOs can combat the loneliness of the job in other ways, too. "I now have a better appreciation of why CEOs tend to hang with other CEOs," Carol Tomé said. They understand the strange new features of the job you're contending with, and it's okay to open up with them about the difficulty and ask for advice. And other CEOs are of course important sources of business insights. Building a good network of peers is a great means of gaining new ideas for problem-solving and assessing opportunities and threats that might not have come up on your radar, such as a new technology that another CEO is using with great success or a supply chain disruption that is about to affect your company.

Developing good channels of communication deeper down into the company is also important for breaking through the isolation bubble. Tim Guertin emphasized, "You need to find people in the organization who are trustworthy and you can talk to." Although "you can't talk to him or her about everything," he said, you can find different confidants to discuss different matters with. Roger Ferguson, former CEO of TIAA, found an especially strong sense of camaraderie and support, as well as energy, in working with his strategy team. As we'll describe in a later chapter, they launched an ambitious transformation of the company, and Ferguson felt members of the team were close partners. "They believed as much as I did," he shared, and that meant he didn't feel as alone.

These distinctive features of the job continue to shape your experience as CEO throughout your tenure, but they are particularly disconcerting in the early going. Coping with them is made all the more difficult when a CEO is reluctant to open up about their anxiety and self-doubt in those early days. Most CEO autobiographies scarcely mention the emotional challenges of taking over the role if at all, which contrasts starkly with many accounts by company founders, who speak volumes about their doubts and fears. Maybe it's because successful CEOs gained their footing over time and no longer have vivid memories of the emotional turmoil they went through. Indeed, Shantanu Narayen commented, "One of our attributes in these roles has to be the ability to forget your terrifying moments."

A CEO's reticence to discuss doubts and fears may also result from the expectation that CEOs exude *and* feel great confidence. Yet self-questioning is of vital importance, uncomfortable as it may be. Dave Cote writes that "in public you have to convey confidence in the moves you've made," but it is imperative to be "constantly questioning your own decisions."[9] Otherwise, confidence all too readily verges into overconfidence, partly because of social pressure. As Daniel Kahneman cautions, "Society rewards overconfidence. We want our leaders to be overconfident. If they told us the truth about their uncertainty, we would discard them."[10]

The key takeaway: experiencing some fear and self-doubt along with the thrill of taking charge is not only perfectly normal but also a feature of success. It's a sign that you're keeping a critical perspective about how well you're doing, which is crucial in embracing the need for continuing development.

Aspiring CEOs can take heart from the fact that, despite these challenges, so many first-time CEOs have hit the ground running to great success. Striking in this regard is Carol Tomé. She exemplified the core skill of both/and thinking for navigating the particularly intense push and pull of competing demands in this Launch stage.

THE BOTH/AND IMPERATIVE

Alternating between internal and external demands is only one way CEOs must learn to divide their time and energy. They also have to focus on the urgent here and now *and* on longer-term plans. In addition, they must be in command of the "hard stuff" of numbers *and* devote considerable time to the "soft stuff" of people management. Also crucial is striking a balance between taking decisive charge by quickly making some moves *and* engaging in learning more about the company. All require both/and thinking rather than either/or thinking. As skilled as leaders may have become in this over the course of their careers, the challenges of the Launch stage greatly up the ante on getting the balance right. Carol Tomé pulled off this balancing act with aplomb.

Tomé took the helm of United Parcel Service in June 2020 and achieved one of the strongest first years of more than two thousand CEOs whose performance we analyzed. The UPS share price had stagnated for years, but by the end of her first year, it had risen 104 percent, besting the S&P 500 by more than double. With early moves, she quickly generated great market enthusiasm. Bloomberg reported, just two months after Tomé took charge, that she had "made a remarkable amount of progress in a very short time."[11] That was aided by her having served on the UPS board for seventeen years, so she knew a great deal about the challenges the company had dealt with and was currently facing. Yet, as she quickly discovered, she hadn't had any exposure to some issues that were impeding performance, and she needed to do intensive discovery work. She also faced the unprecedented challenges posed by the COVID-19 pandemic, which had spread to the United States three months prior to her appointment.

The volume of packages delivered to households soared because of lockdowns. To meet the demand, the company had to hire forty thousand new employees in the quarter Tomé took over.[12] Those extra deliveries might have cut deeply into profit margins because home deliveries are more costly to UPS than are deliveries to businesses. Tomé immediately applied her expertise in creating operational efficiency from her days at Home Depot, garnering some great quick wins.

She'd been CFO of Home Depot for eighteen years, a position from which she retired in 2019. She agreed to come out of retirement to take over at UPS largely because of her board work, where she saw how she "could get in there and turn certain dials to create more value." She did that in spades. By the end of her second quarter, earnings were twice analysts' projections and profit margins had grown considerably.[13]

But efficiency improvements were only one major focus in her first year. One both/and balancing act she deftly managed was putting in place measures for longer-term improvements even as she was pressing urgently with the short-term operations fixes. Indeed, her grasp of issues farther down the road was so strong in her first earnings call that one reporter wrote, "The level of detail on her longer-term outlook was staggering."[14]

Her longer-term efforts included an important shift in strategy. She set out to build up the company's share of higher-grossing small-business-market deliveries and cut down on lower-margin deliveries to behemoth online retailers such as Amazon and Walmart—with their enormous purchasing power, they had been squeezing the profits of UPS.

Tomé also worked on the long-term mission of culture change, which is a great example of a former CFO broadening her range well outside of finance. Of her personal development process, she told us, "Any new opportunity that came my way, I would take it." One of those was helping lead a culture-change initiative at Home Depot to boost customer satisfaction and employee morale. She didn't know it when she took the UPS job, but she soon discovered she needed to do the same at UPS.

Another both/and juggle she managed well was taking charge with authority while also intensively learning more about the company, openly conveying, even with rank-and-file employees, that there was much she didn't know. To uncover the inevitable lurking problems, a CEO must make clear that they are aware there is much they don't know about the company and that they need people to teach them. Getting the balance right between leading decisively and learning can be quite tricky. For one thing, the pressure to be the person with all the answers can easily lead to "smartest one in the room" syndrome, when a leader comes on too strong and appears arrogant rather than confident. Larry Merlo, who was forthright in sharing that he had a ton to learn when he took charge at CVS, emphasized, "A strong leader takes pride in being both a student and a teacher; you've got to find the sweet spot between them."[15] We'll explore later in the chapter ways CEOs ensured they were doing rapid learning while also decisively leading.

Tomé traveled all around the company, to warehouses and retail operations and out in the field delivering packages with drivers, and in the process, she discovered serious morale problems. Employee survey data revealed that employee satisfaction was distressingly low, which she hadn't expected. This is a telling example of how board directors have little access to internal aspects of a company's operations. Tomé devoted considerable time to demonstrating to employees that she wanted to understand their needs. Walking her talk, she donned the signature brown UPS delivery person's uniform and put herself on the front lines of coping with COVID along with them.

Also, though Tomé well understood that culture change is a "journey, for sure," she rapidly took other steps as well. One was a move that was, in her words, "largely symbolic": relaxing an incredibly strict dress code to allow people to feel more themselves at work. She understood how important such signals of intent can be, and that they can make a good start. She also appointed a cross-functional team to craft an inspiring purpose statement: "Moving our world forward by delivering what matters." That statement could not have spoken more appropriately to the vital deliveries of vaccines and medicines UPS's army of essential workers carried out, risking their lives during the pandemic.

With so much to do internally, Tomé also did a good both/and job of attending to the interests of outside stakeholders. When it came to shareholders and analysts, who always love to see efficiency, Tomé greatly impressed, even though she had to ramp up spending enormously to serve the exploding customer demand. She also appreciated the importance of addressing the public's environmental concerns, increasing efforts to reduce the company's emissions by increasing its contributions to carbon offset programs. She also invested more in green technology, including alternative-fuel vehicles, and issued a commitment that the company would be carbon neutral by 2050.[16]

In addition, during her first year, when Georgia passed a controversial election law that was widely seen as intending to limit the voting rights of African Americans in the state, she understood that she had to respond. UPS is headquartered in Atlanta, and she appreciated that the company had to take a stance even though it was a delicate matter. Corporations struggled to respond to the law, and as the *New York Times* reported, weighing in on voting rights was "a head-spinning new landscape for big companies, which are trying to appease Democrats focused on social justice, as well as populist Republicans who are suddenly unafraid to break ties with business."[17] Indeed, one of the other largest Atlanta-based companies, Delta, fell under intense criticism from both sides of the political spectrum, being criticized first by the Left for staying silent and then by the Right for too strongly condemning the law. Tomé issued a judicious statement that prevented UPS from falling under attack and that affirmed the company's commitment to efforts to increase voter participation. The statement read, "UPS believes that voting laws and legislation should make it easier, not harder, for Americans to exercise their right to vote. UPS will continue to work with elected officials across the country to strengthen our democracy by facilitating equitable poll access and voting." The statement also explained that UPS contributes funds to organizations that lead get-out-the-vote drives.[18]

All this dexterity was vital to the incredible results Tomé achieved in her first year. She probably also benefited from a general lift in enthusiasm for new CEOs that was clearly reflected in our Life Cycle analysis.

THE CEO HONEYMOON

As enormously challenging as these early days are, they're also a period of great opportunity. The transition to a new CEO is a rare natural period of malleability for a company. A new CEO is usually seen as a force for rejuvenation, whether by bringing new energy and fresh ideas or by leading a needed turnaround.

A new CEO often enjoys what's referred to as a *honeymoon*, both within the company and outside. David Novak said, "In the first year, you come in and everybody wants the CEO to be successful. So, there's a lot of positive momentum for a decent start." The board feels confident in their new pick. Many employees are energized about new leadership. Analysts and investors are enthused too.

We found in our CEO Life Cycle study that this often leads to a boost in the share price. In the twenty-year period we analyzed, firms on average outperformed the S&P 500 by 10 percent in a CEO's first year. George Paz, for example, received a boost from enthusiasm during his first year at Express Scripts. He drove change impressively, with a successful acquisition in his first three months. The market swooned, driving up the share price 109.26 percent during his first year, which significantly beat the bumps up of the two key Express Scripts competitors. That was true even though they both also made strong acquisitions that year. Shares of the number one firm in the business, Medco, rose 34.13 percent. Those of the number two competitor, Caremark, increased 20 percent despite the fact that the acquisition Caremark closed was viewed so favorably that the company was described as "the phoenix of a flourishing industry." It also came in as number twenty-two on the *Businessweek* list of fifty top corporate performers for the year. Yet it was Express Scripts stock that truly shot through the roof.

More evidence of a lift from exuberance during the Launch stage is that the lift in the stock price is often followed by a sophomore slump. Of those CEOs who enjoyed a honeymoon period, 73 percent realized lower results in their second year. The CEOs caught in such a downdraft on average relinquished 21 percent of TSR. For Paz, the share price slid 14.56 percent, despite the fact that no significant problems arose to trigger concerns. Also, market growth overall was strong that year, with the S&P 500 rising 12.34 percent.

An interesting aspect of the honeymoon lift is that although some CEOs felt it, many said they didn't think they'd gotten one. Certainly, it's true that not every new CEO gets this lift of enthusiasm, at least not from all stakeholders. Market players may not be convinced that a CEO is the right pick, for example, as was true for Dave Cote at Honeywell. But even in cases when a CEO experiences this wave of support, the Launch stage is so challenging and anxiety provoking that it's likely quite hard to feel the exuberance. Tellingly, by contrast, board directors, who don't experience anything like a CEO's pressures, readily concur about the existence of a honeymoon. When we shared our CEO Life Cycle findings, Chris Coughlin, who has been a director at five companies, commented, "The honeymoon period doesn't surprise me. I've seen that in a lot of companies that I've been involved with."

As we'll explore in the next chapter, CEOs say that the roller coaster from share price spike to slump can be a quite difficult ride. Randy Hogan shared this about his first year at Pentair: "The stock overshot. But you can't have the CEO go out and say, 'The stock's too high.'" In his next year, the stock took a bad tumble. "First I was a hero, then I was a bum," he mused.

Hogan's comments speak to one important takeaway about the honeymoon spike. In communicating with market players and the media, CEOs should practice the fine art of what David Novak calls "sober selling." "When I first became CEO," Novak told us, "I hadn't really worked with Wall Street. I was very enthusiastic and very passionate about the company. But I was overenthusiastic, too much of a salesman. Investors would say, 'You're so optimistic,' but things can't all be good, right? So I started talking about the things that could go wrong, and I saw they really loved that. Yeah, you want to be positive about the company and the opportunities, but you get more credibility when you talk about what could go wrong. Then Wall Street will be more likely to believe you when you talk about what could go right."

Practicing sober selling from the beginning of your tenure will stand you in good stead if a honeymoon lift gives way to a slump. The market will always make its own judgments. But if you've noted possible headwinds before they are widely apparent, your credibility will grow all the stronger.

The other key takeaway about honeymoon enthusiasm is the importance of being wary about tailwinds of support that may be short-lived. Working intensively in your first year to build a strong foundation of trust with the board and key stakeholders inside and outside the company is vital. A good first step is demonstrating that you know you have a great deal to learn.

LEADING BY LEARNING

There are going to be surprises no matter how well you know a company. Learning about them early is challenging because employees, even at the highest levels, are reluctant to share troubling information. Learning what you need to know requires rigorous questioning while conveying in a compelling way that you absolutely want people to speak openly.

A CEO coming in from the outside needs to emphasize getting a good fix on the full range of business operations, the strengths and weaknesses of the leadership team, and the nature of the culture. Insiders, even those with broad experience of divisions and functions, will still encounter areas of little knowledge. Going on a listening tour shortly after stepping into the CEO job—or before if possible—by getting out of headquarters early and into the field to observe, ask lots of questions, and listen intently is widely understood as an important way for CEOs to start their tenure. It's vital to observe and question not just the top leadership team but also, as Ajay Banga says, "everybody above you, below you, beside you."

Chris Nassetta, when appointed to the helm of Hilton Hotels in 2007, made vital discoveries by traveling to a large number of hotels to talk with employees. The company had just been purchased in a high-stakes leveraged buyout by Blackstone for $26 billion, one of the largest LBO deals ever. For his first three months, Nassetta traveled to Hiltons in the United States and abroad, talking to workers on the front lines, such as bellhops and cooks, in addition to hotel managers, and questioning customers. He discovered that, as he put it, "the culture was a wreck."[19] Among many problems, the company's standards for service were subpar. To kick-start rapid improvement, he instituted a requirement that every company manager spend three days working in a hotel, at the front desk or in the kitchen and doing housekeeping. He also implemented an employee evaluation process, emphasizing quality of customer service provided.[20] Those were early steps in a many-years-long process of creating a culture of excellence, which, as we detail in Chapter 7, drove a remarkable turnaround in Hilton's fortunes that made the LBO one of the most successful in history.

This discovery work is important not only for making quick operational improvements, thereby scoring some quick wins, but also for pressure-testing a longer-term strategic game plan. This agenda usually is agreed upon through the course of discussions with the board during the interviewing stage. A good succession process makes developing a clear strategic agenda a priority. But it is imperative that once a CEO is in the role, they make a renewed assessment of the strategy's carrying power. All the discovery work you do may point to needed refinements of the agenda or even a more substantial change of course. Clarence Cazalot, who helmed Marathon Oil for twelve years starting in 2002, decided to make a dramatic change in strategy. The company had invested heavily in an oil and gas drilling development based on Sakhalin Island in Russia. As he delved into the project, he determined it was too risky and that the company should offload its stake, which he rapidly did by trading it to Royal Dutch Shell for some other properties in the North Sea and Gulf of Mexico.[21] In subsequent years, the costs of the Sakhalin project surged, and Shell sold off its stake at a massive loss of $1.6 billion.[22]

Questioning so many people early on is also a powerful way to convey respect for people's knowledge, showing them, not just telling them, that you respect them. It also harnesses the enormous power of demonstrating humility. Mark Hoplamazian, who took the helm at Hyatt Hotels Corporation in 2006, credits his great success to fulsomely owning up to his ignorance and asking for help in understanding the business. When he took over at Hyatt, "My experience was within finance: I did not have a lot of managerial experience. On paper, I was seemingly unqualified for the role." He had never worked in the hospitality industry, having spent the prior seventeen years at the privately owned Pritzker Organization, which comprised just ten employees, where he rose to president. The Pritzker Organization owned Hyatt and was looking for a new CEO. Because of the Pritzker family's long relationship with Hoplamazian and their trust in his good judgment, they asked him to step into the role on an interim basis. Unexpectedly, Hoplamazian fell in love with the company and the opportunity he perceived to grow such a well-respected brand. But as he told us, his "learning curve was vertical for an extended period of time."

What's more, his key competitors, Marriott and Hilton, both much larger than Hyatt, were run by leaders with long careers in the business and had been making bold growth moves. Under Chris Nassetta, at the start of the year, Hilton announced a $1 billion investment in brand enhancements.[23] Marriott embarked on a massive renovation of its hotels, described as an "extreme make-over."[24] Both Marriott and Hilton were gunning for Hyatt's lucrative higher-end luxury travel and business customers.

Talk about a stretch move—Hoplamazian "approached the challenge from a very public announcement of my ignorance," he said. Showing so openly how much he needed people to guide him led them to be generous in teaching him. "Reactions were humbling, and I was grateful for members of the Hyatt family helping to guide me," he recalled. Within two years, he led Hyatt through a highly successful IPO—in the second year of the 2008 financial crisis, no less—and his tenure was so successful that, in 2015 when he shared with the Hyatt board that he did not want to stay past his "due date," the board informed him they did not see any evidence of him approaching such a date. Hoplamazian continued to lead the company through transformative growth, including Hyatt's largest acquisition, Apple Leisure Group, in 2021.

One important benefit of outreach work is that it makes all the hard work more meaningful. It makes the impact of your moves on the daily lives of so many people palpable. "My most powerful motivator," said Enbridge CEO Greg Ebel, "was the five times a year being in the field for several days, if not a week, of going around to different locations and meeting with rank-and-file employees. You feel the awesome responsibility you have. I would tell myself, I cannot screw it up for these people. Each one of them is building their own castle, whatever that is, whether it's a playhouse in the backyard for their kid or a brand-new car."

Ebel's routine of five annual field visits speaks to how important it is to do this deep and broad discovery work not only in the early days but also throughout your tenure. The time has proven so valuable that many leaders incorporate various listening and observing practices into their ongoing agendas. Chris Nassetta said, "I am talking to customers and our team at all levels all over the world all the time to make sure that I'm learning and understanding what's going on inside our business. I spend as much time with team members on the front lines in a hotel as I do with the corporate people. Probably even more with the frontline team." Many also implement regular opportunities for exchanges with employees. Terry Lundgren, for example, scheduled a monthly breakfast with fifteen Macy's employees to discuss issues they were concerned about and to give them the opportunity to ask him questions. He found these sessions so valuable that he extended them from thirty minutes to an hour.[25]

By establishing a set of ongoing listening practices in your first year, you build trust that you're not just putting on a show of wanting input. Over time, as people see you acting on their input, you will encourage leading by listening throughout the organization.

PARTNERING WITH THE BOARD

Building strong relationships with your board members is another top priority of a new CEO. Yes, you've gone through an intensive interview process with them, and they've just selected you. But in the words of one CEO: "You won't know if you were selected by an inch or a mile." Some directors may disagree with your vision and plans; some may even be dead set against you, but won't share those sentiments with you.

The complexity of board relations and regrets about managing them were hot-button topics in our interviews. Many lamented not working harder early on to get to know directors. David Steiner, former CEO of Waste Management, cautioned, "You ignore board members at your peril. I underinvested in board relations because I did not have the operating model or the mental and emotional energy to focus on the board. But if you are not invested in the board, they may begin to behave differently, and meetings will become like the lion's den."

It goes without saying that strong support from the board for key moves, especially when they involve significant change, is imperative. "My experience," Darren Walker, CEO of the Ford Foundation, said, "is that boards will say, 'Yes, we want change.' And then when change starts to happen and blowback occurs, the CEO has to be able to say, 'Remember, we agreed that this is what change would look like.'"

Cheryl Grisé stressed the importance of quickly getting clarity about board buy-in. "What I tell every CEO is, 'You don't want to be out on a limb by yourself. You want to make sure that you and the board are in alignment, particularly in these early days.'" The amount of time needed to build alignment varies considerably because, as Ann Hackett, a director for Capital One and Fortune Brands Innovations, highlighted, "there are very big differences between boards." In David Novak's case, he recalled that "our chairman put together a great board, everyone was accomplished, and I had their full support." But another CEO described intensely challenging board meetings: "The board was not collegial. Not because they didn't like me, it just wasn't their style. Their style was to be critical, which I think was helpful. But at the same time, it made board meetings terribly unpleasant."

Boards are like a team of star performers. Directors are appointed because they're highly accomplished. Most have been successful executives. All have a depth of leadership experience. Directors are also selected because they have expertise the company needs. They have strong views about where the company should be heading and what's going well and what's going wrong. They can be of enormous assistance. But they can also be agitators against the CEO. Or the CEO might have the opposite problem, a board that is far too passive, that does not engage deeply enough in company issues and strategy setting or that focuses too much on narrower governance functions of financial oversight.

Board relations is another area where the new CEO can do deep discovery work to find out how the board operates. The "social system" of each board is greatly complex. Particularly tricky are boards in which directors have been working together for many years, with some in their seats for over a decade. They've had many debates among themselves and disagreements about all manner of issues. They have strong opinions about the prior leadership of the company. Often a few key influencers act like a board within a board. Or there may be factions that are at cross-purposes. The chair or lead director, who's charged with acting as the primary liaison to the CEO and developing meeting agendas, among other responsibilities, may or may not be the lead influencer. One director recalled, "I've seen situations where the chair or lead director has been passive. Then, other board members try to step into the void and it gets messy. You know, each board is its own little psychosocial drama." In one case, a board was divided into factions over what the company's top priority should be and, accordingly, what expertise a new CEO should have. One group was pushing for digital transformation, and it supported a candidate with great credentials in that area. The other group wanted someone with really strong brand-development experience. They split their votes, and the candidate with digital expertise just barely edged out the other. But the new CEO was not able to win the support of those who'd voted against him, and he was ultimately forced out during his second year.

When you step in as CEO, you'll know little to nothing about these board issues. Even if you've been working with the board as

CFO or president, you will have limited exposure to how directors interact. We've seen many CEOs overestimate their understanding of how to partner with the board.

Another tricky aspect, which we'll explore in Chapter 8, is that your predecessor CEO may be sitting on the board as executive chair. Transitioning outgoing CEOs into this role has been on the rise in recent years, with the number appointed increasing by 50 percent from 2010 to 2019. The idea is that the former CEO will act as a stabilizing source of continuity and an invaluable guide for the new leader. But the presence of your predecessor can also loom large, increasing the difficulty of taking firm charge of the helm.

New CEOs can get off to a good start by spending quality one-on-one time with board members, ideally right after they have been appointed. Doing so makes the initial board meetings much less intimidating. Charles Lowrey, CEO of Prudential Financial, recalled, "Limited previous exposure to the board made me very nervous and stiff during the initial board meetings. But then I went to their hometowns and broke bread by having lunch or dinner with every one of them. That took our relationships to a completely different level. I asked lots of questions and learned about both what they were thinking about the company and who they were as people. The experience turned out to be so much more than I had expected. It was a game changer, because then when you walk in the boardroom you really know everybody."

Doing spadework learning about directors is crucial. It's best to start by talking with the chair or lead director because helping a CEO develop a good relationship with the board is part of their remit. Focus on getting a good read on this person. Then ask about each director and their history. What contributions have they made? What issues are particularly important to them? Which top three questions should you pose to directors? It's important to do this discovery early on because, further down the road, it may come across as political gamesmanship rather than genuine discovery work.

Then, when you speak with the other directors, ask them to share their observations about the company through their time on the board. They have voluminous knowledge about the history of issues the company has faced. Find out their views. They'll also have their own storehouse of knowledge about other directors' perspectives and can share valuable nuances, such as how you can best approach working with board colleagues. Outside advisers such as legal counsel, bankers, and strategy consultants are also good sources of insight about the board.

Once you're attending board meetings, you can strengthen your relationship with the group if you don't do too much talking. Instead, prompt discussion by asking directors plenty of questions. The boardroom is one room where the temptation to prove you're the smartest person in the room can be especially strong but especially off-putting.

Above all, let full transparency be your guiding principle. Piyush Gupta, for example, said, "I told the board and my management team day one that I never want to ever hear that the board was surprised by anything. So, we have completely open communication with the board and, as a consequence, I've wound up with twelve advisers, not policemen, on the board."

The peril of the board being surprised by bad news was dramatically revealed in John Flannery's ouster as GE CEO. As reported by the *Wall Street Journal*, Flannery was fired in October 2018 "after 14 months in the job as deeper problems in the conglomerate's troubled power unit blindsided the board and caused GE to warn it would miss profit and cash targets."[26] The company was forced to take a $23 billion charge against the power business despite Flannery assuring investors and analysts throughout his tenure that, as troubled as the power business was, good progress was being made in turning it around. His firing was likely the culmination of multiple factors. The stock took a terrible tumble that year, and some analysts were criticizing him for moving too slowly with the company's turnaround strategy. But the day after Flannery apprised the board of the charge, the directors met again to discuss firing him.[27]

Always be a step ahead in gathering and sharing bad news. As discussed in the next chapter, do that with the board and with investors, analysts, and, really, all stakeholders. Your workforce will also resent being blindsided, as will community leaders regarding effects on their constituents. Dave Cote tells a powerful story of getting out ahead of bad news when he started at Honeywell in 2002. "I was hit almost immediately with a bombshell: our finance team informed me that we'd have to significantly reduce our earnings commitment for the year."[28] He decided to lower the company's earnings projections, and then did so again within a few weeks when more information became available, even though, by his account, "analysts and investors already lacked confidence in me." Over time, though, as he acted so forthrightly, they developed great confidence in him.

If you've built strong relationships with directors early on and keep them well apprised of emerging difficulties, they can shield you from market pressures, such as analyst criticism or activist investors' campaigns against you. Ann Hackett highlighted, "If you can create a relationship of deep underlying investment from the board, in terms of really feeling they understand the strategy, they're deeply committed, they will be your staunchest ally."

DRAFTING THE TEAM

The other great source of support is your executive team, so be extremely rigorous in evaluating the team you inherit and deciding who to keep and who to bring on. Letting go of the people who are clearly underperforming or in disagreement with the strategy or key operational changes is relatively straightforward. The situation is more challenging and the decisions not as easy when, as one CEO recalled, "we had to get rid of people who had not failed, who had actually had some measure of success in the company, and who were widely known. But they weren't going to be right for the company going forward." Many CEOs shared that they held off replacing team members because they knew doing so would be unpopular. "I knew my first week," one said, "that my team was not up to the task. Later I kicked myself, why didn't I move faster? I didn't want to rock the boat. But I should have been more brazen."

The discomfort many CEOs feel about letting members of their team go is more than understandable. You know how hard being let go will be for them. What's more, sometimes they are colleagues you've worked with for years. You may have even spent time with them outside of work and know their families. Maybe they are well liked around the company, so you worry that their allies may react badly or follow a leader out the door. In addition, evaluating whether a person is right for a role is sometimes as much a matter of intuition as of empirical data. As mentioned, their performance by the numbers may be solid, but they may lack the skills needed for the growth plan you're implementing. A CFO, for example, may not have the experience with digital transformation that you need. Meanwhile, in replacing them with someone who does have that experience, you're making a bet that the new person will perform well. What if they don't? Your decision will become a mark against you.

In wrestling with these concerns, it's important to keep in mind that many key stakeholders will respect such tough decisions. Pat Kampling, who led Alliant Energy Corporation, told us, "I didn't want the reputation of being the hatchet person. But it turned out that the personnel changes I made early on gave me more credibility in the organization because people knew I'd take action on personnel problems, whereas in the past things moved slowly." Difficult changes can also score you points with the board, which is often aware of the need for them. When a new CEO let several of the executive team go immediately, one director said, "He made all those tough decisions and the board was thrilled."

One pitfall of making changes is that new CEOs potentially shake up their teams more than is optimal because they want to work with like-minded people. "I have seen a lot of good leaders who surrounded themselves with people who they were comfortable with or thought like them," Susan Story, CEO of American Water, cautioned, "and it significantly reduced their effectiveness."

Once you have built a strong team, you will have to relinquish considerable control to them—more than is comfortable for many new CEOs. Tim Guertin recalled what a challenge this was. He had greatly enjoyed the hands-on work of running one of Varian's businesses, being directly involved in designing new medical equipment that would help patients. Varian specializes in cancer therapy devices, and he found the company's focus deeply meaningful. He also loved working closely with customers. The shift in his responsibilities when he became CEO was very discomforting at first. He told us that about two or three months after he became CEO, "I went to see the chairman, who had been the CEO before me, and I said, 'I don't feel like I'm adding value.' He started laughing and asked me, 'Why do you feel that way?' I said, 'Well, because I'm used to running a business. I was making decisions about what projects to invest in, what products to do, what service lines to add. I was talking to customers all the time. I was invited into sales opportunities. Now that's all gone. The business unit heads do that.'" The chairman responded, "That's the trick. You don't have to get involved in those business unit decisions like you did before. You have to give up doing things that you've spent your whole career learning to do."

Otherwise, you will not only undermine the authority of those who are responsible for running the businesses but also run yourself ragged. With a strong team in place, you can, and should, focus on a few key responsibilities that only you can take the lead on. One is to clearly and powerfully articulate your enterprise vision.

INSPIRING HEARTS AND MINDS

Even CEOs who take over a well-established and effective strategy for the company must articulate their own powerful statement about the course they are setting. For those coming into a turnaround situation, the urgency of doing so is obvious. But optimizing your effectiveness in this crucial Launch stage requires inspiring followership throughout the organization, at all levels. That, in turn, depends on crafting motivating and memorable communication of your distinctive enterprise vision and, ideally, expressing it in a short and highly impactful phrase.

Crafting this statement is inspiring and energizing, forcing a highly concentrated consideration of the core purpose around which you want to rally the whole organization. The more compelling the statement is, the more readily this direction setting will cascade throughout the organization.

Ajay Banga masterfully crafted a powerful enterprise vision for Mastercard. He had not formulated a strategic plan for the company before taking the helm. But within the first three months in the job, having done a great deal of discovery work, he gained clarity about a deeply motivating purpose he would align the company around: financial inclusion. He became impassioned about Mastercard setting its sights on bringing access to capital to the two billion adults around the globe who were unable to open bank accounts or obtain credit cards, which excluded them from the formal economy.

His realization of the massive potential of this mission grew out of his experience spearheading the microfinance business at Citigroup. He'd also seen that, despite the ubiquity of credit cards in some parts of the world, cash still accounted for 85 percent of all transactions, and cash facilitates illegal economic operations, such as drug dealing. He calculated that even in the developed US economy this market activity accounted for a quarter of transactions. What ignited his excitement about Mastercard's potential was that by making financial inclusion fundamental to the business, "my entire balance sheet and my entire technology, all my people will view this as something they want to do." He articulated a powerful vision, summarized by the simple and forceful phrase "Killing cash." "That," he shared, "was the holy grail that got unlocked," propelling the explosive results he achieved.

Many other CEOs affirmed how important crafting a punchy and potent statement of vision was to their success. When Larry Merlo took over at CVS, the company had produced both a mission statement and a vision statement, each several paragraphs long, and neither at all inspiring. He pulled a group of leaders together and they hashed out one powerful phrase: "Helping people on the path to better health." He knew how well the message was working when one day he saw a CVS store employee help an elderly woman to her car. When Merlo called out to say kudos to the employee, he responded, "This is my way of helping people on the path to better health." Vision statements done right can be extraordinarily powerful.

This set of priorities for a CEO's first year is incredibly demanding. But doing all this early spadework is so important to flourishing as you move forward. The more effectively you engage in the Launch stage, the better prepared you will be for the distinctive challenges of the next stage.

3

CALIBRATION

*"Market sentiment is seldom
reflective of reality."*

The phenomenon of the sophomore slump is common in the music world, with critics often judging a second album as disappointing after a fabulous debut release. The Who, The Police, and Jay-Z all fell victim. In fact, a study of *Rolling Stone*'s list of the one hundred best debut albums showed that 66.25 percent of groups' second albums fell victim to the slump.[1]

In sports, players with exceptional first-year performance often slump in year two. One study found that out of the twelve Rookies of the Year in baseball from 2010 to 2018, nine slumped badly. Cody Bellinger had "a monster season" for his debut with the Los Angeles Dodgers in 2017.[2] His hitting was so impressive that, as one reporter wrote, "He was so feared at the plate that he led all of baseball in intentional walks."[3] That year, he hit thirty-nine home runs and had ninety-seven runs batted in, but the next year those numbers slid to fifteen and twenty-eight. At one point, he'd connected for only five hits in fifty-three at-bats.[4] Ouch.

The term *sophomore slump* originated with the performance of college students. Many lose enthusiasm or even fall into a deep malaise in their second year. Often, that leads to sinking grades or dropping out. The severity of the slump seems partly to result from how lavishly "you are feted as a freshman."[5] Some hard reality setting in is also at play, such as realizing your ability or inability to do the work or discovering you actually dislike courses in a field you've expected to major in. One professor reflected, "We enter college with all of these dreams about what we're going to be, and we have to put some of those to rest in the second year."[6] Many CEOs know the feeling all too well.

Of course, just as with many college students, an individual CEO may have a sophomore year of great performance. But even so, this year generally presents distinctive and very difficult challenges. One is that the bloom is off the rose, so to speak. The first year's tailwinds of enthusiasm abate, and board directors, analysts, and investors become more intent on seeing tangible results. They often want to see improvements at a faster clip, and that may be true even if results are quite good. When results are lagging, the blowback can be fierce. If the share price shot up honeymoon style the year before, a dramatic slump often ensues. And if that occurs, the second year may be quite a rocky ride.

Recall that our CEO Life Cycle analysis found that three out of four (73 percent) CEOs with a successful start that beat the market in year one did worse in year two. On average, the dip in TSR was a whopping 21 percent, underscoring that a slump should be taken very seriously. That said, it's also important to keep a clear head about why share price is being battered. Often, the slide—as with the honeymoon spike—is a market overreaction. Analysts and investors often overshoot in punishing shares, mainly due to sentiment rather than the facts of performance and company initiatives being undertaken. A strong indication that market overreaction is at play, rather than company results, is that, for the average CEO in our data, many of the key metrics remained stable between years one and two. Revenue continued to grow, profitability margins remained steady, and return on invested capital slightly increased. Yet for many, share price fell.

Other times, the adjustment is a slowing of growth rather than a reversal. That was true for Carol Tomé. UPS continued to beat or exceed its guidance every quarter of her sophomore year. Nonetheless, the growth in share price nearly stopped dead, falling from 104 percent to 1.8 percent. While that still bested the S&P, which slid 6 percent, it was clear that market enthusiasm had cooled.

During the Calibration stage, perception is still out of alignment with reality. Those experiencing a sophomore slump in any field should take heart because slumps are usually quickly reversed. Dodger Cody Bellinger, for example, boomed back from his 2018 slump to be named National League Most Valuable Player in 2019 and to win a World Series ring the next year.[7] The Who, The Police, and Jay-Z, of course, not only went on to put out many platinum albums but also were inducted into the Rock and Roll Hall of Fame.

So, too, for many CEOs who experience a slump. Consider the case of Jim Craigie and his tenure at the helm of consumer-goods stalwart Church & Dwight, owner of the flagship Arm & Hammer brand. He'd demonstrated his talent for revitalizing leading brands at Kraft, turning around the fortunes of two icons: Jell-O pudding and Maxwell House coffee.[8] When he took over at Church & Dwight in 2004, he was viewed as a good pick, and he enjoyed a strong honeymoon spike. Shares rose 27.5 percent, against a 6 percent lift for rival Procter & Gamble and a 13 percent downturn for Colgate Palmolive. In his second year, he oversaw many successful moves. One was exercising an option to purchase full control of a joint venture that brought in substantial new and highly profitable revenue. Some great innovative products were launched, such as the first enamel-repairing toothpaste.[9] Profits steadily surged that year, ultimately by 24 percent, and net income rose nicely, as did earnings per share, both somewhat exceeding analyst expectations. In short, the company was thriving. Yet, the share price boost stopped dead and then reversed course. Meanwhile, share price rose for both P&G and Colgate.

By the next year, with continued strong results and smart acquisitions, the Church & Dwight share price went on a new tear, rising 39 percent. That also again handily outperformed both the key competitors. One headline cooed, "Forget Gold; Take a Look at Church & Dwight."[10] Craigie racked up ten more years of remarkably consistent growth, and along the way, as he recalled, "we became darlings of Wall Street." Indeed, in 2022, contrasting the poor performance of Colgate and P&G vis-à-vis the stellar results of Church & Dwight in recent years, one analyst wrote that, of the three, "only Church & Dwight has managed to increase its returns thanks to ex-CEO Jim Craigie's exceptional leadership."[11]

Our analysis shows that many of the CEOs widely regarded as among the most successful in the past two decades saw the stark swing from honeymoon to sophomore slump. That includes Hubert Joly, credited with taking Best Buy through a brilliant turnaround.

When he took charge in September 2012, the company was facing what he described as an "all-you-can-eat menu" of problems.[12] Amazon was a black hole sucking away market share. Many analysts predicted it would crush Best Buy. Meanwhile, Apple, Microsoft, and Sony were opening their own retail stores, which Joly recalled "could have become lethal."[13] Profits had dropped 91 percent in the prior quarter.[14] He had to move fast.

Two months into the job, he introduced a detailed turnaround plan, Renew Blue. It included major investment in improving both online sales and store sales. A key component of the strategy was improving the in-store experience, which was dismal. A focus was creating "mini-stores" within the stores in partnerships with the major electronics brands.[15] Joly quickly made a deal with Samsung, and by the end of his first year, the company had opened 1,400 Samsung mini-stores. It had also installed 600 Windows stores. In parallel, the company advanced the transformation of its online platform, improved its price competitiveness, increased its Net Promoter Score by more than 300 points, and reduced costs by $765 million.[16] In a striking example of a honeymoon lift, the share price went from a low of $11 in November 2012 to about $40 at the end of 2013.

Then in January 2014, the share price cratered by a third in one day after the company reported it had missed its sales target during the holiday season.[17] A difficult holiday sales period—which the competition experienced as well—shook market confidence in the turnaround. That was despite the fact that Best Buy actually gained market share in the period. As his second year progressed, press reports changed their tune from "Best Buy charges ahead"[18] to Best Buy "claims to have made significant progress."[19] Meanwhile, the Renew Blue strategy produced more signs of working. Pivotal was that by the end of Joly's second year, in-store sales had begun increasing. The big bet on enhancing store experience was paying off. Revenues spiked nicely, and profits doubled in the last quarter. Analysts began their questions on the earnings call that month with "Congratulations." One headline cheered, "Best Buy Tells Amazon: Take That!"[20] But, although the share price recovered after the January 2014 dip, the company had to wait until the latter part of 2016 for the share price to exceed its 2013 high.

Perception and reality were beginning to align.

DON'T OVERREACT TO OVERREACTION

Analysts' and investors' tougher questioning about results you're producing can raise your hackles. Some are like pit bulls with a particular concern, pressing relentlessly for answers in each earnings call. When they press to see immediate results, they're often showing a lack of understanding about the time required to produce those results. Few, if any, have experience actually leading the kinds of performance initiatives they're judging. Laurie Siegel, director for Century Link and FactSet, highlighted that "it's easy from the outside to underestimate the time it takes to pursue some of these value creation paths."

What's often not adequately considered is that getting results with low-hanging fruit in the first year—cutting costs, implementing familiar operational efficiencies—is so much easier than driving top-line growth initiatives. This makes a CEO's second year a juncture when the market's pressure for short-term gains is especially fraught.

One director reflected pointedly on market impatience. The company's CEO was experiencing a slump at the time, even though a turnaround process was progressing well. "I think market sentiment is seldom reflective of reality," she shared. "Right now, there's an emotional discount to our stock. As we deliver to customers, as the results materialize versus being our rhetoric, that emotional value discount will disappear." She also put her finger on a key reason for the discounting: investors and analysts aren't privy to information about the company that the CEO and the board have. "They know what they know based on our publicly filed information. I sit in the boardroom and I have access to information they don't have."

Sometimes that inside information can't be shared for competitive reasons, to the frustration of many. Tim Guertin, for example, recalled having a groundbreaking new piece of medical equipment in development at Varian when he took over that he couldn't talk about until three years later when it was ready for launch. "You know there is a great story to tell," he said, "but you just can't tell it." He took a beating from the market, and then the share price soared when that product was released.

Although extremely clear and compelling communication about results is always imperative, it's especially important as recalibration unfolds. Actual results are, of course, paramount in assessing performance. But the *perception* of those results and of whether the CEO and leadership team are on top of the situation is at least as important.

Nothing is more vital to managing fallout when under fire than respectful transparency, no matter how off-base or lacerating critics may be. The arrogance of some market players can be staggering. Indra Nooyi received a tsunami of market criticism when she presented her strategy for growing PepsiCo's repertoire of healthier foods, which she dubbed Performance with Purpose. "The most memorable comment," she reflected, "came from a portfolio manager in Boston. 'Who do you think you are?' he asked me, 'Mother Teresa?'"[21] Nooyi refused to take the bait, instead restating her case that the public was demanding healthier products and this was a huge potential growth area for PepsiCo.

Defensiveness or dismissiveness will get you nowhere. The best response to tough questions is to express appreciation, a response that jumps out in the earnings calls of high performers who weathered this period particularly well. "I appreciate the question" is a steady refrain. They treat being asked a tough question as a great opportunity for demonstrating how well they've assessed and addressed issues. Key here is answering with detailed responses that clarify the logic behind the company's decision-making or the reasons for a different assessment of results. Earnings call transcripts for public companies are available online, and they are brimming with examples of deft market management. We recommend any aspiring CEO dive into them. A great place to start would be with listening in on Hubert Joly, who stands out as one master of the craft. For example, on the earnings call for the third quarter of 2013, in November, just over a year into the turnaround, with sales still lagging, one analyst asked him the following:

> You've talked a lot about what's working. Could you talk about some areas possibly where you feel that you've been a little slower, things are running a little bit behind, and what you're doing to deal with that?

In a long response—much too long to include all of it here—Joly didn't try to downplay areas where progress was sluggish but instead forthrightly acknowledged them while also reaffirming that the company was on the case. One was the revamping of the company website, about which he said:

> Candidly, there's a lot of obsession on how to further drive this, drive the customer experience on the site in a very meaningful way. How we address certain customer segments, think about millennials, think about buying occasions. As an example, we don't have a registry as a retailer. We're probably the only one who does not. So, I think that we are very pleased and proud of the progress we've made, but there's so much more to come.

DEEPEN BOARD RELATIONS

Continuing to build your relationships with directors is crucial to maintaining their support as you go through a slump. So many CEOs are ousted because boards have lost confidence in them, and often the seeds of doubt have been sown in this period when perceptions outweigh fundamentals. Of course, sometimes the loss of confidence is merited. But, as Jeffrey Sonnenfeld, who runs leadership programs for CEOs, says, there are also times when boards "go for the symbolism of sacrificing a CEO. Many, many good people have been forced from office."[22]

Transparency about problems encountered is vital. Mahesh Madhavan, CEO of Bacardi, reminded us that "when you talk about confidence in your leadership, it does not happen in the first ninety days or in the first year. It happens over multiple interactions. It happens through the way you and the team around you interact. Remember, the board is not involved in the business day-to-day. . . . It takes years to build confidence and only a moment to break. So it takes courage, consistency of performance, and ability to be transparent no matter how bad the news is to maintain that trust and confidence."

Directors need to know that you're on top of the near-term problems. They're under enormous pressure to ensure shareholder interests are being served. But it's also important to convey that you're not getting caught up in the weeds of short-term issues. Bill Kennard, who served as director for AT&T, Ford Motor Company, and MetLife, cautioned about communicating with the board: "If you tell a story, quarter to quarter, you die by it. You need to put results into a larger picture." Director Ann Hackett also highlighted that "a board is charged with long-term value creation" and that when the CEO–board relationship is working best, directors along with the CEO take ownership of problems being confronted and the solutions pursued.

To get the PepsiCo directors solidly behind her long-term strategy of growing Pepsi's healthy foods offerings, Indra Nooyi wrote a long memo outlining the extensive research undertaken by several senior executives in the company, with the help of outside consultants. This memo covered the "megatrends" that would be influencing consumer behavior in the coming decades. One was a continuing shift toward healthier eating. She met with each director to discuss the memo and answer all their questions about the strategy in sessions that went for two or three hours, and she recounted, "They were all extremely engaged, and from then on out, I felt the board's support."[23]

As Nooyi did, deepening your partnership involves going well beyond just reporting to the board at meetings. Ann Hackett advises really engaging directors in ongoing problem-solving. "A CEO should share their biggest challenges and want the board's thinking about them." She's seen some make the mistake of thinking "they have to have solved everything, and they shouldn't bring problems to the board." But for the relationship to work optimally, "you have to be able to go to deep places and challenge one another." You want to be doing all you can to ensure that the board is, as she put it, "a learning organism." She recommends regularly providing them high-quality information about what the company, and the industry, is facing. Also help them "get close to the business and customers," which a CEO can facilitate in many ways, such as by setting up factory visits or meetings with members of the management team. If you do this extra work, she advises, "then a board thinks differently about everything they're doing. Governance becomes more strategic. Risk becomes more strategic." This creates "a relationship of deep underlying investment from the board"—not only in the strategic agenda but also in you.

Steve Cooper, who took charge of workforce solutions firm TrueBlue in 2006, had an extremely difficult sophomore year. The 2007–2008 financial crisis hit, and the business was pummeled. The share price tanked. He told us that what got him safely through the turmoil was working hard to keep building his relationships with board members. "It took a lot of outreach," he recalled. "I did one-on-ones with board members, not just board meetings. I went to all of them, on their turf, and I did it twice a year. I would be out with one or two of them every quarter. That was one of the most valuable things I did those first two to three years."

We've found that apprising boards of our findings about the common honeymoon-to-slump pattern has also been helpful. In one instance, we were advising the board of a Fortune 50 company. The freshman-year CEO was enjoying a huge spike in share value. The board had selected her because of her long experience in executive roles in the company's industry, and the market agreed with the board's enthusiasm. The board was over the moon about the response. But having seen the high likelihood of a honeymoon-to-slump pattern in our modeling for this firm, we advised the board that they should expect a correction. When, sure enough, the share price dropped precipitously starting early in her year two, the board credited it to the predicted swing back from a honeymoon lift and didn't turn up the heat on her as they might have. She's gone on to thrive for five more years in the role, and counting.

INTUITION WELL-INFORMED

The market so often over- and undershoots in valuations because evaluating company performance is anything but straightforward. Even state-of-the-art analytics can only produce lagging or leading indicators. Market conditions are always in flux, often in ways that are as yet indiscernible. Although numbers may not lie, there are truths of which they may not speak. They can sometimes clarify with exquisite accuracy what transpired in the last quarter. Their read on the current moment will be imperfect. And when it comes to the next quarter, you're in uncharted territory. Commodity price swings, interest rate spikes, disastrous weather, sometimes of unprecedented nature—the list of unknowables is long and always growing.

The best models will always fail at some point. CEOs must combine information with intuition in decision-making. They must deploy *informed intuition*. This is not simply going with one's gut. A good definition of informed intuition is "the process of blending existing information and data with one's experiences, educated assumptions, and instincts to arrive at a logical conclusion."[24] Relying on it is always important, but it becomes even more so in the second year, as you're moving further out from the initial assessment of your strategic agenda. Informed intuition also requires taking the people component into account. Call it the social side of strategy: marrying the people and performance components. Numbers and analysis and logic only get you so far when you are in the fog of war.

Of course, making good decisions with informed intuition is much easier said than done. Yet many of the CEOs we interviewed shared stories of using informed intuition masterfully.

George Paz shared a great one. When he was appointed CEO of Express Scripts, he was chosen largely because of his success with acquisitions as the company's CFO. "When I came in," he told us, "I had a lot of experience in mergers and acquisitions. Express Scripts was a small company. Nobody had ever heard of us." Within his first year as CFO, he led two acquisitions, which quadrupled the size of the firm. "It took us from being an itty-bitty, little company," he recalled, "to joining the Fortune 500."

As CEO, he continued on the acquisitions roll. Within three months, he made a deal to acquire Priority Health, a smart move that contributed to the strong honeymoon share spike he enjoyed. Then he set his sights on Caremark. This was big-game hunting.

Caremark was much larger than Express Scripts and the number two competitor in the sector. The purchase would vault Express Scripts beyond market leader Medco. Paz moved boldly, making a hostile bid. Several months prior, Caremark had come to an agreement with CVS for a purchase. Paz thought the price drastically undervalued Caremark. "CVS was getting the company for a prayer. For nothing. It drove me crazy," he shared. "I worked hard to convince my board that we should be the buyer." He had a great deal on the line.

Then he had to come up with his offer. Rather than rely on number crunching alone, he came up with a great way of marshaling informed intuition. He assembled his executive team to make a final judgment about the bid. "We were at the lawyers' office. The bankers were in the room. We were going to announce our offer at six o'clock in the morning." Discussions extended throughout the night. "At two in the morning, we were all sitting around a table and I asked everybody to write down what they thought Caremark was worth on a blank piece of paper. I also wrote my number down. Then I went up to the whiteboard and wrote all the numbers down but mine. It was a pretty big array of figures. And I said to them, 'Okay, let's talk,' and after another hour and a half, we came to a number, and I never did turn over my own paper. I never said what my number was. Everybody on that team owned that number." It was aggressive: the CVS deal had valued Caremark at $21 billion. Paz and his team offered $26 billion. Then the games began.

CVS raised its offered price. Both companies lobbied with major Caremark shareholders. Months went by. Finally, "a consortium of the shareholders got me on the phone," Paz said. If he would raise the Express Scripts bid by one dollar per share, they'd force acceptance of the offer, they said. "So, I'm not naive. CVS could raise their price again too. I went back to my group, got them all together in a conference room again, and asked, 'What do you think about this?'"

About half of them wanted to give the extra dollar. Paz then said, "Let's put up that original number and talk about all that's happened." They discussed positives and negatives for quite a while. "I had the guys that really knew how to do finance put numbers on it." He was determined: "If it wasn't worth more, we weren't going to bid more just for the sake of trying to win. We weren't going to be emotional." Ultimately, he decided not to raise their bid. CVS prevailed.

Excruciating as the outcome was, Paz told us, "I'll be honest with you, it was one of the best things that ever happened to us because they had a tough go of it." Indeed, Larry Merlo, who took over the task of integrating Caremark into CVS when he became CEO of CVS several years after the acquisition, recounted just how tough making the merger work was. By reining in their emotions, Paz and his team avoided a common trap of bidding for acquisitions: convincing themselves that they could reap more gains through synergies in integrating the companies than they'd initially estimated. Unrealized synergies are a major reason that so many mergers fail. Paz recalled, "We had that discipline of not going above the price as adjusted by what we knew. You could go over the price, but only by what you knew, and not what you conjured up or thought you knew." A better example of using informed intuition would be hard to find. Paz's skill at leading with informed intuition stood Express Scripts in good stead, to underplay the results he achieved. During his eleven-year tenure, he led growth from a $6 billion valuation to $46 billion, and the rise in stock price beat the S&P 500 during that time by 500 percent.

Rigorous data analytics should inform intuitive thinking. Shantanu Narayen, for example, stressed its role in his decision to move

Adobe to cloud-based service. The process involved "a lot of discipline," he said. "We ran pilots in some countries. We got feedback. People give us credit for bold decisions. But we put in a lot of work."[25] Yet, when asked how he evolved as a CEO, he said, "I got much more comfortable with pattern matching." Discerning a pattern you've seen before in a new situation is one of the signature abilities of informed intuition. But spotting patterns, as Narayen cautioned, can be "both a plus and a minus." Doing it well requires building up a robust mental archive of patterns seen through time. With that strong repertoire, pattern matching can be remarkably powerful. Without that archive, it can go badly awry. But even with good experience, it's easy to fall into the trap of confirmation bias—seeing a pattern because you expect it to be there. It's essential to rigorously challenge your intuitions.

Narayen emphasized that to ensure you're both listening to your intuition and checking it, it's important to create a process for combining your informed intuition with that of others, as Paz did. "You should make that a structured approach," Narayen advised. "I include my team in every decision. Sometimes, they wonder 'why did you invite me in for this?' But I know I need their input. I will go around the room and have everybody weigh in with their point of view. Allowing people to do that is amazing. Sometimes it's the people who are perhaps the least vocal who have the most insight."

Of course, with major decisions, ultimately the CEO must make the call. Once it's come down to you, and you know what you want to do, a great practice is to impose a wait time on yourself. Dave Cote made a rule for himself about this. He forced himself to wait three days after a long meeting to discuss the decision with his team. "We had an opportunity to sell an underperforming business. . . . Although we would be selling at a $50 million loss . . . I gave the deal my blessing." But having become aware of his tendency to make decisions too quickly, he decided to hold off and reconvene his team for another discussion. Even though they had "been through the deal exhaustively" before, that new meeting revealed some new information, which made clear that Honeywell would actually be losing $75 million in the deal. He decided to back out. Then, several months later, he was able to sell the business to that same buyer with only a $50 million loss. He'd saved Honeywell $25 million. After that, Cote applied the "wait three days" rule in many other ways.[26]

Using time to gain some distance is one of four key steps in a simple but powerful decision-making framework called WRAP. In their book *Decisive*, Chip Heath and Dan Heath introduce this method of making decisions with informed intuition:[27]

Widen your options.

Reality-test your assumptions.

Attain distance before deciding.

Prepare to be wrong.

KEEP GETTING OUT IN THE FIELD

Strong informed intuition requires that qualitative observation complement data. Even the best data analytics can't provide the insights that observation yields. CEOs have to keep doing fieldwork.

In 2016, Rear Admiral Michael White, the head of training for the US Navy, reintroduced a class in celestial navigation. In this era of GPS, who would think this ancient technology would be necessary? Yet, GPS is vulnerable to "spoofing," a type of cyberattack when a radio transmission throws satellite signals off-track with falsified information. In fact, anyone can buy a GPS jammer on the internet. Satellites can also be shot down with missiles. But the possibility of system failure is only one reason Admiral White reinstated the training. Navigating by stars teaches vital fundamentals of developing a reliable sense of where you are, of whether you're heading north, south, east, or west. He cautions that relying solely on modern technology is like "blindly following the navigation system in your car"—"it takes you to places you didn't intend to go."[28]

Getting out of the C-suite down into the company and out into the field pays great dividends and allows you to see and hear for yourself how moves are unfolding. Frontline employees may have a very different view from what's included in the assessments being shared with your team. All sorts of discoveries about how products and services can be improved can result. Indra Nooyi got "out in the marketplace almost every week."[29] She was a great anthropologist. One day, she even spent some time sitting in a car in the parking lot of a Publix store with the head of Pepsi's American Foods division. She wanted to watch shoppers enter and exit, and her observations led her to a great insight. She made note that many elderly shoppers would stop to chat with one another. "Shopping was clearly a happy occasion for them," she recounts. Then inside the store, she had a major realization. The Pepsi soda and Aquafina bottles were all being sold in twenty-four-pack cases. How could those elderly people load those into their cars? She subsequently sent a team of product people to the MIT AgeLab, which specializes in working with organizations to improve elders' quality of life, such as through product engineering sensitive to their needs. The Pepsi team came back with many ideas, which they used to redesign product features, such as making twist-off drink bottles easier to open.[30] Nooyi was brilliantly combining her intuition with expert information.

CALIBRATING THE PACE OF CHANGE

By their sophomore year, CEOs have learned a great deal about the organization's ability to execute the strategic agenda. A major imperative at this juncture is assessing whether you're pushing change at the right pace. The market exerts enormous pressure on companies to show results faster than might be feasible. In fact, moving too slowly is cited as a main reason CEOs are ousted within their first few years. Succumbing to the pressure can lead to making moves too quickly, and debacles may result. CEOs must work hard to determine the correct speed of change. Pat Kampling of Alliant Energy cautioned, "An organization has a pace. The CEO can't be outrunning that." Shantanu Narayen highlighted, "You have a cadence of execution in a company." If you've been with the company for some time, you may have a good understanding of that cadence. If you've joined from outside, developing that knowledge is vital. And those with long experience in the organization won't have this awareness about some teams or whole divisions and must develop it.

Carefully calibrating expectations according to the type of change initiative is also important. Some types of operational improvements can be done rapid-fire, but others should be more gradually implemented. Dave Cote recalls learning this about manufacturing-process improvements. "One of my greatest regrets from my time at Honeywell concerns how we implemented Six Sigma."[31] He reflected, "I rolled out the program too quickly and hadn't refined how we presented it to workers and managers so that their mindset would change. . . . We were a mile wide in how much training we had delivered." The company had invested a great deal in the implementation but saw mediocre results. He corrected for the mistake a few years later, more gradually phasing in the adoption of the Honeywell Operating System, "a comprehensive system for operating our plants," which produced powerful results.[32] He recounted, "Go slow to go fast became our mantra when it came to process change."[33]

Whereas tensions over the speed of change will flare up periodically through the course of your tenure, the sophomore year tends to be rife with them. Investors and analysts are breathing down your neck to see clear indications of progress. Within the organization, stresses almost certainly will emerge.

Darren Walker has instituted bold new programs and strategic initiatives at the Ford Foundation at a cadence of about one a year. He described how big change initiatives "cascade across the entire organization." One of his most innovative and daring moves was issuing the first "social bond" in 2020, which the *Wall Street Journal* named the innovation of the year. The foundation's charter restricts it from soliciting donations to add to its many-billion-dollar endowment. As the COVID pandemic began raging, Walker wanted to find some other way to greatly increase the $500 million to $600 million its endowment allows it to distribute for social assistance causes every year.[34]

He drew on his earlier career experience as an equity salesman for UBS and convinced Morgan Stanley and Wells Fargo to offer thirty- and fifty-year bonds, which raised $1 billion in one hour on the market. That money allowed him to double the distribution of Ford funds. What he said he hadn't fully appreciated were the effects on staff. "We were going to give away not $500 million, but a billion dollars a year for two years. That meant the lawyers were reviewing many more legal documents, the grant managers who had a portfolio of thirty grants now had a portfolio of fifty grants. And I wasn't saying go hire more lawyers and more grant managers." He wanted to keep costs down. "That was exhausting for them," he reflected. When he announced at a company meeting in 2022 that he would not institute any big change initiative in 2023, the staff burst out in applause. That made a powerful impression on him, helping him to appreciate just how taxing his continuous push for change had been.

The story has another takeaway, though. Sometimes there are very good reasons for pushing your organization to the max. That additional $1 billion of funding that Ford distributed during the height of the COVID crisis was surely of great importance and the first of its kind. Walker even convinced other foundations to follow the practice and raise additional funds, thereby scaling the initiative to provide badly needed help at the time. As was true in this case, pushing people right up to or—for a time—past their max may sometimes be called for.

Clearly, calibrating the cadence of change is a complex calculus. It must be highly sensitive not only to the demands of investors but also to the needs of customers, employees, and external stakeholder groups.

PROTECT YOUR FLANK

In warfare, one of the biggest blunders is exposing one's flank in the process of leading an attack. This can be a grave danger in business transformations too.

As change initiatives are implemented, it's vital to shore up revenue from existing operations. When Randy Hogan took over at Pentair in 2001, he quickly set forth a strategy of getting out of the power tools business, which was a large component of Pentair's revenues, and getting into manufacturing water filtration systems. That "was a much more attractive business," he explained, "with more stable returns and better growth prospects, where we could control our own destiny." But he held off selling the power tools division for three years. Analysts were pushing for the sale, but he made a strong case for his strategy, and the market listened. Share price grew at a good clip of 65 percent over his first three years.

Meanwhile, he directed improvements in the tools business so that by the time he put it up for sale, "we were actually doing well," he recalls. That helped him make a good deal when he sold it, freeing him to buy a water company that doubled those operations. The market sent the share price soaring 93 percent for that year.

Another CEO who handled this balancing act well is Chuck Robbins of Cisco. Taking charge as the successor to John Chambers, who served as CEO for twenty years, was never going to be a cake walk. Chambers was considered a business legend, having grown Cisco from four hundred employees to seventy thousand, with annual sales exploding from $70 million to $47 billion a year.[35]

As a leapfrog appointment who'd beaten out two well-known company leaders, Robbins confronted a complex challenge, especially because Chambers stayed on the board as executive chair for two years, and his presence loomed large in the company. Some members of Chambers' executive team who'd been passed over for the job also made it clear they were opposed to Robbins assuming the role. Meanwhile, some market pundits cried foul about the Robbins pick because they thought an outsider should have been brought in to execute a major overhaul. For years, the company had been losing market share in its core computer networking business to Amazon and a number of competitors who were dwarfs in comparison to Cisco, such as F5, Inc. Cisco was characterized as a "big, old dog among technology stocks," and its share price had significantly underperformed the S&P 500 for the prior five years. "This company is fat and insular," said one chief investment officer. "It screams for change."[36]

The Cisco board, however, saw the urgency for change differently. Carol Bartz, who is on the board, told us, "Yes, the company had been flat. But it wasn't as though we were in a really bad situation." A change strategy had already been set in motion under Chambers: to build up Cisco's software business and cloud computing services to complement and eventually overtake its long-standing strength in hardware networking technology. That part of its business had been suffering in recent years. When Robbins took over, he immediately communicated loudly and clearly that "We need to move faster across every piece of our business." He emphasized again and again in communicating with analysts and investors that, while moving fast to develop new software, the company would also "continue to build massive, high-performance hardware."[37]

Robbins moved quickly out of the gate on both fronts. He replaced the heads of engineering and restructured the function, combining two groups into one and breaking down silos within them. The company launched several new hardware products his first year, along with new software services, and made fifteen acquisitions. The market responded with a strong honeymoon share boost of 21 percent, which outperformed the S&P 500 by 8 percent.

In his second year, though, he faced increasingly pressing questions from analysts about continued softness in the hardware business. The company was still seen as sluggish, underperforming the S&P 500 by 8 percent. But in year three, with better progress to be reported for both hardware and software, the stock shot up 42 percent. He'd done a great job, it turned out, of calibrating the pace of change. Underscoring how well he'd balanced efforts, he was praised for, in the words of one analyst, his "surgical allocation of resources."[38]

A striking contrast is the case of the turnaround effort at Bed Bath & Beyond. Mark Tritton was appointed CEO in late 2019 to execute an urgent turnaround. The company's fortunes had been sinking badly, with expectations that it would soon face bankruptcy. Tritton was brought in after an impressive stint as chief merchandising officer at Target. In his three years in that role, he had spearheaded the introduction of thirty private-label brands, which were integral to revitalizing Target's fortunes.[39]

Following that playbook and introducing private-label brands for Bed Bath & Beyond was a key part of his remit, along with increasing in-store sales by "decluttering" and remodeling stores.[40] Another goal was reducing reliance on coupons to attract customers. For decades the chain had sent out slews of large printed 20 percent off coupon mailers, affectionately known in the retail business as "Big Blue." It was adored by customers, largely because the coupons never expired. Customers would bring handfuls of them into stores to shop.[41] But with Amazon, Walmart, and Target competing heavily on lower prices, the chain wanted to decrease its "coupon attachment rate" and focus more on offering list prices for goods.[42]

Tritton moved with great speed. Within his first two years, he'd launched eight private-label brands and had seventy stores remodeled. He reported to analysts that they were "performing above plan."[43] After the first few months of the COVID pandemic when stores were closed, store traffic rebounded well, and as a COVID-fueled boom in the purchase of home goods ensued, the chain enjoyed a strong boost in sales. But, then, in the latter half of Tritton's second year, sales declined. Although he characterized the slide as "a disruptive moment along our multiyear transformational journey," the moment turned out to be protracted.[44] Many factors contributed to increasingly dire results for the chain, but among them was that, as reported by the *Wall Street Journal*, "Mr. Tritton ushered in changes faster than the retailer could build systems to support them."[45]

One such change was a drastic cutback on the mailing of the Big Blue coupon flyers that customers loved, especially the most loyal customers. Although the strategy was meant to drive growth in website sales by transitioning to almost exclusively online deals, website improvements he'd instituted hadn't increased traffic enough to offset the loss of sales driven by the printed coupons. Tritton admitted on an earnings call that this was "one of the critical missteps" of the turnaround efforts.[46]

Another was that many popular brand-name products were taken off store shelves to make room for the new private-label products. Tritton reported to analysts some indications that customers were liking the new brands, but sales showed they were hardly falling in love with them. Meanwhile, customers were driven away by the absence of the brands they expected to see. One store manager recalled, "My customers would look at the private label and say, 'What is this?' [When I] tried to persuade them to buy [our private-label] dishes, they'd say, 'Where is Mikasa?'"[47]

In 2021, even as key competitor Home Goods reported a 34 percent increase in sales, Bed Bath & Beyond sales decreased by 10 percent. Then, in the first quarter of 2022, physical store sales plummeted 24 percent and online sales also tanked, by 21 percent.[48] Tritton was ousted in June of that year.

While Tritton was absolutely right to move with great urgency, the changes made to core features of the business that had driven success were not well calibrated.

EARLY MOVES OF HIGH PERFORMERS

To develop guidance about moves CEOs should focus on in their critical first two years, Spencer Stuart joined forces with the Boston Consulting Group to conduct a study. We know that every new CEO of course faces a distinctive set of key issues, with a unique mix of optimal moves to make. But we thought that some patterns might emerge suggesting major categories of initiatives, such as seeking operational efficiencies and undertaking acquisitions. They did.

The study analyzed the fortunes of nearly four hundred CEOs appointed to the helm of S&P 500 companies within the decade of 2004 to 2014. A set of the fifteen most effective early moves was identified. And out of those, the highest performers relied most on these five: operational improvements, launching new products, improving customer relationships, increasing employee engagement, and culture change.

When we later performed analysis on our Spencer Stuart database of CEOs who were in office between 2000 and 2022, we corroborated the original study's findings and made a number of additional findings about the long-term effects of these moves. Those in the top quintile of performance increased company efficiency at a much faster clip in their first two years than lower performers. In fact, they cut costs at twice the pace as those in the lower performance groups. This allowed them to achieve, on average, gains of 10 percent in operating income in their first year and 20 percent in year two. Top performers also engaged, on average, in fewer acquisitions in these years, and those they did were typically smaller scale.

Our analysis also revealed striking patterns in how quickly the results achieved by top performers began to exceed results produced by low performers. ROIC jumped significantly higher during year two for top performers. What's more, ROIC continued increasing through years three through six for top performers, whereas it decreased dramatically for low performers starting in year three and then leveled off at a much lower rate than that of high performers. Growth of revenue also diverged strongly beginning in year three. It shot up for high performers but began a long slide for low performers.

Successful CEOs who took over companies in a challenging situation were quick to divest sizable chunks of their business in the early years. They moved with urgency to shed investments and subsidiary businesses in their first two to three years to refocus the business on its core, reduce debt, and free up cash flow. Often burdened with bloated capital expenditure, they rigorously rightsized their investments in the assets they chose to keep. They reduced investments in plants, buildings, technology, or equipment during their first three years. Only by the fourth year did capital expenditures relative to sales begin to rise. Their judicious financial moves paid off in impressive bottom-line improvements. They increased earnings before interest, taxes, depreciation, and amortization (EBITDA) margins within the first two years of their tenure to comparable levels as those of their peers who took over healthy organizations. These often drastic changes in the operating model during the Calibration stage allowed them to shift from defense to offense, free up resources, and fuel the future growth of the company.

Finally, the data underscored how tricky taking over from a long-serving CEO perceived as quite successful can be. CEOs stepping into such illustrious shoes lagged their peers in the first two years by a sobering 4 percent TSR year-over-year.

These findings offer a stark picture of how pivotal the first two years are to a CEO's overall success. Those who safely navigate the roiling waters and remain in the job—about 88 percent of new CEOs—generally move into several years of improving results. Moves made early increasingly pay off. But the next stage, Reinvention, also presents its own distinctive challenges.

4

REINVENTION

"When you guys made me the
CEO, you didn't think I'd have a
strategic bone in my body."

"I can't believe how disappointed we are in you," an investor
said to Larry Merlo in the second month of his tenure at the
helm of CVS. "We've known you for years. We're big supporters of
you, and I can't believe that you're sitting here defending the CVS
Caremark combination."

Merlo had inherited an extremely vexing integration challenge.
After CVS bid so aggressively to acquire Caremark four years prior
to Merlo's appointment, in 2007, fending off the eleventh-hour
charge by George Paz and Express Scripts to swoop in and claim
Caremark, CVS had been struggling mightily to realize anticipated synergies from the deal. Caremark earnings had plunged.
Then, in 2010, the company lost a whopping $5 billion from con-
tracts that weren't renewed. A chorus of Wall Street analysts called
for CVS to sell off the "albatross."[1] A *New York Times* article pro-
nounced just two months after Merlo stepped into the CEO role,

"The merger that created CVS Caremark never made much sense. The $50 billion company could be worth $13 billion more carved up. Undoing the deal would be an easy win."[2] Merlo recalled, "We had investors who were kicking and screaming that shareholder value had been destroyed."

But, "I believed in the strategy" behind the purchase, he told us. He also believed he could solve the problem because it was "very operationally focused." Solving operational integration issues was his forte. He applied his expertise leading integration from several earlier acquisitions and, finally, after two more years, Caremark "began to prove its value," he recalled. The CVS Caremark share price surged. "By the time we got to the end of 2012, people were not questioning the strategy," Merlo said. He, meanwhile, launched a deep interrogation of the longer-term strategic game plan for CVS.

He hadn't been seen as a "strategy guy." Indeed, he recalled that he'd once told CVS Executive Chair David Dorman, "When you guys made me the CEO, you didn't think I'd have a strategic bone in my body." Merlo was appointed as the "execution guy," the best candidate to get the Caremark acquisition finally working. But when he started, he shared, "I put my balance sheet together, of things I'm good at and things I'm going to have to grow into," with strategy being prime among those he'd need to work on. Then, with a 23 percent spike in revenue and tremendous 43 percent growth in operating income in the first quarter of 2013, he saw that he should seize the day and tackle a pernicious problem looming in the years ahead for the pharmacy business.[3]

For the next few years, the large pharmacy chains would be enjoying a boom in profits as a raft of high-cost drugs lost their patent protection and generics flooded the market. Pharmacies would actually earn higher margins on the sale of generics because the chains had more negotiating power with generics producers than they did with Pfizer, Merck, and the other patented drug producers. But, within a few years, that burst of growth in generics would dramatically slow, and pharmacies would face an economic crunch. "The business had become commoditized, with a Walgreens, Rite Aid, and maybe a CVS, too, at any given busy intersection, and there's a food store with a pharmacy and Walmart just down the street," Merlo reflected.

Foreseeing this conundrum, his predecessor, Thomas Ryan, had initiated a strategy of growing CVS beyond the retail pharmacy business. The Caremark purchase had been a centerpiece of the diversification strategy. Also key was the 2006 purchase of a controlling stake in MinuteClinic, a chain of retail health clinics. But CVS hadn't integrated the clinics into its pharmacy business. Merlo envisioned a much bolder, truly transformational development of the company into a new kind of health-care provider. "How can we take our very successful pharmacy franchise and plug it into the broader health care delivery system? That was the strategic question," he recalled.

To find the answer, he drew on his early career experience as a pharmacist behind the counter at a Peoples Drug store. A longtime neighborhood establishment, Peoples still had a soda fountain counter at the time he worked there. In those days before commoditization, he recalled, "I did a lot more than fill prescriptions. I loved the customer interaction. I got to know my customers. I got to know their families. With the advice I provided, I felt that I became a trusted resource for them." He also realized that "it's much easier for people to talk to their pharmacist than for them to talk to their doctor." Some customers even asked him to call their doctors about their issues. Merlo believed that CVS could capitalize on this trust and accessibility to offer a broader range of medical services. By actually incorporating MinuteClinics into its stores and greatly expanding its staff of nurse practitioners, the company could provide wider access to quality care for a host of ailments at lower cost than private practices and hospital ERs charged.

The need for greater access and lower-cost care was pressing, and in the coming years, with a tsunami of baby boomers reaching old age, the nation faced an outright health-care crisis. The transformation from pharmacy to health-care provider would surely be a daunting challenge, fraught with controversy, such as questions about conflicts of interest if a seller of prescriptions also managed care. It would also take many years to bring to full fruition, which was why, he perceived, he needed to light a fire of urgency now, when the company was flush with capital and had a runway for ramping up.

Launching an intensive strategy-development process that involved both his executive and his strategy teams, Merlo wasted no time in getting started executing plans even as longer-term moves were analyzed in great depth. In his year three, CVS purchased nutrition services firm Coram for $2.1 billion and paid Target $1.9 billion to buy its eighty walk-in clinics as well as 1,600 pharmacies, which CVS would operate in Target stores and eventually expand into clinics.[4] But the biggest move that year was the decision to stop selling all tobacco products in CVS stores, which amounted to $2 billion in annual revenue. His chief medical officer had shared that tobacco sales had been a major obstacle in efforts to build partnerships with health insurance providers, physician groups, and hospital systems. It always came up: CVS couldn't be a health-care provider if it sold a deadly product. The idea of removing tobacco products had been discussed for years; Merlo finally acted on it despite "a lot of angst" about the decision. He shared that the clear and powerful articulation of the purpose statement his team had crafted, "Helping people on the path to better health," was a strong motivator. "The words were easy to remember, but importantly, I felt like that purpose talked to me," he recalled. It turned out they spoke powerfully to the board as well. He had socialized the move ahead of time with the chairman and some of the directors, and he expected a lively discussion at the meeting in which he formally proposed the move. "I could not have been prouder of our board," he shared, "because that discussion lasted probably thirty minutes; there was uniform agreement that this was the right thing to do."

In evangelizing the move with investors, Merlo had anticipated pushback, yet in every meeting, people shared their own family stories of loved ones addicted to smoking or who had died of lung cancer. Despite great trepidation about how Wall Street would react to walking away from $2 billion of revenue, the share price surged with news of the move. By the end of Merlo's fourth year, share value had risen 200 percent since the beginning of his tenure versus a rise of 56 percent for the S&P 500.[5]

The same day tobacco removal was announced, the company changed its name to CVS Health. The creation of an unprecedented new model of health provider was well underway. Merlo immediately engaged his team in an even bolder pursuit. He proceeded to lead a two-year-long strategic review of the entire health-care industry, evaluating how best to take a major next step, a truly disruptive acquisition that would bring CVS into a whole new domain in the industry. They considered every possible type of business that would do so and arrived at the decision to make a bid to merge with health insurer Aetna. "The board was skeptical," recalled CVS chairman David Dorman. "When he first brought up managed care organizations and health insurance, the board thought, What? Insurance? We don't know anything about that. How are we going to do this? But Larry did a great job of laying out a vision for reinventing health care." That involved hard work, starting with months of research and including a two-day offsite to introduce the board to the strategic review process. Merlo also visited all the board directors at their homes for long one-on-one meetings.

In December 2017, at the end of Merlo's sixth year, CVS and Aetna announced they'd reached an agreement at a cost to CVS of $69 billion, the largest acquisition in the history of the US health-care industry to that date.[6] Merlo had not only driven phenomenal growth but also ensured that the next several years of his tenure would be anything but complacent.

Larry Merlo exemplifies what the highest-performing CEOs do with the credibility they've gained by successfully navigating the challenges of their first two to three years—leverage it to push vigorously for big advances. That may be moving "pedal to the metal" with the existing strategy, or it may involve a pivot to a new strategy. Sometimes it involves both: full speed ahead with initiatives that are succeeding while turning increasing attention to addressing challenges and opportunities further out on the horizon.

By this time, the CEO fully owns the strategy, whether it's been inherited or newly fashioned. Most often, if the former CEO moved over to the board, they step down by the end of year one or two so that in this new phase, their lingering influence, which can be so challenging to contend with, dissipates. Corporate memories are long, and the influence of a former CEO won't simply vanish, especially if he or she had a lengthy and highly successful tenure. But many CEOs describe a decisive shift at this juncture, generally about year three or four, to feeling more fully in charge. At this point, as Indra Nooyi expressed it, "I really had my legs under me as CEO."[7]

Lew Hay, who led NextEra Energy for eleven years, from 2001 to 2011, shared that it was only after his first few years, having successfully steered the company through some rough headwinds and built his own team, that he felt he could forcefully make the case for his strategic vision: transforming the company into a leader in production of renewable energy. When he took over in 2001, the company was called Florida Power and Light (FPL), and it was a highly conservative utility business, generating electricity from fossil fuel and nuclear power plants. Though Hay planned from the beginning to transition the company into largely renewable production, he shared with us that at the time, "The vast majority of the players in our industry thought it was a fool's errand. There was still skepticism as to whether renewables were just a fad and government incentives would go away." In his first few years, he focused on bringing in a team of innovative thinkers with entrepreneurial experience. "We had some of the best utility people around," he shared, "but they were very risk averse." No wonder. "The culture I inherited," he continued, "was one in which, if anybody stepped out and tried a new initiative and it didn't work, they got their head chopped off."

He started building renewables capacity right away, but with small steps. "In the very early days," he recalled, "I had to downplay what we were doing and say, 'Hey, it's kind of a nice little niche for us, and we're making some money, but it isn't a core element of our strategy.'" In his first few years, he had to focus heavily on addressing crises. The Enron scandal broke in his first year and led to a massive downturn in the energy industry. After steering through that admirably, Hay faced an annus horribilis his third year, in which Florida was devastated by three successive hurricanes that caused major damage to FPL facilities. Once he led the company through those shocks to the system, he stepped up renewables investment considerably. "It was easier to make bigger steps over time, because we had a successful track record and I felt I really had the board backing me." So vigorous was the execution from then on that, by the end of his tenure, the company, renamed NextEra Energy, had become the leading producer of wind and solar power in the world and had been named three times to *For-tune*'s top ten list of the world's most innovative companies.

We found this initiation of a big new strategy push at this year three to four juncture again and again in the journeys of the most transformative CEOs. Mary Barra took charge at GM in 2014, and in her first two years largely focused on urgent short-term issues. She had to steer the company through the tumult of a scandal that broke just three weeks after she stepped into the job: GM had failed to disclose that ignition switches in some models were causing cars to suddenly shut off, resulting in the deaths of more than 120 people. Meanwhile, she strengthened the balance sheet, plugging massive leaks in revenue by shutting down longtime money-losing operations in Europe and laying off 157,000 employees, 27 percent of the workforce. "All that was about getting the company in better financial shape to actually start, then, on the next journey," board director Patricia Russo recalled.[8] Under the radar of the press, Barra had also been researching and laying the groundwork for an ambitious new commitment to electric vehicle production. Midway through her third year, in September 2017, she announced that GM was aiming to launch at least twenty new all-electric vehicles by 2023, with an ultimate goal of not only overtaking Tesla and other competitors to claim the lead in EVs but also catalyzing a transition to a world of "zero crashes, zero emissions, and zero congestion."

The scale of that vision was not forced by the current market conditions. Demand for all-electric vehicles was comparatively minuscule. Even sales of the one all-electric model GM had brought to market by that time, the Chevy Bolt, which was released in 2016, though promising, were tepid. Barra could certainly have aimed for fewer new models going to market on the timeline announced. But she was putting forth a powerful narrative, forcefully planting a flag, as Shantanu Narayen would say, about how serious GM's commitment to transformation was. She was clearly demarcating a new era for the company. And the timing of the declaration of this new phase was tied not only to the progress made in developing the EV technology required to achieve that goal. The timing was also tied to Barra's successful journey through her first stage.

Hubert Joly's timing in announcing a next-era strategy emphasized how the mindset he'd developed, of thinking of his career in terms of chapters, helped him seize the day to explicitly launch a next-phase strategy for Best Buy. "The length of my chapters is typically three or four years," he told us, "because it takes a few years to get where you're going. Then you pause and say, Where do we want to go next?"

Having achieved results by the beginning of his third year that showed the turnaround strategy was succeeding, Joly and his team pivoted to developing a next-phase strategy focused on accelerating growth. "After having saved the company," he said, "the big deal was, Were we going to be able to grow it? With the shift to online, the store footprint would be shrinking." He recognized that they needed to get ahead of that, and he moved on several fronts. "We had been looking for ways to grow, but it was hard to get traction. The dominant mindset was still 'let's not take too many risks.' Our planning process was quite risk-averse. We knew that we needed to find a different modus operandi." He solicited input from consultancies, asking, "Tell us how we should organize to go after growth." One result: "We created a Strategic Growth Office with about fifty people focused purely on refining the strategy and crafting specific initiatives that we could then go pilot." They did intensive work on market segmentation and identified the core consumers they wanted to target: "high-touch technology fans, who love technology but need some help with it." That led them to focus intensively on new services they could offer, which included, for example, providing technology and customer support for home health care, building on the success of the Geek Squad service model. They also introduced agile product development processes, which facilitate faster and more flexible design through continuous collaboration, testing, and improvement. Agile development is also important in encouraging more risk-taking.

Joly additionally turned the executive team's focus to organizational development, with an emphasis on establishing a clarity of purpose and leading cultural transformation. "We then did work on framing our corporate purpose," he recalled. They formulated a clear and concise statement of purpose that was open to wide-ranging possibilities for growth: "to enrich lives through technology." Then, as we'll describe more fully later, they developed methods to "enable every employee at the company to write themselves into that story and connect what drives them with their work and with the purpose of the company."

In this process, Joly demonstrated his receptivity to input. For example, Patrick Doyle, then a board director who went on to become chairman, suggested in a board meeting that Joly should, officially and publicly, declare the turnaround was over and announce the new growth phase. In March 2017, in the middle of his fifth year, Joly did just that. He announced the completion of the Renew Blue turnaround and introduced the Building the New Blue strategy. "I believe that you cannot have a strategy if it doesn't have a name," he shared, emphasizing that announcing the new strategy helped the company "more clearly close the door on Renew Blue and start the new phase."

PRESCIENCE GENERALLY MEETS PUSHBACK

Hard-won credibility by no means ensures all-around support for big next steps. The hero mythology obscures one aspect of the actual CEO journey: even after great initial success, even after building a strong team that's in alignment, and even after garnering strong support from investors and much of the wider stakeholder community, CEOs cannot depend on unity of support for initiatives they spearhead. That's true no matter how well-founded their case may be and even despite how persuasive they are.

Terry Lundgren ran into stiff resistance while executing his strategic plan in the years of his Reinvention stage. As noted earlier, he was appointed CEO of Federated Department Stores in 2003 with the express mandate to make bold moves to expand the business. After just three months at the helm, Lundgren faced a golden opportunity: purchasing the legendary Marshall Field's chain. The acquisition would take the company a grand leap forward, and he would become the steward of another of the nation's most beloved retail brands. But his only competitor in the bidding, the May Company, was fierce. Months of intense and elaborate bidding machinations ensued, and in June 2004, Lundgren got word that Gene Kahn, the May CEO, had swung for the fences with an offer one investment banker said "took my breath away." Lundgren immediately backed out. He vividly remembers the difficult phone calls he had to make to his board. His first major move had failed.

But then, in January 2005, a mere eight months after May bought Field's, the May CEO resigned; Kahn was under fire for vastly overpaying to clinch the deal. Lundgren immediately seized the opportunity to buy all of May—much bigger game purchased for a fabulous price. "After selling assets that were part of the bigger $11 billion deal, we ended with a net purchase price of $3 billion," he recounted, "which is $200 million less than what May paid for Marshall Field's. I got Marshall Field's plus all of the May Company assets that we wanted in order to expand our brand." He sealed the deal at the end of February, capping his second year with this remarkable coup. The purchase of May allowed Federated to become a truly national brand, the only department-store chain to have that reach.

The May Company demise resulting from heavy debt burden in overpaying for Marshall Field's shined a bright light on Lundgren's wisdom in walking away from the bidding. He shared with us, "I think the confidence the board gained in me for not overpaying and walking away from the Marshall Field's bidding process was one of the best things that happened to me very early on." He was lauded in the press, with one headline declaring "Lundgren at Top of Retail Heap."[9]

Yet, as he did in executing on a main part of the strategy for going national, he faced stiff pushback from the board. Some years earlier, Federated had snapped up the venerable Macy's chain, and Lundgren proposed that as part of going national, Federated should change its name to Macy's Inc. and change the names of its regional stores—Burdines in Florida, Lazarus in the Midwest, Robinson's May in Los Angeles—to Macy's. Some shoppers loyal to the Marshall Field's chain were outraged, especially fans of the beloved flagship Marshall Field's store in Chicago. Customers marched in protest, carrying placards calling for a boycott and jeering "Macy's Is Just Wal-Mart with Pretension."[10] Chicago native and famous film critic Roger Ebert warned Lundgren in an editorial, "Don't mess with the name Marshall Field's. You will generate rage beyond your wildest nightmares."[11] Many of the board directors balked in response. "I had at least half of my board disagree with me that I should change the names," he told us. "It was very controversial. They were particularly concerned about Marshall Field's, about the PR aspects and the local community and that customers would stop shopping. All good reasons."

But Lundgren was acting with well-informed intuition. "We tested the name [Marshall Field's]," he recalled, and "it did not register on the East or West Coast."[12] To create a truly national brand, the only option was the Macy's name. What Lundgren intuited—which took a good deal of persuasion to impress upon stakeholders, both within and outside the company, over the course of the next several years—was that the more online sales challenged brick-and-mortar retail, the more important a truly national brand following would become. Federated had launched a retail website back in 1998, when Amazon's business model was still a matter of much dispute and Amazon hadn't yet branched out into broader department-store categories. Federated's efforts to build online sales had thus far faltered. But with Amazon beginning to encroach on market share in many department-store mainstay categories, Lundgren foresaw that the website could, and must, be developed into a true contender, with the Macy's name driving brand awareness online. He forged ahead. "I ended up having to say [to the board], 'I've got your opinion, and I recognize I don't have all of you voting in favor of this, but I'm making a very strong recommendation that this is better than the status quo. I'm not saying this is not risky, it is risky. But the status quo is more so.'"

In the next year, 2005, he moved with alacrity to earn back capital from the deal, selling marquee chains Lord & Taylor and David's Bridal, along with many other assets purchased in the May deal, and raking in $8 billion. With that capital, he launched a major brick-and-mortar revamping and invested heavily in boosting online sales, to the tune of $230 million in 2006 and 2007.[13] With these dual investments, Lundgren was leading Macy's in developing the retail strategy that would obtain a name only in 2011 in a *Harvard Business Review* article: omnichannel selling.[14] Omnichannel leverages technology to provide shoppers with a seamless buying experience across all channels, from in-store to laptop and smartphone. Not until well into the next decade would the prescience of vigorously pushing innovation in omnichannel selling become vividly clear.

Lundgren's embrace of the strategy proved a major differentiator in the fate of Macy's versus two of the nation's oldest formerly successful national retail department-store brands, Sears and JCPenney. By 2010, Macy's had become the fourth-largest online retailer. What's more, in that year, the profitability Macy's achieved from online sales began to soar, increasing by 257 percent over the next three years.[15] As for the other major department-store chains, having failed to cultivate effective omnichannel operations, Sears, which had once been the nation's premier retail brand, filed for bankruptcy in 2018 and dwindled to just fifteen stores. JCPenney filed for bankruptcy in 2020. "The difference between Sears, JCPenney, and Macy's," an analyst highlighted, "is that Macy's found a way to get ahead of industry trends by investing heavily in technology."[16]

The more prescient a new strategy or shift in strategy is, and the more substantial the change in course, the more a CEO will have to battle inertia and pushback. Executing that strategy is also likely to require more time. Making the case and then keeping up support through the course of years, continuing to address skepticism, stoke motivation, and stay vigilant about detecting any inevitable subversion and backsliding, can be a real grind. That's especially true when the payoffs won't be quickly manifesting.

Roger Ferguson shared with us the years-long process he had to persist with in order to gain board approval for a brilliantly forward-looking strategy to diversify the conservative investment manager into a much broader financial services company. TIAA manages the retirement savings of many millions of Americans. When Ferguson joined as chief in April 2008, the financial markets were just about to take their historic dive off the subprime meltdown cliff. He started with the expectation that he was stepping into "a role filled with positive upside challenges," and then three months in, he was "thrust into cost-cutting, emergency actions, changing the portfolio drastically." He deftly navigated through the crisis, and then, rather than revert to the norm of conservative portfolio investing, he launched into a hard-fought campaign to get out ahead of another crisis, but one of a very different nature. "Not the shocking crisis of 2008, but rather a longer and more dangerous challenge of low interest rates," he explained. TIAA's performance was heavily dependent on interest rates, and Ferguson foresaw a long period of extremely low rates, which would drastically reduce customers' earnings.

He proposed a bold acquisitions strategy, which was such a departure for the then almost one-hundred-year-old organization that, he shared, "it took two years to convince the board to do it. Trying to create a sense of purpose and coalition at the board table was really hard." As he recalled, "The company had just come through a crisis. There was a sense of relief. It's human nature to want to take a pause and breathe. The challenge I had was to convince them that there was really no going back to where we were. I had to bring to life the slow challenge of low interest rates versus the shocking challenge of 2008. It felt grinding." He made the case at every board meeting, "doing and redoing analysis, reminding them why we wanted to make a move, taking two steps forward, then one back. You get a few allies. At one meeting, a few speak in your favor. A bunch are quiet. You come back to it for the next meeting, moving patiently as opposed to moving quickly." Working to address the board's concerns, meanwhile, gave his leadership team pause. "It was a funny dynamic," he said. Concerned he was going out on a limb, they'd ask him, "in many, many meetings, does the board really want to do this?"

Here he highlighted a core issue that CEOs raised about the shift in these years as they more fully assumed strategic leadership: "The energy around the need to change had to come from me." How did he keep his own energy up despite all the resistance? And how did he fuel it in his team? This is all the more challenging, Ferguson said, when progress isn't clear to see.

Some of Ferguson's personal drive came from having "a problem-solving mindset, so chomping down on a really interesting problem is for me what the job's all about." This was a constant theme in our research and interviews with the highest-performing CEOs. Ferguson, using the analogy of being the architect of a building, was also energized by the challenge of championing his own strategy. "It was very exciting because it is a vision, and I will take all the time necessary to go from rough sketch to blueprint, to bringing in the team, the subcontractors, to actually seeing the building. There's nothing like it; it's so very rewarding." Ferguson also shared that he is comfortable with a "gradually making progress mindset." "The key to my success," he shared, "is my ability to keep at it every day." Sustaining his energy through the long haul of these years also was an appreciation for small wins. "There are small wins even in big marathons. You chunk up these big, long journeys into steps. Sometimes it's just a board meeting in which you finally got someone to agree."

Creating awareness of small wins, and celebrating them, was also key to sustaining his team's energy after initially exciting them with the vision. "First, they needed the belief that the goal was worth the journey. Why does it matter? Then it was celebrating the small victories. So getting the document ready, finishing the analysis, getting the vote, all those steps." For the company as a whole, "there were some metrics that we could share about in every town hall, having to do with asset flows, client wins, and our win-loss ratio. People could keep track. We had quarterly town halls, and a report card that was consistent, and that showed progress." He also injected energy through his personal presence. "At town halls, I'd go shake everyone's hand as they were coming in. You have to make yourself readily accessible." He emphasized that this was relatively easy for him in comparison with many corporate heads, given the comparatively small size of TIAA's staff, which grew from about six thousand to seventeen thousand employees during his tenure. But we heard the same commitment to being accessible and making regular appearances at company functions from leader after leader.

All of Ferguson's campaigning began to bear fruit with a string of major acquisitions starting in 2012. TIAA made a bold move every year for four years straight. First was a joint venture with UK asset manager Henderson, after which Ferguson invested $125 million to buy out Henderson's share and take 100 percent ownership. This acquisition included a large real estate investing fund and made TIAA one of the largest global real estate asset managers, with approximately $70 billion of assets under management in 2013. Then came the acquisitions of Nuveen Investments, a mutual fund company, for $6.25 billion and Everbank Financial Corp, an online lender, for $2.5 billion, followed by starting TIAA Global Business Services in India, which provides technology and operations support to TIAA and its associates. This was the company's entrance into offshoring. Along with those successes came plenty of failures. The road was rocky.

"There was an acquisition I wanted to make for a mutual company," Ferguson recalled. "I must have pursued that company for a year and a half. We put in a bid, then another one and another one. And I thought the whole strategy is going to blow up if I don't get this company." He didn't, but he made another purchase not long after. "I had a bunch of ideas that didn't work," he emphasized. "We entered a couple of businesses that we just couldn't make work." These are the stories that mythologizing narratives of heroic CEOs gloss over, and along with them, the truth of the individual's inner experience. Ferguson readily described the bite of disappointment and the drumming of doubts in his mind. "Should I have moved more quickly? Did I offer too little? Did I miss a signal? I know I did in one case," he said of an acquisition bid that failed. But he also expressed a foundation of resilience that carries CEOs through these mid-tenure downdrafts: the love of how much learning they're doing. Those who thrive relish the personal development they're forced to undergo. "This whole middle period was one of incredible growth," Ferguson said, "where I had to learn how to communicate more broadly, run a different kind of company, describe to everyone what the vision was, and try to knit together all these cultures into something that hearkened back to the great strengths of TIAA while imagining what the future was going to be." The excitement and satisfaction he had felt were palpable. The results of the transformation he drove were striking. Under his leadership, TIAA added a million new participants in its funds, a 20 percent increase, and more than doubled the assets it managed. It had several years of record net inflows and was recognized with numerous awards for superior fund performance.

In their proactive drive to get ahead of upcoming challenges and their persistence and resilience in pursuit of their goals, all these CEOs exemplified what psychologist E. Tory Higgins has named a *promotion focus*. Higgins describes it as focus on personal growth, attaining desired outcomes, and realizing ambitions. He contrasts it to a *prevention focus*, which directs attention to preventing losses, avoiding mistakes, and maintaining safety and security.[17] CEOs with a prevention focus are primarily motivated by the desire to fulfill their responsibilities and avoid negative outcomes. They tend to prioritize risk minimization, seeking stability, predictability, and the avoidance of disruptions. They also generally adhere to established guidelines and procedures. In short, they're playing not to win but to avoid losing.

Promotion-focused CEOs play to win. They take calculated risks and vigorously seek novel opportunities. In that quest, they foster a culture of creativity. They also demonstrate impressive resilience in the face of setbacks or unexpected challenges, allowing them to stay committed to their goals even during trying periods. This orientation toward proactive problem-solving is always a major asset for leaders. In the Reinvention stage it's particularly advantageous in driving them to capitalize on the momentum of successes achieved. Our data on performance over time shows in stark relief how this translates into strikingly divergent results for high performers in the next several years compared to those achieving middling or subpar results.

THE GREAT DIVERGENCE

As noted earlier, the data we included in our CEO Life Cycle study database includes a wide range of metrics for performance, including total shareholder return (TSR), revenue growth, capital expenditure, and investment in innovation. We identified the high performers and low performers among all CEOs in the S&P 500 from 2000 to 2022, comparing the statistics for these variables between the two groups, and found stark differences. On many significant measures, by year three, high performers' results spike up and continue to improve for the next several years, through about year six, whereas low performers' results increase at a much lower rate, stagnate, or turn downward. For revenue growth, our analysis shows a steady annual increase for the high performers, from 9 percent to 11 percent, over the course of the first five to six years. Over those same years, the low performers' revenue growth slows during the first three years and then remains stagnant at between 4 percent and 6 percent the next three years. The average for all CEOs over that same period is 8 percent growth. When it comes to operating margins, whereas earnings before interest and taxes (EBIT) rise steadily by 0.5 percent a year in the first five years for high performers, they steadily slide for low performers.

High performers invest in growth vigorously. First, they fund growth by investing more in acquiring, upgrading, and maintaining their physical assets, such as property, plants, buildings, and technology. Their capital expenditure (CapEx) relative to sales rises considerably higher, from 12 percent in year one to 17 percent in year five. The low performers, by contrast, cut their CapEx spend from 9 percent to 6 percent in the corresponding period, attempting to save their way to prosperity. The high performers also invest more in innovation by driving up their R&D spend by 40 percent, from 10 percent to 14 percent by year five; the low performers' R&D spend remains flat. Finally, after doing fewer M&A activities in their first three years, the high performers do more in year four, averaging roughly one acquisition annually from then on. The low performers engage in more M&A in the first three years, but it tails off, and the high performers overtake them in activity in year four. The values of these transactions follow the same pattern: the value of high performers' M&A deals done in the first three years is relatively moderate and increases in year four; the value of low performers' deals is higher in the early years and then decreases.

The divergence in investment payoffs is also glaring. The high performers increase return on invested capital (ROIC) at a much faster rate, by about 60 percent (from 5 percent to 8 percent) over the course of their first five years, after which returns plateau at that higher level. For the low-performing group, ROIC drops by 50 percent (from 4 percent to 2 percent) during the first five years, after which it continues to slide.

A particularly intriguing finding from our analysis has to do with the multiple at which a company's stock is trading beginning in year three. This metric can be considered a good measure of the market's confidence in a company's leadership. Starting in year three, the multiple becomes higher for the high performers but decreases for the low performers, and the degree of divergence increases over the next several years. This indicates that, by year three, the market has begun to differentiate which CEOs to put its faith in. Perception and reality have converged.

These findings underscore why 25 percent of CEOs are out of office by the end of their year three and why the highest year-to-year "dropout" rate is in year four, with 10 percent leaving then. It's safe to assume that the vast majority of these departures are forced: by this time, boards have determined from a wide range of indicators that the CEO is not making the decisions needed to drive strong growth. Tough as the first few years are, the several years after are their own proving ground, where CEOs who aren't driving satisfactory performance face increasing scrutiny. Underscoring how hard flourishing in this stage can be for many CEOs is the fact that, by the end of year six, 50 percent of CEOs have departed. Many departures may be voluntary exits, but that figure speaks powerfully about how tough the demands of the job are.

Those who flourish once again stretch themselves to learn new information and skills to drive a new phase of reinvention for their company.

REJUVENATION THROUGH REINVENTION

The CEOs who are most successful in this middle stage come to understand that they won't be able to lead the transformation envisioned for the company without a personal transformation. Larry Merlo had never spearheaded strategy. Terry Lundgren came up in retail as a master of in-store merchandising, with no experience in online sales or in technology generally. Roger Ferguson had never led an acquisition. Lew Hay had no previous experience in renewable energy production; his expertise before joining NextEra Energy (formerly Florida Power & Light) was in the food services industry. The need to embrace personal reinvention remains the same even for CEOs who have spent many years in their company and industry.

Recall that when Indra Nooyi took charge at PepsiCo in 2006, she had a number of pressing company issues to address, including operations in China and the profit squeeze from bottling companies. In the first several years of her tenure, she had to focus intensively on them. "I would say from 2007 to about 2010, that's all we did, fix every one of these issues," she recalled. Then, four years into her tenure, she immediately turned her attention to reinvention.

She targeted learning about design and the emerging discipline of design thinking, a powerful process for driving innovation, setting her sights on creating a leading-edge innovation hub for the company. "We needed an in-house design studio," she said, "where designers would work side by side with innovators and marketers."[18] She immersed herself in how design could invigorate all aspects of Pepsi's business, from the conceptualization of new products to more powerful branding and enhanced customer experience. This included a sit-down with Steve Jobs, who perhaps more than anyone else proved the case for the remarkable value of great design. (Being a CEO does, after all, have its perks.) Realizing she'd need to bring in a top expert to lead design development, she lured Mauro Porcini away from his role as head of design for 3M and appointed him to the new role of chief design officer. She also opened a Design and Innovation Center in New York City. The design team was made available to all units within the company, and they were expected to consult with the design group about all new products in development.[19]

One hugely successful new product developed with the design-thinking principles the design team introduced is Mountain Dew Kickstart, tailored specifically for women. Research showed that few women were drinking traditional Mountain Dew, in part because it was so sweet and perceived as a guy's drink. The product developers worked with the design team to create a fruit juice–based drink with only sixty calories per can in flavors that would appeal particularly to women, such as watermelon, pomegranate, and blood orange. The design team also created a sleek can, thinner and taller than the standard soda can. The launch was one of the most successful for the company in a decade. Over time, the infusion of design into all product development has been so effective that the company has opened twelve design hubs around the world, from São Paulo to Shanghai and New Delhi.[20]

Personal reinvention may also involve changing one's leadership style, as was true for Hubert Joly yet again in this stage. He had challenged himself repeatedly before to evolve his approach to leadership, having started his career, as he put it, as a "hard-charging McKinsey consultant all about problem-solving and performance optimization." By the time he came to Best Buy, he was devoted to a purpose-driven, human-centric approach to management. That led him to get out into stores and elicit the views of the frontline employees, to immediately empower the salespeople on the floor with the authority to price match, and to limit job cuts in the turnaround. He also drew on his expertise in leading turnarounds and took a firm hand in decision-making. "I made lots of decisions fast," he recalled. "But now we had an extraordinary team of highly talented people who respected and trusted each other. Decisions did not have to be made by me all the time."[21] The 360-degree input he received the year he and his team embarked on defining the Building the New Blue strategy helped him understand that, "in this second phase, if I made too many decisions, I would become a bottleneck."

He worked with a consultancy to clarify the decision-making he should have responsibility for, "which was really only for the strategy, who's on the team, capital allocation, and culture. That's it. Then we could spin out, so who's in charge of the mobile phone strategy or the supply chain strategy. That was a big unlock." He described the transformation as learning "the role of the leader as a gardener, not a decision-maker," focused on creating "an environment in which others could blossom and flourish."

The opportunity to devote more time and energy to culture change is an important source of drive during the Reinvention stage. Vast quantities of advice have been written about methods for driving cultural transformation. We won't showcase any one methodology here because the circumstances within different companies vary far too much for any given formula to be deemed best. What we can highlight is that CEOs revealed the depth of their personal commitment and how much skin they had in the game when embarking on a change initiative—and how energizing it was for them. They understood and embraced the fact that no initiative will reap any appreciable rewards without the CEO's intensive devotion to the mission. That inevitably involves contending with a good deal of skepticism that results from how flawed so many culture-change initiatives are, full of the sound and fury of declarations of corporate values and purpose statements that signify nothing truly being done to enact behavioral change.

Yet research finds that when done effectively, culture change produces impressive results. Key is that specific desired changes in behavior are articulated and in clear alignment with the company's strategy, not treated as separate from the core drivers of the company's success. A recent survey of five hundred CEOs of global companies found that "most [of them] aren't particularly intentional in their pursuit of culture as a driver of financial performance."[22] Those who said they did see culture as a core driver of financial results, however, led companies that saw significantly greater revenue growth over a three-year period, a compounded annual growth rate (CAGR) of 9.1 percent versus 4.4 percent for the firms led by respondents who indicated they didn't see culture as key to improving results.

Hyatt CEO Mark Hoplamazian shifted his focus to culture building once he successfully negotiated a host of pressing near-term challenges in his first few years. Recall that he made a huge stretch move in stepping into the role, transitioning from seventeen years with the ten-person Pritzker family organization. Hyatt was a global corporation with eighty thousand employees. For his first few years, he focused intensively on learning about the organization while also applying his deal-making skills to strengthen the balance sheet, buy and sell many properties, and then in 2009, his third year, lead a successful IPO. Flush off of that achievement, Hoplamazian turned his attention to a feature of Hyatt that was the reason he'd decided to make his big leap. In his months as interim CEO, working closely for the first time with the Hyatt executive team, he realized that "there was something so special about the culture of Hyatt. I couldn't quite put it into words, but nobody was showing up just to punch a clock." He felt deeply that he'd had "a true emotional experience of joining the Hyatt family." Now he decided to delve into the power behind that strength of connection he felt as fuel for growing the company.

Many of the company's general managers from around the world had been with the company for twenty-five years or more. At a meeting in the Grand Hyatt in New York City, Hoplamazian asked each manager to answer this question: "What led you to join Hyatt to begin with and why are you still here?" He was sure they'd all had plenty of opportunities to move elsewhere. "I was the scribe at a whiteboard," he recalled, and in their answers, one word "came up over and over and over": *care*. They felt cared for by the company, that there was a genuine "interest in their advancement." They also articulated that "they felt fulfilled when they got to care for others." That was what made working in Hyatt feel so special. In the year ahead, he surveyed the broader employee base as well as customers and learned that "we didn't have that same emotional connectivity with our guests." Or with Hyatt colleagues out on the front lines. Hoplamazian dedicated time to meeting with many of them. Through his own and others' probing into the colleague experience, he realized that the company evaluated employees largely based on their compliance with an elaborate set of rules and that "we tracked success in our hotels by compliance with a list of brand standards, not guest feedback."

He and his team articulated a clear and highly motivating statement of company purpose: to care for people so they can be their best. They also developed an extensive data-driven plan to align company practices with that purpose. Hoplamazian stressed that he saw this as the key strategic differentiator for Hyatt going forward. "My feeling was that we really needed to articulate what was so special about Hyatt. I thought it was the most effective way for us to compete against much larger players and to make sure we didn't become a commoditized brand." They didn't need to grow bigger to compete; they needed to provide the highest quality of care for their core customer base, higher-end business and leisure customers. This flew in the face of what analysts were urging. "The Wall Street analyst community were constantly asking, 'Aren't you too small to survive?'" he said. He also initially received pushback from the board and from within the company. But he made a strong case for how the initiative would lead to concrete results.

"It's important to clarify exactly how purpose translates into better performance," he highlighted. "You have to hear the critics because there are going to be a lot of critics. I don't think you can get distracted by them, but you need to listen carefully and make sure that you're addressing what the underlying nub of the criticism is. And in our case, it was, What's the payoff?"

He didn't sugarcoat what dealing with the resistance was like. "It was really hard," he told us. "There were many times when my frustration level boiled over." The deep emotional commitment Hoplamazian felt to the value of the purpose was instrumental in sustaining his energy to forge ahead. That commitment, he said, has "been personally incredibly important for me." It has also been integral to the transformative growth of the company, but growth on Hyatt's terms, maintaining its differentiation. "Without our purpose of care and what we did to commit ourselves to it, we would be a shadow of what we are today as an organization," he said. In the last five years, "we have doubled the number of our luxury hotel rooms, we've tripled the number of resort rooms, quadrupled the number of lifestyle rooms—the Hyatt portfolio has grown across luxury and lifestyle."

We could hear in his voice how energizing the clarity of purpose was for him, and this was true of other CEOs who made articulation of purpose central to their leadership. When we asked Indra Nooyi how she coped with Wall Street analysts' vociferous and sometimes quite nasty opposition to her Performance with Purpose strategy, she said, "You have to feel it [the purpose] in your heart. Everywhere I traveled in the world, I didn't just go to the Pepsi offices, I went to people's homes, I watched what they ate and drank. I tried to understand the issues they faced." She recalled being in towns that faced severe water shortage and seeing people lined up at diabetes clinics. That depth of concern also drove her proactive Playing to Win mindset and led her to encourage her industry peers to get out ahead of the problem as well. "Let's not act after we are told to act," she recalled that she said in one speech at the annual meeting of the Food Marketing Institute. "Let's act before we are told to act because we know the problem in front of us."

CEOs also told us about the deflating effects of not feeling a strong connection to purpose as their tenure progressed. One CEO, who had loved his role as divisional manager of a health-care company, struggled mightily with a lack of enthusiasm in his new role. As manager, he'd found great sustenance in being out in the field, visiting doctors, talking with patients in hospitals, and seeing the wonderful results of the services the company provided. As CEO, he stopped making those visits, and his enthusiasm suffered. The job became a real slog for him, and he decided to step down in year five.

CONSIDER WHETHER YOU'RE A SPRINTER OR A MARATHONER

If a CEO is unable to stay energized and continue vigorously driving change at the company, moving on is the right decision. But there might be a strong temptation to "retire in place." It's not hard to understand why, given the perks of the job and the opportunity to throw oneself into activities outside the company, with all the conferences to attend, speeches to give, roundtables to take part in. "Suddenly, you're part-time at your CEO job," a successful longtime CEO observed of others he'd seen falling into this behavior. Stephen Schwarzman, CEO and chairman of Blackstone, who cofounded the firm, has seen plenty of this behavior and commented, "It's like a bad marriage. It just goes on because you don't want to end it. Why would you? You lose half your net worth, you lose your house, you're out on the street.

You think, maybe we can get through another year, maybe it'll change." Before long, company performance begins to suffer. CEOs who hang on despite having lost their zest for the job are likely heading into the Complacency Trap we describe in the next chapter; they are just getting there ahead of time.

Because continuing to perform to a high standard in the job requires continued fortitude and enthusiasm, when moving through the Reinvention stage it's important to consider whether you lean toward being a marathoner or a sprinter. Marathoners are leaders with a longer-term vision. Their passion about that vision is critical to their staying in top fighting form. This is the orientation Indra Nooyi expressed in her memoir. She wanted "to set up PepsiCo to be successful for decades and decades." She was well aware that developing the healthier food offerings and growing them while also driving continued strong results for the legacy brands would be difficult. And she knew that she would take plenty of flak for it from Wall Street. Yet she kept finding new ways to further the mission, and by the end of her twelve years, 50 percent of the company's brands were in the healthier-foods categories, and they were a great contributor to profitability.

Another marathoner, David Novak, found taking over the newly formed Yum! such a tantalizing opportunity because, as he told us, "we were going to create the Yum! dynasty." He emphasized "dynasty-like performance" of "consistent growth year after year," with a target of at least 10 percent growth in earnings per share annually. Under his leadership, the company achieved that thirteen years in a row.

When Dave Cote took over at Honeywell, he knew getting the company into good shape would require many arduous years of process improvement and a transformation of the company culture, and he relished the challenge "to build an institution for the long term."

Other CEOs are more like sprinters: they prefer to run a shorter race. Their greatest excitement in stepping into the job is about righting the ship. They're especially energized by fixing problems that they can see a clear route to correcting. Their passion might also be about a particular strategic challenge, such as executing a big acquisition or managing the integration or the launch of a new product line. The challenges involved in longer-term strategic transformation aren't as appealing to them. We worked, for example, with a CEO who, in his first five years, did a stellar job of executing on a plan to reignite growth. He then realized that if he were to stay on, he would have to pivot to developing a longer-term transformational strategy because market conditions were evolving. He wasn't interested in that mission, and he moved to another CEO role to lead a turnaround.

In addition to leaders with a preference for shorter- or longer-term focus, there are mid-distance "runners." In our Life Cycle study we looked at how many of the top one hundred performers were sprinters or mid-distance or marathon runners, with a range of measures for performance. Note that in the full set of CEOs, there are roughly equal numbers of sprinters (38 percent), mid-distance runners (31 percent), and marathoners (31 percent). Yet, top performers tend to be sprinters and marathoners. And there are important differences in the nature of their performance success.

When it comes to TSR over their full tenure, marathoners were hands down the strongest performers, accounting for eighty-eight out of the top one hundred. But when it comes to CAGR, the sprinters were the winners, with forty-five out of the top one hundred. The mid-distance group trailed on both of these measures. These findings reinforce the observation that during the years of the Complacency Trap, years six through nine, CEOs' performance may be less than stellar, dragging down the overall performance numbers for CEOs who stay on through those years. Only in the longer term do they reap the rewards of reinventing the company.

Sprinters and marathoners use very different strategies to drive their success. It's important for CEOs to consider these approaches early so they know what type of athlete they are and whether it might be best to step down by or before year six. Our data shows that sprinters' success results from a focus in their approach to business improvements that is strikingly different from successful marathoners' approach. From the start, sprinters rely more on efficiency gains and increases in profitability to create value. This results in superior improvements in EBITDA margins, raising EBITDA from an average of 22 percent in their year one to 27 percent by year five. Marathoners, by contrast, take fifteen years—three times as long—to raise their EBITDA margins from an average of 20 percent to 25 percent.

When it comes to organic revenue growth, however, sprinters invest less in it, and in fact they achieve lower rates of revenue growth, which on average decreases from 9 percent in their first year to 4 percent by year five. By comparison, marathoners, from the start, focus more on revenue growth, boosting it from an average of 10 percent in their first year to 15 percent by year five. They also maintain stronger revenue growth throughout their tenure, with it barely dipping below 10 percent in any of their other ten-plus years. Another striking difference is that marathoners invest more in innovation early on, in keeping with their longer-term strategic horizon. They also engage in less M&A activity in their early years and make smaller acquisitions, then gradually step up their M&A activity as their years progress. Sprinters tend to focus more on M&A early on, and they pursue larger deals.

As CEOs head into the Reinvention stage, it behooves them to consider whether they are a sprinter. Should that be true, staying in the role longer may present especially tough challenges because efficiency gains will almost surely become harder to achieve. Meanwhile, their lesser focus on innovation and revenue growth may become an increasing drag on overall performance. Boards should also consider whether a CEO moving through this stage might have their best years of performance behind them. A tenure length of four to five years may be optimal for some CEOs regarding company performance, and this data may provide insights to assist in making that determination.

CEOs who stay on and move into the Complacency Trap stage will face distinctive new challenges that threaten their ability to stay agile and continue evolving themselves and their company.

5

COMPLACENCY TRAP

"You have to be changing faster
than the world is changing."

Shortly after sunset on November 29, 2014, the sixty-five-foot sailing sloop *Vestas Wind* was speeding through the choppy waters of the Indian Ocean, 268 miles from the nearest coast, that of the island of Mauritius. Captained by sailing ace Chris Nicholson, *Vestas Wind* was competing in the grueling Volvo Ocean Race, which traverses thirty-nine thousand miles over the course of nine months and presents some of the globe's most treacherous navigational challenges. Each boat is required to carry a body bag because of the number of deaths that have occurred in previous races.[1] But Nicholson and his navigator had determined this stretch of ocean posed no grave danger. Except, that was, for the thousand-mile-long string of coral reefs the *Vestas Wind* had unwittingly sailed straight into. At 7:10 p.m., the sloop slammed into a reef, which ripped through its hull and crushed its rudders. Seawater flooded in and shorted the electrical system. The *Vestas Wind* was stranded; only two days later would the crew be rescued.

The maneuvering required to reach the racing team was extraordinarily tricky due to the great danger of being swept into the reef.[2]

The *Vestas Wind* was "one of the best-equipped, best-crewed, best-skippered boats in ocean racing," one assessment of the accident heralded.[3] How could this have happened? Especially given that the captain and navigator had access to a remarkable array of high-tech navigational equipment. The official report concluded that the navigator had misread some data and failed to access other sources that would have alerted him to the danger. He had come to believe that the reefs they were fast approaching were underwater mountains—called sea mounts—the peaks of which were some forty meters below the surface. In making that assessment, he had not attended to a signal given by one important piece of equipment called a C-Map. This electronic mapping program displays a notification mark that alerts navigators to zoom in and get a more detailed picture of the area, warning them that there are obstacles. The navigator hadn't zoomed in to get the scoop. Meanwhile, he had not consulted paper charts, which were onboard and showed the string of reefs in stark relief.[4] Had the sun not yet set, of course, the debacle would have been averted when the crew saw the reef spreading out before them. It isn't small, stretching thirty-five nautical miles. But the ocean at night is like the ever more fast-paced and complex world of business: easily disorienting and harboring all manner of hidden dangers.

The story speaks to how even the most talented and experienced leaders, who've successfully navigated through many challenges, may overlook or misinterpret arising threats or fail to perceive them at all. That may be true even when they've instituted good monitoring systems, with the best data gathering and analytics, and have crackerjack strategy and operations teams supporting them. Ironically, the more success they've driven, the more they may be given to misreadings and a slackening of vigilance.

A great deal of attention has been paid in recent years to seemingly out-of-the-blue external shocks, as with Nassim Taleb's best-selling *Black Swan*. The COVID pandemic and wars in Ukraine and Gaza have reinforced the need to enhance risk-assessment measures and crisis scenario planning. Much less focus, however, has been put on the problem of more gradual deterioration, or stagnation, of performance. Our Life Cycle research reveals that this is a particularly common development beginning approximately after the first five years of a CEO's tenure. Company performance was lower on many fronts in years six to ten for two out of three CEOs than in their first five years. The rate of revenue increase slowed in these later years. Both EBITDA and ROIC slackened relative to earlier years, companies often became less efficient, and growth in operating income stalled. Commonly during these years, the tempo of innovation slowed. Companies may miss opportunities to jump on new technologies. They may stick with a strategic plan that's becoming obsolete. And they may fail to detect or may misinterpret warning signs of customer discontent, new competitive threats, operational dysfunction, or any other myriad means by which performance erodes. As results begin to betray to the market that problems have been brewing, TSR is dragged down, with the average performance during these years often below market returns. Our research into the performance of more than two thousand CEOs found that a plurality have lower-performing years during this period relative to the other stages of the CEO Life Cycle.

When CEOs depart during the Complacency Trap stage of the life cycle, generally from years six to ten, inefficiencies that have crept into the organization and problems that have been festering—such as an underperforming unit or product line—constitute much of the low-hanging fruit their successors immediately go after. This invites the question: If those problems are so apparent to new leaders and to the boards that appoint them, why haven't they been more effectively addressed?

Part of the answer is that a CEO's sheer load of responsibilities is so demanding. In attending to the most pressing concerns, it's inevitable that one focuses less intensely on problems that are slowly simmering or that are apparent but less impactful on results. In setting their initial priorities, CEOs must consciously place some issues on the figurative back burner. The more time that passes without tackling these issues head-on, the more corrosive they may become.

Signals of trouble brewing can also be devilishly difficult to detect and to interpret, even for those closest to the problem, let alone from the distance of the C-suite. They may also be covered up and may take years to come to light. This was infamously true with the ignition switch problem that ultimately forced GM to recall thirty million cars and pay over $2 billion in lawsuit settlements, with the greatest cost being the 124 lives lost as a result of accidents caused by the problem.[5]

We delved into the dampening of performance in this period to see whether additional factors are at play, ones specifically related to the experience of being in the CEO role for this amount of time. One we homed in on is, ironically, the success a CEO has achieved.

SUCCESS AND REVENGE EFFECTS

As former Intel CEO Andy Grove wrote in his influential book *Only the Paranoid Survive,* "Business success contains the seeds of its own destruction."[6] CEOs who make it to the Complacency Trap stage have navigated the rough-and-tumble of the Launch, Calibration, and Reinvention stages of the first few years. One unintended consequence of leading their firms adroitly can be an overly assured attitude about the course they've set and the organizational improvements they've made. They may let down their guard and delay drilling down into areas of lagging performance and scanning the horizon for threats and emerging opportunities. Grove famously warned, "Success breeds complacency." Many CEOs and directors we interviewed named complacency as a cause of lower performance in these years. "You get a little bit full of yourself, and the board's really trusting you," Greg Ebel cautioned. Director Ann Hackett shared, "I've seen over many years, both in my consulting career and my board experience, that companies that are successful start to think about success in a less daring way, which can actually breed complacency."

Of course, CEOs likely do not see that this is happening as it's happening. Given the intensity of the daily demands of the job and the punishing hours CEOs devote to it, it's easy to understand why they might not perceive themselves as complacent. Another factor at work here, though, is the *status quo bias*, a powerful and widespread psychological force in business. The concept was introduced by researchers William Samuelson and Richard Zeckhauser, who showed in studies with many kinds of decision-makers, including managers, that "when making an important choice, people are more likely to pick the option that maintains things as they are currently."[7] When you're enjoying success, your status quo bias is reinforced, which might be just fine. But given that after five, six, or seven years, market conditions will surely have evolved, it usually won't be fine to stick with the status quo later. When responding to those changes would involve making a substantial alteration to or even reversal of a winning strategy or to operational engineering you have orchestrated, the status quo bias makes recognizing the need for change and making the case for it to your team and board a good deal more challenging.

Nigel Travis, who led Dunkin' to strong revenue growth in nine years at the helm, observed in his book *The Challenge Culture* that companies "can quickly go from success to trouble . . . because the culture does not allow for challenging the status quo."[8] He shared with us that finding ways to break the spell of satisfaction with success was a main focus of his leadership. That was in part because of what he'd witnessed as a senior executive at Blockbuster.

The prevailing wisdom is that Netflix drove Blockbuster out of business because the leadership at Blockbuster failed to appreciate the potential of the Netflix mail-delivery and subscription business model. Blockbuster CEO John Antioco totally blundered when he declined to purchase Netflix for Reed Hastings' asking price of $50 million in 2000. But the story is more complicated, and more interesting.

Missing from that nutshell narrative is that John Antioco had pulled off a stunning turnaround. The year he was appointed, 1997, one analyst said of Blockbuster, "According to many on the Street, Blockbuster is worth zero."[9] The company had been purchased by Viacom three years earlier for $8.4 billion. Myriad leadership errors plagued Blockbuster, from problems with its distribution system to a badly misguided diversification into selling T-shirts, toys, books, and magazines, forcing it to take a $300 million charge chiefly for bad inventory. Two-thirds of its employees had left the prior year, including a third of upper management. Antioco was the third CEO appointed in a year. He'd just achieved great success as CEO of ailing Taco Bell and returned the company to strong growth, and he turned Blockbuster's results around fast. A leading entertainment-industry expert wrote, just two years into Antioco's tenure, "A year ago, that chain was a C-minus operation. Now, it's really quite a powerhouse."[10] Revenue and profits soared. As Nigel Travis recalled, "The company skyrocketed to the very top of its game in 2004."[11]

Antioco had by then sustained great success for seven years. That success reinforced Antioco's confidence in his strategy to put off building an online delivery business. "I didn't believe," he wrote later, "that technology would threaten the company as fast as critics thought."[12]

Had Antioco decided to build a mail-delivery business during those years, while whipping the brick-and-mortar business into shape, Blockbuster might have withstood the Netflix onslaught. Another cautionary tale about both/and thinking. Antioco did decide in 2004 to make a huge plunge into online ordering and mail delivery, spending $400 million to develop the business, which was his downfall. Due to his prior years of success, Viacom decided to sell its stake in the company. Activist investor Carl Icahn scooped up shares, gained control of the board, and he and the new directors imposed their own status quo bias on the company, firing Antioco and cutting back dramatically on investment in the online service while refocusing on brick-and-mortar stores.[13] Revenue immediately declined. The company stuck with the strategy as the ship inexorably sunk, and Blockbuster declared bankruptcy in 2010.

The problem of opting for the status quo, or perhaps only moderately tinkering with it, is not uncommon; it's just rarely so glaringly on display as with Blockbuster. Roger Martin, former dean of the Rotman School of Management, writes, "A rampant underestimation of the perils of the status quo is something I have observed consistently over a career of attempting to foster change and innovation as a strategist." Often he is brought in as a consultant by management teams who have become "sufficiently unhappy with the status quo to want to consider options for change." And yet, after he leads them through a rigorous consideration of possibilities, such as significantly broadening their product offerings or reengineering their manufacturing processes, they opt not to pursue any of them. He puts his finger on another strong force inducing status quo bias: risk aversion. "Having spent an intense amount of effort on understanding and 'marinating' in the risks of the proposed new initiatives, the management team would come to view all of the options for change as 'too risky.'"[14] Success provides cover for risk avoidance.

Another cause of status quo bias is the concentration of time CEOs spend with a comparatively small group of executives and directors. In a breakthrough study of how CEOs spend their time published in 2018, Harvard Business School colleagues Michael Porter and Nitin Nohria tracked the activities of twenty-seven CEOs for thirteen weeks and interviewed hundreds of other CEOs about their allocations of time.[15] The data indicated that 55 percent of a CEO's working time is spent in meetings or one-on-ones with their direct reports and other senior company managers, and another 15 percent is spent in discussions with board directors. But the longer these individuals have been working together on analyzing the company's business and developing strategy, the more difficult challenging their conclusions and decisions becomes.

Director Laurie Siegel shared, "Certainly, there are CEOs who maintain their change agent role over long periods of time, but there is more energy around being a change agent early in tenure and less later, when they tend to look at the culture and strategy as having their own imprint and therefore conclude it's great." Dan Garton, former CEO of American Eagle Airlines, made this point vividly: "You're no longer calling somebody else's baby ugly. It's a lot easier to do that."

Advice on combating status quo bias by methodically rethinking business assessments and gaining perspective from outside the firm is not new. But the problem is that far too few leaders develop a rigorous and continuous discipline of doing so. And if CEOs don't impose that discipline on themselves, nobody else will.

The imperative to challenge yourself becomes more difficult to achieve the longer you have been doing the job successfully. Nigel Travis said, "Being a CEO for longer is tougher because you have to find ways to keep improving." Some CEOs recalled feeling less engaged in this stage, with boredom creeping in. "When you get into years six to ten, the intellectual stimulus is less," one shared. "You come in with lots of ideas," another commented, "and then run out of them." Someone else said, "Years six to ten is a period of time when the luster is off the rose and what was new and exciting is no longer new and exciting."

Contributing to complacency is that boards generally become a good deal more deferent to CEOs by this point in their tenure. Directors are reluctant to act against less-than-stellar performance. In other words, complacency also creeps into boards, which our data demonstrates. We wanted to know the odds that a CEO would depart after underperforming the S&P 500 for one, two, three, and four consecutive years. In a CEO's first six years, the odds of departure after consecutive years of underperformance steadily increase. By the end of year five, the odds of departure spike up to 40 percent for those who've underperformed for three years in a row and to 50 percent for those who've underperformed for four years in a row. But then there is a steep drop-off in years six and seven, even if the CEO has underperformed for such an extended period of time. For CEOs who manage to get to year seven after three years of consecutive underperforming in the market, the odds of being forced out drop to 27 percent and continue to fall with every additional year to 16 percent.

In short, if they've made it to these later years, the data indicates that they are under considerably less board pressure. But it is difficult to discern how much of the lag in results can be attributed to the moves made, or not made, by the CEO versus so many other factors that drive results. That's just all the more reason for boards to be vigilant in exploring the causes with CEOs and pressing for solutions.

Sometimes boards can act like deer caught in headlights when a company is wrestling with thorny issues. That was true for a retailer that suffered from board indecision. The company faced increasingly tough competition from Amazon and other leaders in online sales, as virtually every retailer on the planet has. Costly missteps were made in replicating the behemoths' innovations, such as curbside pickup, and a number of store openings were delayed, further punishing revenue. The company was also hard-pressed for more investment in order to integrate online and brick-and-mortar sales channels. A succession-planning process had been underway for some time, and yet when a particularly strong candidate was presented to the board, the directors decided not to initiate a transition. As the company's fortunes deteriorated, a number of strong leaders left, further impeding the effort to turn the company's fortunes around.

Of course, any given board may well be extremely active, in these years and throughout a CEO's tenure, in working to address problems. But many of the directors we interviewed argued that, as Elizabeth Tallett put it, "boards need to take responsibility for evaluating the CEO in a far more forceful way." Tallett has served on multiple boards, including Moderna and Qiagen. A number of directors also reported, though, that more boards are becoming tougher and more proactive in taking action if CEO performance is flagging. Cheryl Grisé, a director for MetLife and ICF, told us, "There's more and more pressure on boards and less patience." That's coming from many fronts: activist investors, large institutional investors such as pension fund managers, and the court of public opinion. As we'll explore in Chapter 7, CEOs can use increased board vigilance to their advantage if they are proactive in communicating about arising issues and partnering with the board on solutions.

Investors and analysts may also communicate directly with CEOs, providing well-founded criticisms and good arguments for changes needed, or at least challenging a CEO's current views. Nigel Travis highlighted that "I've always loved dealing with investors and analysts because it gives you that outside-in perspective. Who else could I talk to who'd studied and gone into Starbucks, into McDonald's?" his two leading competitors. "It really enhances your understanding of the competition and broadens your external perspective enormously." He shared that before leaving any investor or analyst meeting, he'd say, "I've listened to all your questions. Now, I'm going to ask you one: Tell me what we're doing wrong. What would you do differently?" Being receptive to and actively soliciting such critique was only one way he combated status quo bias at Dunkin'.

He implemented a number of methods for challenging how he and his team were leading. One drill to force reexamination was this: "About once a year I would say, 'Okay, we've been taken over by a PE firm, what are they going to do?'" Travis had been appointed while Dunkin' was under the ownership of not merely one but three PE firms and had to work closely with them for two years to position the company for its IPO, so he was very well equipped to lead such discussions as these. "Every year," he recalled, "we'd reinvent some of the process." He also regularly put his team through an exercise he called "define your demise."[16] They would consider possible disruptions not limited to those common in risk-assessment planning, such as catastrophic weather events, terrorist attacks, and, because Dunkin' is a food business, breaches in food safety, such as a salmonella outbreak. They would also analyze possible longer-term developments, such as shifting population demographics, nascent technologies such as autonomous vehicles, and yet-to-be envisioned uses of current technologies such as customers sending their personal drones to pick up online orders.

Travis found a number of additional ways to regularly tap into the perspectives of those outside the firm. He would appear at Q&A sessions with MBA students, which gave him access to the views and attitudes of younger people. In addition, twice a year he attended CEO Summits held by Yale School of Management professor Jeffrey Sonnenfeld. These are vigorous debate events in which leaders across industries and from around the globe, as well as government figures, research analysts, and journalists, are challenged to engage in wide-ranging discussions of topics, from global political issues, such as competition with China, to leadership style. Attendees are often put on the hot seat, for example, to defend a statement they made in the press. Travis recalled that at one summit he was pitted against an investor who had very publicly shorted Dunkin' stock and whom Travis had strongly rebuked in a press interview. As he wryly commented about the encounter, the sessions ensure that "you can't fall asleep."

The single most helpful source of outside perspective Travis found was gained by joining the boards of other companies. "If you asked me about the one thing I've done in my career that really helped my development as a CEO," he told us, "it was sitting on another board. Every time I go to a board meeting, I write down more about the company I'm running than I do about that company." Acknowledging that many CEOs say they don't have time to serve on another board, he stresses that not only does it help to see how other companies operate but also the other company has "got a plethora of experiments going on that you can utilize for your company."

In our work with executives, we've seen that joining another board early in a CEO's tenure may be too large a demand on time, but after the CEO has achieved success, their middle to later years should afford more time for valuable external activities. The key is to make sure a board opportunity is truly valuable in terms of insights to bring back inside.

Other high-performing CEOs shared ways they challenge the status quo. Dave Cote had his assistants allocate two to three "X days" on his calendar every month when he'd have no meetings. He used that time to contemplate new ideas for the business, jotting them down in a blue notebook, and he established a self-discipline of regularly revisiting those notes about every six months. "The process of working through my blue notebook," he writes, "allowed me to break free of my daily context and look at our businesses from something approximating an outside perspective."[17] He also designated twelve days a year as "growth days" when he and his team would engage in intensive interrogation of opportunities and assessment of current operations.

Reed Hastings developed a discipline of staging formal debates with employees. He'd ask a few people to prepare arguments both for and against a possible change to make and present their findings to the whole team in the Netflix theater, and then they'd break into small groups to debate the positions. At one such meeting, the question was "Should we spend more money, less money, or no money on kids' content?" Hastings recounts, "There was a tsunami of support for investing in kids' content. . . . One director who is also a mom got up onstage and passionately declared, 'Before working here I subscribed to Netflix exclusively so my daughter could watch *Dora the Explorer*. I care a lot more about what my kids watch than what I watch myself.'" The debate led to the decision to hire a VP of kids and family programming, as well as to begin creating original animated shows. "After two years," Hastings reports, the company had "tripled our kids' slate, and in 2018, we were nominated for three Emmys for our original kids' shows."[18]

For Nigel Travis, keeping the need to challenge the status quo top of mind served well as he headed into this stage of his CEO Life Cycle. In his first five years, he grew the business impressively, introducing the leading-edge digital innovations of a mobile ordering app as well as an order delivery service, expanding considerably overseas, raking in a revenue bonanza with the launch of Dunkin' coffee K-Cups, and instituting a successful customer loyalty program. By the end of 2014, three years after the IPO in 2011, the share price had risen 85 percent, and with a multi-year plan to more than double its number of franchises—Dunkin' being an entirely franchised business—prospects looked strong. Then, in 2015, he recalled, "comp store sales hit a wall."[19] He launched an intensive strategy-evaluation process through a series of meetings with franchisees, and in 2016, the company introduced a new strategic plan that rebranded Dunkin' as primarily a coffee and breakfast chain. This involved dramatically paring down food offerings to focus on breakfast sandwiches rather than donuts, though donuts remained a staple. The plan also upped the ante on offering fast service. They ambitiously aimed at their eight-hundred-pound-gorilla coffee competitor, Starbucks, which at the time operated twice as many stores, while also clearly differentiated through lower pricing and order fulfillment speed. Comp store sales quickly rebounded, and the share price spiked, rising 107 percent from 2016 to 2020, when Travis stepped down, versus a 66 percent rise in the S&P 500 during that time.

Another irony of a string of successful years is that good results can provide cover for bad ones. And eventually, underperforming operations can become an overwhelming drag on overall performance. Success in areas of focus can obscure the need for more rigorous action elsewhere. And, again, it's all the more true the more success a CEO has achieved.

A. G. Lafley was massively successful in reigniting growth at Procter & Gamble during his first five years in charge. When he was appointed in 2000, the company was reeling, as described in one article: "the sort of ink-stained mess you'd find in a Tide commercial"—Tide being P&G's strongest brand.[20] During the tumultuous seventeen-month tenure of his predecessor, Durk Jager, the share price had dropped by half and the company had given up $50 billion in market capitalization. An attempted acquisition to bring the company into the pharmaceutical business was botched, and sales growth slowed.[21] Lafley had been with P&G for twenty-three years, most recently as president of Global Beauty Care and P&G North America. Among his earlier standout accomplishments were the launches of Liquid Tide and Tide with Bleach, which helped solidify the brand's dominance.

Lafley moved fast. He believed the company hadn't been focusing sufficiently on its leading brands, and he redirected resources to marketing and development of the ten biggest sellers, which together accounted for more than half of the company's revenues.[22] He explained at the time, "It's a basic strategy that worked for me in the Navy."[23] As a supplies officer, he'd actually run a store for servicemen during the Vietnam War. "I learned there that even when you've got a complex business, there's a core, and the core is what generates most of the cash, most of the profits." He also divested some of the company's food businesses, selling heavy hitters Jif peanut butter and Crisco oil to J.M. Smucker in 2001, because he'd determined they weren't good strategic fits. The market loved the moves, and the share price soared by just over 50 percent in his first two years, despite a general economic downturn in which the S&P 500 slipped 40 percent.

In 2005, after conducting an analysis of the past thirty years of failed acquisitions by the company, Lafley applied the lessons learned to lead the $57 billion Gillette acquisition, the largest in P&G's history. In one fell swoop, he increased sales by $10 billion and restored $50 billion in market cap.[24] Warren Buffett described it as "a dream deal."[25]

In 2006, Lafley was named CEO of the Year by *Chief Executive* magazine, and by 2007, he could report that he'd more than doubled the number of P&G brands that brought in $1 billion or more in sales annually, from ten to twenty-three, and the market cap had reached $200 billion.[26] Impressive growth by any estimation.

But during those years signals of increasing threats to P&G's model arose. Lower-priced private-label brands produced by leading grocery chains, such as Kroger, and big-box stores, including Walmart, Costco, and Target in the United States, had been taking market share from consumer-goods producers. Lafley and his team were acutely aware of the trend, but they decided not to get into that game, instead competing on the strength of their premium brands.[27] Enhancing marketing of those brands and increasing the pace and quality of innovation in those lines were their chosen competitive responses. Lafley had overhauled the company's innovation processes early in his tenure, notably introducing open innovation, but as P&G's chief technology officer Bruce Brown recalled, "We weren't getting the results we wanted. We were relying on a lot of small, incremental innovation as opposed to large, breakthrough innovation that transforms an existing category or creates new markets."[28] That had been P&G's great differentiating competitive edge, and the edge had worn down. In 2004, Lafley initiated another redesign of its innovation processes, which increased the success rate of new-product launches from 15 percent to 50 percent. More impressive success. Yet, those good results belied the fact that no truly transformative new products emerged.

When the 2007 financial crisis kicked off the Great Recession of 2008 to 2009, P&G fared worse than its leading rivals as consumers shifted to lower-cost products. After Lafley stepped down in 2010 and moved into the executive chair role, his successor, longtime P&G executive Robert McDonald, struggled mightily to renew growth, in part due to the long tail of the recession. But McDonald was also criticized for several missteps. An underlying problem, however, weighed on the company's results: it had held on to a large number of underperforming brands. Lafley recounted that when he became CEO in 2000, "55 percent of our revenue came from P&G's core strategic businesses. By 2010, 80 percent came from core strategic businesses."[29] He'd boosted select product lines brilliantly, but he hadn't continued to vigorously divest of the large number of other businesses that were contributing little profit or that were actually unprofitable. One analyst wrote, "Procter & Gamble has succumbed to its own success over the last several years. . . . P&G was supporting far too many brands. Mediocre brands took resources from the company's most dominant brands."[30]

In 2013, under pressure from activist investor William Ackman, the P&G board ousted McDonald, and Lafley was brought back as CEO for two years. Impressively open to making a major pivot, Lafley focused intensely on selling off or shutting down a hundred brands in a "shrink to grow" initiative. He pared the company down to its sixty-five best-performing brands. A much leaner P&G continued to face strong headwinds, but by 2016, the company began a march toward renewed growth.

Combating complacency becomes more challenging once a model for success has been developed. The case of Jim Craigie, who achieved one of the strongest and steadiest records of performance in all the S&P 500 during his tenure at P&G competitor Church & Dwight, highlights this fact. Craigie led strong continuous growth at Church & Dwight straight through the Great Recession and to the end of his twelve-year tenure in 2016. The share price rose 678 percent in those years versus an 84 percent rise in the S&P 500; it was in his middle years that the stock really took off. He also raised the company's dividend payouts every year. He shared with us that "complacency was my biggest concern," in part, because he and his team had crafted such an effective growth strategy. He knew that to achieve those goals, they would have to stay hypervigilant.

In his first two years in the role, Craigie conducted a deep strategic analysis and homed in on gross margins as the lynchpin to sustainable growth, the "gas in the engine," he said. "They drive everything—revenue, profits, share price appreciation, our valuation multiple, and TSR."[31] He implemented a rigorous standard for acquisitions to ensure improvement in gross margins and created a new product development team to enable a steady stream of product innovations for organic growth.

For acquisitions, he shared, "We would look at almost anything that came up within the industry for sale, and we had four factors that drove our decisions. One, we only would buy number one or two share brands in their category. We did not believe we could take a dying brand and turn it around. Two, we wanted to buy businesses that had higher gross margin than our company average, so would help our gross margin. Three, we looked for asset-light companies. We didn't want to buy a company with lots of factories or ones for which we'd have to build new factories. We preferred to bring operations into our own facilities. And four, we went for products that had some sort of advantage versus the competition that we could leverage with our marketing, sales, and operations muscle to make better." That formula guided the well-measured acquisition of numerous leading brands during his tenure, including Spinbrush, OxiClean, Orajel, Batiste, and Vitafusion. These were businesses that his own business leaders had the expertise to run, and he folded them into Church & Dwight's existing operations. Focusing on employees with R&D expertise, they kept, on average, only 10 percent of employees, many of whom joined the team at headquarters. "We doubled the size of the company," he reported, without adding substantially to the number of employees.

As for organic growth, Craigie insisted on each business launching strong new products every year. "We constantly harped on it," he said. Business heads worked with the new-product team he'd established, and the company implemented open innovation, tapping a large global network of scientists and inventors.[32] Church & Dwight became a leader in brand extension, for example, building its flagship brand, Arm & Hammer, from a business with products in three categories and sales of $135 million to offerings in over fifty categories and $1.2 billion in sales.[33]

Achieving such results, however, led to a dangerous sense of assurance. "I worried about complacency," Craigie recounted, "because in the company we got to the point where people were thinking we didn't need to worry, 'Of course we're going to deliver great results.' I'd say, 'No, you have to keep finding new ways of doing things.' It was a constant challenge for me to challenge all the employees that we couldn't rest on our laurels." He credits the bonus structure he set up with helping to keep the drive going. The bonuses "for my C-level team were all based on the same four factors: 25 percent based on revenue growth, 25 percent on meeting the gross margin target, 25 percent on hitting the earnings per share goal, and 25 percent on making the cash flow target. Like a Musketeers approach. It led to such a great team dynamic, because we all knew we won or lost together." This led to strong cross-silo collaboration. "My marketing people spent lots of time talking to the supply chain people because they knew holding down costs to improve gross margins was as important as revenue growth. They found ways to reduce costs without hurting the quality of the product."

Achieving the consistency of results Craigie and his team racked up is extraordinarily rare. Wall Street was dubious that they could keep it going. Analysts would say to him, "You can't possibly have another good year." After eight good years in a row, however, the Street was convinced. The stock then truly skyrocketed.

KEEPING CONFIDENCE IN CHECK

Craigie's ability to consistently succeed with acquisitions is the exception to the rule: a wealth of research studies indicate that between 70 and 90 percent of acquisitions fail to add value to acquiring firms.[34] Research has also shown that the high failure rate is attributable largely to the cognitive bugbear Daniel Kahneman, the author of *Thinking Fast and Slow*, cites as the most pernicious of all: overconfidence.[35]

Overconfidence is another cause of performance dips during the Complacency Trap years. Success tends to breed confidence, and the longer success is sustained, the greater the risk of overconfidence rearing its head. And that's true not only for acquisitions. Researchers conducted an extensive empirical analysis of strategy successes and failures made by several thousand of the world's largest companies. Their findings show that "the more your confidence grows, the higher your risk of arriving at the wrong conclusions."[36] Or, in the words of Bill Gates: "Success is a lousy teacher. It seduces smart people into thinking they can't lose."[37]

The trickiest thing about overconfidence is that it's fiendishly hard to know when you've crossed the line from healthy confidence to hubris; it's not exactly a line in the sand. What's more, showing great confidence is a powerful advantage in business because it leads people to evaluate you as more competent, which can make you more influential. The allure of confidence even appears to be embedded in our brain. Studies have found that when we encounter someone exuding confidence, an area of our brain involved in feeling positive emotion, the ventromedial prefrontal cortex, is stimulated. Scientists conjecture that we've evolved to fear uncertainty, and confident people come across as having good reason to be certain.[38]

After a number of successful years, keeping confidence in check may be made harder by the media. Hero worship may begin.

George Paz recalled that one of the most important pieces of advice he ever got in his career from one of his bosses was, "The worst thing you can ever do is start believing your own press." The boss had just orchestrated a deal that Wall Street was going crazy about, and Paz had said to him, "You must feel great!" He was, by contrast, circumspect. "You better understand," he told Paz, "that only you know how well that deal is actually performing and where the shortcomings came up so that when you do your next deal you see where those went wrong and focus on getting those things right. Because if you sit there and swim in your own accolades, you're going to drown at some point."

Invitations to give speeches, to join prestigious committees, and to hobnob at global leadership gatherings all may pour in. The job is fraught from the start with ego-inducing dangers. A CEO once commented to our colleague Ellen Kumata, "The corporate jet is the crack cocaine of CEO leadership." Within the company, people tend to fawn over you. In a discussion about how important it is to stay cognizant that all this special treatment is about the role rather than about you, Carl Bass, former CEO of Autodesk, recalled, "When I first became CEO, I joked that I became a lot funnier and smarter." He then cautioned, "The attention that's paid to you is not about who you are, it's about the position." He loved riding on San Francisco's public commuter railway, BART, because he'd be elbowed by other riders, whereas in the office "everyone holds the door for you and bows down."[39]

The more accolades that come your way, the more challenging tamping down your ego can become. It's simple human nature.

One remedy: actively cultivate confident humility. Wharton School professor Adam Grant writes in his book *Think Again*, "The most productive and innovative teams aren't run by leaders who are confident or humble. The most effective leaders score high in both confidence *and* humility."[40] How to get the balance right?

Probably the best means is to remain highly cognizant about mistakes you've made but also mindful about what you learned from them.

Piyush Gupta exemplifies confident humility. He was quick to share with us a number of mistakes he and his team made at Singapore's DBS Bank. In accounts of his career at DBS, those missteps are almost utterly obscured by the company's strong growth. Recall that DBS was in the doldrums when he took charge. One key problem was that the bank's technology systems were antiquated. "In my first phase, one of the main things that I had to focus on was fixing the plumbing of the company," he shared. When it came to data analytics, he recalled, "We had nothing. We were flying blind."

He hardly lacked confidence, however, in setting a strategic vision for DBS: to become the best bank in Asia. By 2013, four years in, that goal had been achieved. He did not rest on his laurels. "When we started getting all of these accolades as the best bank in Asia," he said, "I started getting very worried about complacency for the company. It's at times like this when you've got to reinvent, you've got to set new goalposts, because if you don't, then the system starts getting complacent." Again demonstrating bold confidence, at a company convocation in 2014, he set the bank's sights on becoming the best bank in the world. "I created a presentation depicting DBS as on our way up Mount Everest. We had reached base camp one, and we were going to keep ascending to base camp two, three, and four." He also had a slide created of a masthead of the *New York Times* dated May 2020 with a headline proclaiming that DBS had just been voted the best bank in the world. The bank was actually voted the world's best bank by *Global Finance* magazine in 2018, two years ahead of schedule.

He's clearly remained highly cognizant, nonetheless, of the value of owning one's failures, rapidly recounting three to us that he's kept top of mind. In 2012, he and his senior team "missed the fact that we had big capital exposures in India. Eventually, we wound up writing off several hundreds of millions of dollars, which was more money than we'd made in a decade. All the way to 2015, we kept writing off money." About losses incurred on investments in oil and gas ventures in Singapore, he highlighted that they "weren't due to lack of knowledge" but because he and his team had miscalculated their prospects. Regarding the launch "with a lot of fanfare" in 2016 of a digital-only bank in India, he recounted, "It became quite clear to us the strategy wasn't working." Although the bank rapidly signed close to two million customers, they weren't creating sufficient cash flow, "so we had to course correct."

Gupta wasn't pummeled by the market for these misjudgments. "I never got criticized by shareholders or analysts." For them, he shared, "I've got a clean sheet from an outside view, whether of shareholders or the media. We've been a lot more critical of ourselves," he said of himself and his senior team. "I kick myself a lot." That self-recrimination wasn't disempowering because he was also so vigorous in learning from missteps. For example, within a year of the failure of the India-based digital-only bank, DBS launched the successful digibank in Indonesia, a mobile banking app that allowed for signatureless transactions and incorporated cutting-edge biometric and AI technology.[41]

Gupta also demonstrated another tendency that helps keep success from leading to overconfidence: being tough-minded about the causes of your success. That involves being cognizant about situational factors that contributed, such as a bull market lifting virtually all boats. When reflecting on the great results of his first few years, Gupta shared, "We had fixed a lot of the fundamentals, but I got lucky, because China opened up in 2010. For the first time, the Chinese Central Bank allowed Chinese companies to go to the financial markets of Hong Kong and Singapore" for funds and trading activity. "That gave us a strong tailwind, and our results in those years were driven by China." Of course, had the fundamentals not been put in good order, much of that business might not have come to DBS. The success resulted from both leadership and luck.

Keeping overconfidence in check is helped when you coach yourself to give credit due to rivals and to emerging competitors that might otherwise be dismissed as insignificant threats. As Piyush Gupta headed into his Complacency Trap stage, he reached outside the banking domain to explore the emerging world of fintech, and what he learned, he told us, "scared the daylights out of me." He and his team had attempted to acquire a bank in Indonesia, but regulators nixed the deal. He concluded that he'd be forced to pursue a primarily organic growth strategy. The trouble, though, was that the traditional avenues for that growth "would require very deep pockets and long periods of time." He wanted to move faster. This was in 2014, and Alibaba founder Jack Ma had just launched Ant Financial. Gupta requested a meeting with him. By going entirely digital, "they were completely redefining how banking could be done," Gupta recalled. Acknowledging their entrepreneurial prowess, he saw fintech as a potentially existential threat to traditional banking. His response was to lead a radical transformation of DBS, turning it into a technology leader. This is why three years later he was able to launch digibank. Many more leading-edge innovations have followed.

In driving the transformation, he drew on earlier career experience with technology, both in operations and e-commerce for Citibank. As noted, he left Citi to start his own dot-com. In that venture, he had the opposite of luck: he launched it in 2001, just as the dot-com bubble was bursting. Now he made good on the pain of that debacle. "The perceived wisdom then," he recalled, was that

DBS should create a separate division for digital banking or buy a fintech start-up. "We took a contrary view. We were going to bring everyone along. Our battle cry was that we were going to become a twenty-thousand-person start-up." He invested heavily in retraining existing employees and hired a phalanx of data scientists. To engage employees in the mission, he launched regular hackathons and he set a goal of conducting one thousand experiments a year.

With a strong focus on optimizing the potential of artificial intelligence, he had to pour himself into learning about the technology. One way he did so was to take part in a global competition called DeepRacer hosted by Amazon Web Services. Participants must program a self-driving model car that they race on a track, and competitors with the fastest times then compete in a showdown. From this endeavor, not only did Gupta learn more of the ins and outs of AI development but his participation also inspired employees throughout the organization to embrace the reinvention. Three thousand DBS employees participated, and out of them, Gupta came in nineteenth in the race. DBS won the competition for the Asian region, and three of its employees participated in the grand finale held in Las Vegas.

The result of Gupta's constant push for innovation is that DBS was named best bank in the world by *Global Finance* magazine, not just that once in 2018 but every year thereafter, for five years in a row as of this writing.

Gupta's continued strong performance as he headed into his Legacy years demonstrates a key finding from our Life Cycle study, which we'll explore in the next chapter: the long-standing yet misguided notion that the optimal length of CEO tenure is ten years. Leaders who no longer have passion and energy for the job as they approach the Legacy stage might better move on to a new challenge. But for those who still have a fighting spirit and devotion to a longer-term vision, continuing in the role after ten years may well lead to the enormous satisfaction of seeing earlier moves pay off handsomely and knowing they are leaving their successor a good runway for continued strong performance.

But, of course, as we'll see, the Legacy stage presents distinctive challenges as well as rewards.

6

LEGACY

"One of my goals is to be,
ultimately, dispensable."

With three laps to go in the 1995 Formula One European Grand Prix, the track slick from heavy rain, Michael Schumacher bore down on leader Jean Alesi. Schumacher pulled up wheel to wheel with Alesi just as they rocketed toward the track's treacherous Veedol chicane, a nearly forty-five-degree bend to the left followed almost immediately by another forty-five-degree bend to the right. The Veedol is so tricky to maneuver that most drivers lose considerable time on it. Alesi had lost a full five seconds in the Veedol some laps earlier, having verged off the track into the gravel. Schumacher, who drove so exquisitely on rain-soaked tracks that he was dubbed by German fans the "Regenmeister"—rain master—saw his moment. At the first hard turn of the Veedol, Schumacher surged past Alesi in a move described as "so millimetrically perfect in its execution that only a handful of drivers in Formula One history could have hoped to have pulled it off."[1] The two cars actually touched for a moment. Two laps later, Schumacher streaked to victory.

Schumacher won the World Driver's Championship, the sport's highest prize, that year for the second year in a row. He is the youngest driver, at twenty-six, ever to win the prize back to back. He'd been driving for the Benetton team, and his future there would surely have been secure. But he had bigger plans.

The next year, Schumacher signed on with Ferrari, the most iconic team in the sport's history. Legendary for dominating the sport in the 1950s through the 1970s, Ferrari hadn't kept up with innovation in engine design and hadn't won a championship since 1979. Schumacher relished the challenge of restoring Ferrari to its former glory, but he knew that would likely be a many-years-long quest. About Schumacher's decision to join Ferrari, one sports journalist wrote that he "was risking his best years on a team out of step with the times."[2] Indeed, though Schumacher was widely considered the best driver in the sport, he wouldn't win another championship for some time. But it turned out that Schumacher's best years were yet to come.

With his bold vision for Ferrari, he lured Benetton's brilliant technical director and chief designer to join him, and they collaborated on the intensive work of building Ferrari's cars back into leading powerhouses. Their commitment paid off in spades. From 2000 to 2004, Schumacher led Ferrari to five consecutive World Championships, an unprecedented reign in the sport. What's more, Schumacher accomplished the feat in his years ten to fifteen in Formula One, beginning when he was thirty-one and ending at thirty-five. Formula One had increasingly become a younger man's sport, with few championships won by drivers over thirty.[3] But Schumacher showed that age was not necessarily an impediment to superlative performance.

Michael Schumacher came to mind as we wrote this chapter because he exemplifies successful CEO performance in the Legacy stage. For those who still have great energy and enthusiasm for the work, this stage can be one of especially rewarding payoffs. That's true in terms of not only company performance but also longer-term visions coming to fruition. They can solidify a legacy, secure in the knowledge that they are handing off a healthy company that is poised for continued strong growth, even as their successor will need to evolve that strategy in time, just as they had to do.

One of the myths about the CEO job that our Life Cycle study puts to rest is the rule of thumb that ten years is an optimal length of tenure. Much ink has been devoted to the question of optimal tenure length, and ten years has become conventional wisdom. That was the overwhelming consensus, for example, in a survey of board directors we conducted. The common view is that, past that duration, a CEO loses steam in driving performance and that results tail off. Many CEOs, in fact, adhere to this advice. For example, former Medtronic CEO Bill George gave himself a term limit of ten years when he was appointed, and he stuck to it. Yet, many CEOs who are considered the highest performers year after year in various rankings, such as by *Barron's* and *Harvard Business Review*, have been in the job longer. The *Harvard Business Review* writes about the leaders selected for its annual CEO 100 listing of best performers that they "demonstrate remarkable longevity" having "held their jobs for an average of 15 years."[4] Some interesting quantitative research also indicates that CEOs in the role longer than ten years perform comparatively better, as a group, than those with shorter tenures.

For example, in *Fortune* magazine's 2012 survey of shareholder returns at one hundred public companies during the tenure of their CEO, returns improved the longer the CEO's tenure. For CEOs who departed after five or fewer years, returns were about a fifty-fifty mix of positive overall and negative. Starting with a tenure of about seven years, the number of CEOs with positive overall returns overtook those with overall negative returns. For tenures of between ten and fifteen years, which the authors deemed was "the ideal," the proportion of positive to negative returns continued to increase.[5]

One of the key initial goals of our Life Cycle study was to use our extensive data set to examine this issue. We found incontrovertible evidence that the conventional wisdom that ten years is best is wrong. Our analysis showed that, from 2000 to 2022, 26 percent of CEOs were in the role for over ten years. The TSR performance for this group was stronger throughout that five-year period than in the previous five-year period. What's more, the proportion of CEOs beating the S&P 500 in these years was higher than the numbers in any of the other stages, coming in at 58 percent. Finally, performance in these Legacy years was also a good deal less volatile than performance in any other stage. As opposed to the large spikes up and down in TSR often seen in earlier stages, in the Legacy years results tend to be steadier. Although a CEO's highest performance throughout their tenure might occur in earlier stages, resulting from, for example, the honeymoon lift or the beginning of the Reinvention stage at about year three, the Legacy years are distinctive for their reliability. Leaders in their Legacy stage more consistently deliver strong results.

What accounts for the strong performance? One answer is the wisdom they continue to learn through dealing with ever-evolving challenges. They've gained mastery over the complex demands of the job. Our analysis shows that CEOs in their Legacy years often make more moderate investments in innovation and slow the pace of acquisitions, but that doesn't mean they are slacking off.

Rather, they've developed more precision in allocation of resources and calibration of the moves they make. They're highly prudent stewards.

Exemplary is Mark Hoplamazian, who was in his seventeenth year at the helm of Hyatt when we spoke with him. He emphasized that he can make key decisions more quickly and is more sure-footed in his decision-making. "I get there faster in most cases now than I did before because I know the industry dramatically better. We've been through deals that went sideways, deals that have been amazing home runs, and deals that have failed. That cumulative experience, along with an agile mindset, leads you to be able to make faster judgments."

In fact, he's continued to drive a juggernaut of expansion for Hyatt. Having steered the company through the COVID crisis, he capitalized on a subsequent boom in both leisure and business travel to make the bold move of launching a midrange brand, Hyatt Studios, a pivot from his strategy of focusing exclusively on the luxury high end of the business. The results achieved overall in his Legacy years are enviable, to say the least: "We have tripled our global portfolio of hotels since going public in 2009, while our global development pipeline has quadrupled. Importantly, since we always start by listening, our portfolio has grown to meet the increased demands for luxury and resort accommodations among our guests, with over 70 percent of our rooms now categorized as luxury and upper upscale."

The market tends to be good at perceiving this mastery and places the highest confidence in CEOs in these years, demonstrated by the higher multiple of firm valuation to earnings (measured by EBITDA) that investors assign companies helmed by CEOs in their Legacy stage. Our analysis showed that the multiple increased by 25 percent in these years. Knowing that such an experienced and accomplished leader is at the helm is reassuring, not only for market analysts and investors but also for boards and the CEO's leadership team.

Another key factor is that, early in their tenure, many of these marathoners set in motion substantial transformations of their firms that required at least ten years to bring to fulfillment. Had they been persuaded by the popular notion that they should step down by year ten, they would have deprived themselves of the enormous satisfaction of seeing their transformation work pay off.

BRINGING MOVES MADE TO FRUITION

Consider Dave Cote's fifteen-year run. It wasn't until his tenth year that he finally gained widespread recognition for Honeywell's remarkable turnaround. He knew from the start that the transformation of Honeywell he envisioned would take ten to fifteen years, and he committed himself to staying for the required duration—assuming, of course, that the board didn't ask him to go. He had not underestimated the task before him.

When he took charge in 2002, the company was, in his words, "a train wreck on the verge of failure."[6] A merger with Allied Signal in 1999 and the purchase of Pittway for $2.2 billion that same year had both gone badly. "The three cultures were never integrated," Cote recalled.[7] General Electric's proposed acquisition of the company was blocked in 2001 by the European Commission over concerns about the effects on competition in the sector. In addition, Honeywell had missed numerous earnings calls and had announced write-offs of $8 billion. Many of the most talented senior executives had exited while three CEOs circulated in and out over the prior four years. Cote estimated that about a quarter of leadership positions in the company were unfilled when he arrived.

Ten years after Cote stepped in, Honeywell's TSR had risen in a gradual but steady progression—all but during the 2008 to 2009 recession—by a cumulative 215 percent, even as the S&P 500 rose 88 percent and the performance of lead rivals paled in comparison: 3M achieved an 80 percent rise, and General Electric notched a vastly underperforming 9 percent.[8]

In Cote's tenth year, 2012, market commentators began singing his praises—after largely neglecting to highlight his exceptional improvements for years. Cote was described as "one of the best leaders in business, running one of the best-managed companies,"[9] and hailed by Jim Cramer in *Fortune* as "one of the great CEOs of our time." Cramer also remarked, "Yet he's stayed below the radar."[10] Cote remained solidly on Wall Street's radar thereafter. In 2013, he was named CEO of the Year by *Chief Executive* magazine, which might have seemed an opportune moment to take a bow and exit stage right, especially given that the global industrial economy had just entered a downturn that presented Honeywell with significant challenges. But Cote still had great energy, and he wanted to keep driving the transformation. Impressive as the turnaround had been to date, over the next five years, before he stepped down in March 2017, the share value truly soared, steeply rising another 110 percent.

That was the result of Cote's marathoner "go slow to go fast" moves coming to fruition. Rather than flashy, highly risky, and dramatic moves, he'd made rigorously calibrated incremental improvements in business operations. These were combined with a steady stream of divestments and moderate acquisitions. Indeed, he is a standout example of someone who has mastered programmatic M&A, the systematic, highly strategic, and well-paced acquisition of relatively small companies compared to the size of the acquiring firm. Cote made forty-four acquisitions during his fifteen-year tenure, putting him in the 98th percentile of M&As conducted in our CEO sample. Cote's acquisitions were, on average, firms that were only 1.9 percent of the market capitalization of Honeywell.

Regarding operations, implementing the Honeywell Operating System company-wide took ten years. At a time when many US corporations were rapidly ramping up operations in emerging economies, he focused on expanding operations first in only China and India. He also emphasized slower organic growth of Honeywell's own operations there rather than making a flurry of acquisitions, as some rivals did, often to disastrous outcomes.

When he realized midway through his tenure that Honeywell should begin investing more heavily in growing the software products businesses, he knew that would be another massive transformation that would take many years. The company needed a whole new army of first-rate software engineers. He launched an aggressive recruiting program, competing with the software behemoths for talent, and ultimately transitioned half the company's engineering staff from hardware to software specialists. A centerpiece of the transformation was the years-long development of a cloud-based software-as-a-service data analytics platform, a completely new terrain for Honeywell.

"Analysts wondered when this restructuring would end," he said, "and they didn't like our answer: never."[11] He was highly cognizant that "entropy is the rule in organizations, as it is in the physical universe. Over time, all organized systems evolve toward chaos. Unless you pursue change relentlessly, your efforts will eventually wither away."[12] Cote didn't let that happen.

Indeed, it was in year thirteen of his tenure, 2015, that he made his one swing-for-the-fences acquisition effort: he offered $90.7 billion to take over United Technologies.[13] In one fell swoop, the acquisition would have made the combined company one of the world's largest industrial firms. Cote proposed that he lead the company, but United rebuffed the offer.

Here is another aspect of how the most successful long-termers manage their Legacy years. Even as Cote continued to vigorously pursue growth, and despite his ambition to lead the company through a transformative step-change in scale, he was preparing the ground for his succession. In his Legacy stage, he led the implementation of a rigorous succession-planning process, working with human resources to identify a strong group of contenders and move them into roles that would further build their capacities. Shortly after the United offer was denied, Cote announced that he would step down in 2017. The succession process had identified Darius Adamczyk as a particularly strong candidate, and in June 2016, the Honeywell board announced Adamczyk's appointment.

Cote was adamant when he took on the role that he would not leave his successor anything like the mess he'd inherited. What he did leave to Adamczyk was a company in such strong shape, with such clarity about the road ahead, that Adamczyk could hit the ground running, and during his six-year tenure, the stock price continued on its tear, rising another 67 percent.

A DISTINCTIVE BALANCING ACT

A particularly tricky aspect of the Legacy stage is that, by this time, almost all CEOs know that they will be exiting the job soon. But to keep performance strong, they have to continue to lead innovation. They've got to manage driving full speed ahead while focusing on preparing possible successors. Interestingly, this is akin to a feature of Michael Schumacher's driving technique that accounted for his exceptional performance navigating hairpin turns. Analysis of how he drove through turns showed that he had mastered the difficult maneuver of simultaneously accelerating to top speed with one foot while braking with the other. That allowed him to optimize control, and he was able to fly through turns as much as fifteen miles per hour faster than other drivers.[14]

When it comes to CEOs, the Legacy years present a similar both/and challenge. CEOs must stay very much in command and continue to drive growth, including pursuing new avenues for innovation, making strategic pivots, and capitalizing on great acquisition opportunities. But they must also prepare for stepping down and not neglect the responsibility of cultivating candidates to succeed them. One problem about their length of service is that they may come to be seen as virtually irreplaceable. The flip side of the great confidence they've earned is that investors and analysts, as well as many leaders within the company and the board, stress over whether anyone as good as them can be found. A danger for CEOs in this position is that they may let ego get the best of them and not work to ensure a smooth transition.

For some CEOs we interviewed, deciding when to relinquish the role was straightforward, but for others, it was excruciating. As we'll discuss more in Chapter 8, stepping down can be extremely difficult at any point in your tenure. After so many years, deciding to move on can be a particularly daunting psychological challenge. For some, the decision was facilitated because they no longer had the physical health, energy, or desire to continue doing the job, at least not to their high standards. Some had suffered health problems that were a big factor. Jim Craigie, who stepped down in his twelfth year, when he was sixty-two, realized "in fairness to my company, and in fairness to me, I just can't keep this up." He also wanted to have some time to smell the proverbial roses. "It was time for me to enjoy life," he said, "and turn over the job to somebody who had the energy I used to have doing it." In addition, he felt confident he had a strong successor in Matthew Farrell, who had been his CFO for ten years and whom Craigie had moved into the COO role two years earlier. Craigie didn't depart from the company altogether, however; he remained on the board for several more years as nonexecutive chair.

David Novak stayed on for fifteen years and then stepped down at age sixty-three because he no longer wanted to do the extensive traveling required. "We were in over a hundred countries, and I had to travel all the time." He also considered the work of meeting with franchise owners his greatest strength. "I knew what I was great at was being out in the field, out in the front line, being with the people, understanding what the problems were and helping people solve them." He shared that "you need to step down when you can't put on the uniform the way you used to."

Deciding when to leave may also be facilitated by the completion of some important challenge, such as the integration of an acquisition or the successful launch of an important new product. Such circumstances also assisted Novak in deciding on his timing. He had just orchestrated the spin-off of Yum!'s China business, which had been ailing for several years. "As we target the separation of our China business by the end of 2016," he said in his retirement announcement, "and transition to two powerful, independent companies, it is a perfect time for me to complete my retirement." One reason making the call may be, by contrast, really tough is that there isn't such a clear final achievement to pin an exit to. As Cote's comment about entropy highlights, no matter how many achievements you rack up, the job of a CEO is never fully finished. There is always more change to drive; there are always more fixes needed and new building to do. A CEO contemplating leaving often is in the midst of wrestling with some knotty issue. They might still be struggling with a messy merger. A product launch might not have gone to plan. Any number of moves made are still in progress and much work left to do to leave the company in great shape for a handoff.

Take the case of Steve Ballmer and Microsoft. In 2012, his twelfth year as CEO, the company launched its Surface tablet computer, a huge investment in transitioning into hardware offerings. Sales fell far short of plan, and the company was forced to take a $900 million charge against Surface inventory and faced a firestorm of criticism for lagging behind competitors in design prowess. Many market analysts and journalists covering the industry argued that Ballmer had taken far too long to make the move to building a tablet and now had botched it. One pundit even compared the launch of the Surface to the infamous failure of Ford's Edsel, writing, "The Edsel failed because it was ugly and its design was wildly out of sync with consumer preferences." Similarly, "The Surface is entirely out of sync with what the buying public wants."[15] Ballmer admitted mistakes were made in the launch and committed to improving the Surface, initiatives he quickly set in motion. Microsoft launched an updated Surface Pro early in 2013 to improved customer interest.

Meanwhile, in January of that year, Ballmer announced a major reorganization plan, aimed at overhauling the company's innovation processes. The announcement was met with widespread plaudits. That year, the market was also responding favorably to Ballmer's revamping of the company's foundational product, the Windows operating system. He'd pulled off the successful release of a much-enhanced Windows 8 version at the end of 2012. By late spring of 2013, the share price began rising after a long stretch of languishing. Ballmer seemed poised at long last to lead the company to new heights. But then, in May of that year, he made the surprising announcement that he would be stepping down within a year.

He was only fifty-seven at the time, with plenty of energy and passion for continuing with the mission. He said the decision was extremely emotional for him. He fully expected to get the restructuring well underway before leaving, but the board was pressing for faster progress. In light of that, as he said in a press statement at the time, "We need a CEO who will be here longer term for this new direction. . . . I take this step in the best interests of the company I love; it is the thing outside of my family and closest friends that matters to me most." Making the call was all the harder because he was so highly identified with the company. He'd been the thirteenth employee and had been a lynchpin in solidifying the total dominance of Windows.

That identification with the company, specifically with the CEO role, is another reason deciding to hand off to a successor can be so hard.

NOT LETTING THE JOB BECOME THE SELF

After so many years in the role, a CEO's sense of self can become deeply entwined with the job such that it is hard for the individual to envision flourishing in life after stepping down. Some CEOs, therefore, resist handing off longer than they should, and boards often fail to press the case. This tends to lead to poor succession planning. And when rocky, if not disastrous, transitions follow, the CEO's legacy is badly tarnished, not to mention that poor transitions generally lead to the loss of a great deal of shareholder value.

A person's identity is often too wrapped up in the job they do. The more rewarding and high-status the job, and the longer they are in it, the more powerful that identification with the role is likely to become. Our colleague Ellen Kumata has coached many CEOs through transitions. She shared, "The power of the CEO role is seductive. Everyone is deferential to you. Then there are the corporate jets and the drivers." After ten plus years of that lifestyle, anyone would feel the tug to stay. It's not hard to understand that, by this time, being CEO may have become the key defining aspect of your identity.

Some merging of identity with the job cannot be avoided. Keith Barr, former CEO of InterContinental Hotels Group, went through a challenging process of deciding to step down. He said, "Leaving was really hard. Anyone who says that the CEO job does not become part of your personality is not giving you the full picture." But he and many others managed to keep a strong sense of self apart from the role. They were mindful that, as Carl Bass, the leader of Autodesk for twenty-four years, cautioned, "It's really important to separate who you are from the position."[16]

The sociologist Erving Goffman famously made the case in his influential book *The Presentation of Self in Everyday Life* that it's important to be cognizant that we are playing a role in many spheres of our lives, especially at work. He introduced the concept of "impression management" and the idea of being highly aware of the impressions we're making. In much of our lives, he observed, we are like an actor on a "front stage," where we must tailor our behavior to situational demands. "Backstage," in our homes and out with friends, we can act entirely like ourselves. For the sake of our well-being, he argued, we must maintain a distinction between our backstage and front-stage senses of self.

More recently, Bill George made a related argument in his book *Authentic Leadership*. Much has been written about how important it is for business leaders to be authentic. George is a main voice in the literature. But he warns of the misunderstanding that has grown about what being an authentic leader involves. In his conception, being authentic does not entail always showing up as your unvarnished self or saying exactly what's on your mind. Rather, "Authentic leaders monitor their words and behaviors carefully to be attuned to their audiences. . . . They do so because they are sensitive to the impact their words and actions have on others," which for CEOs, is particularly powerful.[17] Dave Cote writes about how important this varied presentation of self is: "Many leaders tend to evoke the same person in every meeting, but that's a mistake. In one meeting you might need to come across as angry, in another pensive, in another friendly."[18] What this involves, in other words, is a CEO adjusting their "front stage" presentation of themselves to meet the needs of the audience and situation, which is a highly self-aware way of behaving.

George stresses that being authentic is essentially about having good self-awareness, a good understanding of your "backstage" self. Being an authentic leader is not a matter of revealing your inner self at work but of working hard to develop self-awareness through regularly engaging in self-reflection and soliciting critical feedback from colleagues. It's about seeing your behavior more accurately and pushing yourself to be true to the values you aspire to exemplify. Being a great leader also requires keeping your ego in check, and not overly identifying as CEO is a great help with this. It also makes passing the reins to a successor less fraught and helps you embrace the responsibility of developing a strong bench of contenders to replace you.

Hubert Joly is another leader who exemplifies this awareness that, as CEO, you're playing a role and part of that role is preparing to leave the spotlight. He wrote in an article published in the Minneapolis *Star Tribune*, "I am not the chief executive officer of Best Buy. Yes, that is what is on my business card, but the fact is I am not the CEO. While I am honored to hold the job of CEO . . . I am not defined by my job. It is not who I am."[19] He elaborated that as CEO, "One of my goals is to be, ultimately, dispensable. . . . Leaders must keep in mind what legacy they are seeking to build, with an eye toward creating a team to whom they can pass the baton. In the end, any good leader has to be measured in part by what comes after he or she leaves office, which, of course, ties closely to the idea of the leader being dispensable."

He followed through on that ethic of building a strong team and working to ensure he would be replaced by a worthy successor.

Having spotted the talent of Corie Barry when she was several levels down from the C-suite, he put her into a series of challenging roles that rounded out her experience, including chief strategic growth officer, giving her leading responsibility in developing and launching the Building the New Blue strategy. Next he appointed her CFO, from which position she was selected as his successor and proceeded to thrive in the role.

A LEGACY FOR THE COMPANY

Marathoner CEOs often commit to staying longer in the role because they feel such a strong drive to leave a lasting mark on the company. For some, as executive coach Damien Faughnan shared with us, it is "almost a compulsion." The more their drive is about building the company and leaving it in strong shape, rather than about burnishing their reputation, the more psychologically prepared they will be to accept that the end is in sight.

Multiple meanings have been attributed to the word *legacy* over time, and it's often thought of as how one's contribution will be remembered. In other words, it is about looking back, in retrospect, on achievements. But the first-order meaning of the word is "a gift bestowed," such as to one's children. It's this way of thinking about *legacy*, as a gift for those who will lead in the future, that enables CEOs to do the best job of managing the conflicting demands of charging hard while also preparing to move on.

The most effective CEOs in their Legacy stage focus intently on how they can optimally shore up the company's future. How can they give the company an outstanding chance to continue thriving without them? They demonstrate what psychoanalyst Erik Erikson defined as a *generativity mindset*: "the concern in establishing and guiding the next generation." He found that those who have the most rewarding later years in life shift more into this generativity mindset, feeling that they "have a responsibility to invest in others."[20]

Leading researcher of CEO leadership Donald Hambrick and his colleagues concur that the generativity mindset is a powerful aid in making a smooth transition to a successor. In contrast, for those who overly identify with the role of CEO and who are more concerned about reaping the status rewards of the job, the prospect of no longer being CEO can be outright terrifying.[21] Their anxiety about what life will be like once out of the role is so intense that they may subvert efforts to get a transition underway, even if they're not producing the results the company needs from them.

We have seen this subversion in action. One CEO with a checkered performance record who'd been in the role well over ten years drove away a number of potential successors and held the board in thrall to his arguments about why these candidates were inadequate. Despite his mixed results, he argued so convincingly about how one possible successor lacked maturity and how another with poor operations skills couldn't possibly take on the role that the board delayed kicking off a succession-planning process for several years. Meanwhile, the company's performance suffered as several serious issues it was facing were neglected.

Contrast that to the exemplary generative thinking of Lew Hay. Recall that after his first few years, he began to ramp up investment in renewable energy production, and NextEra Energy became the leader in both solar and wind production in the United States during his tenure. He planted many seeds for that growth, focusing on starting small-scale new businesses rather than flashy acquisitions. Working deliberately and managing risk deftly, he and his team launched one new successful business every year. By his year ten, the compounding returns of that steady growth allowed Hay to commit in 2011 to a huge investment in development of wind and solar production: for the years 2011 to 2014, he devoted $5.8 billion to build solar and wind farms.[22] NextEra outperformed the S&P 500 considerably during those ten years, with its share price increasing 110 percent versus 13.7 percent for the S&P 500, yet the price-to-earnings ratio remained about on par with competitor firms that had not performed nearly as well. "It took many years of steady outperformance for the markets to wake up and reward us with a higher PE ratio," Hay recalled. The markets began to do so in 2012, his eleventh year as CEO, when the share price truly skyrocketed. And that was when he decided to step down, at only fifty-six years of age.

He could see that the company's trajectory was looking superb. He knew that probable stellar future would be due largely to the strong foundation he'd built. And he was happy to step aside and allow a successor to take the helm for the truly breakout success to come. "I had a person who was a very good successor," he shared. He was "the one person I could really envision taking the company to the next level. I knew there was going to be a window of time where I could make him the CEO, because if he thought I was going to stick around until I was sixty-five, he would have gotten scooped up to run another company." Hay continued, "There were other things I wanted to do with my life," though he was in no hurry to pursue them. "In my perfect world," he said, "I would have stayed another couple years, but I really didn't want to run the risk of losing him."

That successor, James Robo, did indeed run the company well. TSR rose 500 percent during his tenure. In Hay's second year as CEO, he'd brought Robo to NextEra as vice president of corporate development and strategy, and in recognition of his leadership potential, Hay had promoted him in 2006 to president and chief operating officer, heir apparent. Convinced that he could hand over to a strong successor, Hay began discussing plans for his departure with the board four years before it was announced.

Hay had also attended well to developing the larger management team; there was very little turnover of the team he built through most of Robo's tenure. "In general, they were younger people I had brought in," he recalled, and "the team has really carried the performance through over that period of time."

He expressed pride in what he achieved, highlighting that "we were the nineteenth-biggest company in market cap in the utility space worldwide when I started as CEO, and NextEra is now number one." His use of *we* is striking—he sounded as proud of the team and his successor's achievement as he was of what he accomplished in his own time.

Another striking case of putting what's best for the company ahead of what might boost one's ego is how Randy Hogan exited Pentair. He had joined Pentair in 1998 as president of one of its largest businesses, which specialized in the manufacture of enclosures for electrical equipment. Having driven strong growth in the business, he was selected as CEO in 2001. When he stepped into the role, the company comprised "seven global business units run by really talented people who all wanted to run their own show." Those businesses manufactured industrial equipment ranging from power tools to parts for water and electrical systems, in addition to electrical enclosures. Hogan described the company at the time as "really almost a holding company of disparate businesses with different cultures and different systems." It was like "an unmanaged kingdom made up of different barons and dukes that sometimes war with each other and barely recognize they're part of the same team." He was intent on unifying these fiefs into one stronger Pentair that "was going to use a common language and a common set of tools" based on the lean methods of manufacturing, which he'd learned at United Technologies. He was also intent on crafting a distinctive Pentair culture across all businesses. His goal was to "create a Pentair that's twice as big."[23] That vision for unifying the company and building it into a powerhouse brand was instrumental in him being appointed CEO.

During his seventeen-year tenure, Hogan reorganized the company around two areas of business, water filtration systems and electrical equipment. Both thrived. Nonetheless, the growth of Pentair's share price was sluggish, significantly lagging the growth of the S&P 500 and leading competitors. As his last major move, in 2017, his sixteenth year in the job, Hogan led the way in dividing Pentair into two separate companies: one formed from its water business, which manufactured water filtration and purification systems and which would retain the name Pentair; and the other formed from the electrical business that he'd built up from the electrical enclosures division he'd run, which would be called nVent. He didn't allow his decision-making about what was best for Pentair and its shareholders to be swayed by consideration of what might be better for his reputation as an empire builder. He could see that, as separate pure-play companies, each would benefit from greater focus and could better leverage market-leading positions in its respective domain. Doubling the size of the company had been his initial ambition, but he didn't allow his sense of self-worth to be contingent on that achievement.

Hogan also exemplified a generativity mindset in leading the split. He had groomed leaders to take over as CEO of each company and then announced that he would step down. Pentair CFO John Stauch was named chief of the water business, and Beth Wozniak, whom Hogan had brought in the year before to head the electrical business, was appointed CEO of nVent. In addition, Hogan joined the board of nVent, which was the smaller of the two companies by far. He wanted to do all he could to help Wozniak lead the company in strong growth. And that she did admirably, increasing sales from $2 billion when she took over in 2018 to $5 billion by the end of 2023.[24]

As we'll discuss in Chapter 8, helping CEOs adopt a generativity mindset is one reason, among many, to implement a strong
succession-planning process. It can greatly aid CEOs in feeling
good about handing off and help them set their sights on moving
on to new challenges.

MANY MORE MOUNTAINS TO CLIMB

A final reason that deciding to step down can be fraught is that doing
so may feel like a step into irrelevance. Many CEOs have shared
that they feared their days would no longer be filled with meaningful pursuits. They felt like they were walking off a cliff into a disconcerting unknown. They wanted to continue applying their skills
and experience to important work and to stay vigorous, and worried
that opportunities to make distinctive contributions would dry up.

But leaving a CEO job should by no means be seen as the end
of the road in your career, and that's true even for those who are of
retirement age. Although some who step down in these later years
are more than happy to put the intensity of their work lives behind
them, many embrace the opportunity to take on intriguing new
challenges. They find a new mission.

CEOs leaving the job, especially ones who've achieved successful long tenures, have so many options for new pursuits. A
Stanford study found that only 19 percent of CEOs retired after
leaving the role; the rest took on new work. A substantial 13 percent became CEOs at another company (perhaps being gluttons
for punishment) and 40 percent took director seats. Others dove
into all sorts of other ventures.[25]

Jim Citrin, the head of Spencer Stuart's CEO practice, has
researched how CEOs who've flourished in the years after leaving the role have moved on so well. For some, continuing to do
work much in the same vein has been of great satisfaction, such

as serving on boards. Others prefer to reinvent themselves, taking bold steps into new terrain. The key to charting an optimal path, he's found, is for them to reflect on "what they've loved most about the CEO role and what gives them the most energy, and to look for other ways to find that same fulfillment." He referred to the example of Brad Smith, who led Intuit for eleven years so successfully that he was one of the elite few CEOs in our Life Cycle study who bested the S&P in every year of his tenure. As Smith shared in a post on LinkedIn, he had worked closely with the Intuit board to identify a highly qualified successor and he transitioned into the role of executive chair. Though he found he was just as busy as when he was CEO, he recounts, "something felt off-balance." After a couple of months, "I was beginning to feel rudderless." He didn't regret stepping down, but he realized he needed to craft a new chapter for himself, as he put it. After interviewing a wide range of successful individuals who had made fulfilling transitions to next endeavors, he learned that the common thread was that "each had taken the time to discover their 'why.'" Smith shared four questions he found were powerful in looking back through one's career, and wider life, to articulate your why:

1. What things did I regret having sacrificed to date that I now wish to prioritize higher in my life going forward?
2. When in my life (and not simply my career) have I found myself performing at peak levels, filled with genuine passion and purpose?
3. In what environments do I seem to perform at my best?
4. In what environments do I not perform at peak levels or enjoy the work?

Reflecting on these questions helped Smith realize that he wanted to devote his future years to helping people who are disadvantaged by finding ways to "level the playing field of opportunity." He founded a nonprofit organization, the Wing 2 Wing Foundation, which funds initiatives in education and entrepreneurship in economically challenged regions. He also assumed the presidency of Marshall University in West Virginia, which is his alma mater, because, as he says, along with entrepreneurship, education is a "great equalizer."[26]

As Jim Citrin emphasized, what's most energizing and fulfilling for each CEO will be unique. For David Novak, great joy has come from hosting the *How Leaders Lead* podcast, talking with CEOs, company founders, and even great athletes, like Tom Brady and Peyton Manning, about their experiences and insights. For others, as with Brad Smith, more formal roles in education beckoned. Hubert Joly took on a lectureship at Harvard Business School and leads executive leadership programs for the school as well. Indra Nooyi also embraced teaching, creating a course for Masterclass titled "Leading with Purpose," and joined several boards, including those of Memorial Sloan Kettering Cancer Center and Amazon.

Some, such as Dave Cote, opt to start new businesses. He founded GS Acquisition Holdings, which leads mergers and stock purchases, in affiliation with Goldman Sachs. In 2020, the company merged with Vertiv, a leader in supplying hardware to data centers, in a $5.3 billion deal, and Cote became executive chair. With artificial intelligence applications taking off, Cote saw a great future in Vertiv's business because he understood that the demand for more data storage capacity would be booming.[27] So well positioned was Vertiv to ride the wave that in 2023 Vertiv's share price rose 269 percent.

Roger Ferguson also embraced the possibilities of emerging technologies and dove into a whole new area of business by joining venture capital incubator Red Cell as chief investment officer and chair of the Investment Committee on the board of directors.

The firm specializes in funding innovative start-ups in health care and national security. Among the companies it is incubating is one devoted to innovating new technology for virtual care services for people living in long-term-care facilities.

Moving out of the domain of business altogether, Ajay Banga was appointed president of the World Bank in 2023, where he is empowered to exert enormous influence on furthering the mission of financial inclusion and can spread his wings to drive innovation in fighting poverty and finding solutions to the climate-change crisis, food insecurity, and increasing threat of pandemics. It's an enormous remit and a steep climb up treacherous terrain—the bank having long been subject to lacerating criticism. Indeed, his predecessor was forced out because he was seen as not moving vigorously to combat the climate crisis.

Ever the avid learner, Banga began his new post by going on a global listening tour, visiting numerous countries in every region where the World Bank operates. "There is a diversity of challenges, and countries are experiencing them differently," he explained. "The World Bank Group must reach out to all of them, and we need a new playbook to do it. That is the road we are on."[28] No doubt, his experience with the innumerable challenges of the CEO journey will be of great assistance in navigating these new rocky shoals.

THE PRIVATE EQUITY SPRINT

"We're focused on long-term
value creation in a hurry."

The stages of the CEO journey for a private-equity-managed CEO are substantially different from those we've just described for the public company CEO. Among other things, the PE firm sets a more ambitious timeline for improving results and generally partners more closely with the CEO than a public board does in setting the company's course and executing to achieve those results. A private-equity-backed board is much more closely involved in both strategy and operations than public company boards, and a PE CEO does have one boss: the PE firm partner who spearheaded taking control of the company. In considering whether to make the purchase, the team behind the deal will develop a rigorous investment thesis—a road map for the financial, operational, and strategic improvements needed—that includes an anticipated time for exiting the deal, whether by selling the company or through an initial public offering. That timing typically ranges from a minimum of three years to a maximum of seven, setting the CEO up for a clearly demarcated sprint. A PE CEO may continue in the role after the firm's exit, but for the duration of the deal, the PE CEO experiences a distinctive life cycle composed of three stages: Proof of Performance, Pivoting to Growth, and Executing the Exit.

Understanding the differences in the way PE firms conduct governance during these stages and engage in strategy development and the day-to-day running of the business holds valuable lessons for public companies and their leaders. In turn, PE firms can gain valuable insights from learning public company practices. Meanwhile, for anyone contemplating taking on a PE CEO role, a solid understanding of the differences in the nature of the journey is vital. The PE Life Cycle suits some leaders well, and others struggle mightily with its demands.

OPPORTUNITIES ENTAIL RISKS

Private equity has grown at a remarkable pace over the past several decades: five times faster than the US economy as a whole since 2000. In the early days of private equity, in the 1970s and 1980s, only a handful of firms existed, but the number grew to five thousand in the United States alone and over eight thousand worldwide by 2022.[1] Firms vary greatly in size and amount of assets under management, with the sector heavily dominated by a top tier that includes Blackstone, Apollo Global Management, Kohlberg Kravis Roberts, the Carlyle Group, Bain Capital, and Silver Lake. According to a report by *Forbes*, out of the total $6 trillion in assets under PE management as of January 2024, $3.1 trillion was being managed by the top ten firms.[2] The range of funds available for investment has exploded with the growth of the sector. In 1980, there were just twenty-four PE funds, whereas in 2022, there were at least nineteen thousand.[3] To create these funds, the sector has gobbled up companies at a rapid clip, and by 2012, the number of US companies under ownership of PE firms had surpassed the number of public companies.[4] By 2022, PE firms controlled five times as many companies in the United States as the number of public companies. The share of US GDP accounted for by companies under PE management is much less, however, at 6.5 percent as of 2022, because 85 percent of PE-owned companies are small businesses, with five hundred employees or fewer.[5]

That's not to say that PE firms aren't a major force in the global economy. Although deal activity slowed somewhat during the COVID pandemic, it quickly rebounded, and as of the middle of 2023, PE firms were sitting on a record $2.49 trillion of "dry powder," the term for investment money under their management that has yet to be invested in a deal.[6]

The sector's continued growth will apply increasing pressure on public firms in the war for talent. Whereas public company boards strongly prefer to make internal appointments—recall that we found that 76 percent of S&P 500 CEO hires are from within—it's the reverse for PE firm hiring. One study found that 75 percent of portfolio company CEOs are hired from outside the company.[7] Many public company CEOs and executives with good prospects for advancing to the CEO role at their firm have leapt at the chance to take on a PE CEO position, and this has created headaches for public companies regarding their succession plans. In fact, leaders in the number two spot at public companies, often those groomed to step into the CEO role, are particularly sought after by PE firms. These executives make the jump because of the advantages they see in the PE CEO role, even though they're most often moving to a smaller company with less brand recognition than the company they've left.

Those benefits include being shielded from the intense scrutiny of public markets and being freed from the tyranny of quarterly reporting. Chairman and CEO Stephen Schwarzman, who in 1985 cofounded Blackstone, which was one of the handful of PE firms at the time, shared, "When we were starting out, it was almost impossible to recruit really great people to run portfolio companies, because they thought public companies were the be-all and end-all." Now recruiting is much easier because of the appeal of not having to deal with the "underbrush of a public company board of directors and reporting," as Schwarzman put it. As we'll explore more fully, PE ownership allows a CEO to focus internally on running the company. In addition, the clear and urgent plan for growth that the investment thesis provides appeals to many leaders coming from the public sector. They also benefit from a great deal of expertise, both financial and operational, that PE firms provide. Not the least is that PE CEOs generally earn higher compensation than public CEOs.

PE ownership also means, however, that the CEO has a good deal less autonomy than the public company CEO in setting the direction for the firm. The investment thesis includes a series of benchmarks for achieving results by a given time. It also includes an ambitious target for return to investors, which will be in excess of the anticipated return of public markets. Achieving those results in the time planned is an intense challenge, one that involves considerable risk for portfolio company CEOs. The intense pressure to quickly produce results overwhelms many.

Research has found that 73 percent of PE CEOs are replaced at some point during the holding period, most often within the first two years, because PE boards demand faster proof that the CEO is meeting performance goals.[8] Being replaced may lead to substantial financial loss for the CEO because, in PE deals, the CEO and some of the upper management team are usually required to invest personal wealth in the deal. In return, they're granted a portion of the increase in equity realized at exit, the amount of which varies but is generally between 2 percent and 4 percent. A CEO may receive none of that anticipated payout if they're ousted, though contracts between PE firms and CEOs may make provisions for various amounts of financial compensation in the event of firing.[9]

For those who especially thrive under pressure and welcome close collaboration, the PE Life Cycle can be an exhilarating and highly rewarding journey. That was true for Chris Nassetta, the longtime CEO of Hilton Hotels & Resorts, in working with Blackstone on its buyout of Hilton. He continued at the helm of Hilton after he and Blackstone orchestrated a successful IPO, so he has valuable experience with both public and private models. He shared with us, "What I loved about private equity was a real sense of urgency, and the gritty, scrappy, entrepreneurial aspects of it. If you're buying something that you think is broken and trying to fix it, then you want to get on with it." He has worked to carry that sense of urgency forward for Hilton in the eleven years he's led it in strong growth after taking the company public. His experience with the Hilton buyout is representative of the gold standard of PE deal management.

When Blackstone president and chief operating officer Jon Gray first reached out to Nassetta about becoming CEO of Hilton Hotels in 2007, Nassetta wasn't interested. But he was open to discussions. Blackstone had just purchased Hilton in a leveraged buyout for $26 billion, still one of the largest private equity deals ever. Blackstone's stake of $5.5 billion, a massive investment for a PE firm, is described over fifteen years later as "the biggest private equity check ever written."[10] The remainder of the $26 billion was raised from lenders, including Lehman Brothers, Bear Stearns, Merrill Lynch, and numerous banks, hedge funds, and real estate investors.

At the time, Nassetta was having great success as chairman and CEO of the publicly traded Host Hotels & Resorts, the largest real estate investment trust, which he'd joined in 1995 only to rise to the top spot in 2000. He understood very well why Blackstone had seen a great opportunity in Hilton. One of the oldest marquee brands in the business, founded in 1919, Hilton had lost much of its luster and was seen, as one commentator put it, as the "Granddad's Cadillac" of the business.[11] The Millennial generation was flocking to chic boutique alternatives. In addition, for insiders in the hospitality industry, Hilton had become a "byword for poor, Balkanized management"[12] because the company was divided into ten different fiefdoms, all running according to their own processes.[13] In short, the business was ripe for a turnaround.

Though Hilton had grown considerably in recent years, largely through acquisitions, including DoubleTree, Embassy Suites, and Hampton Inn, it had taken on a heavy debt burden, and the stock was trading at a lower multiple than its competitors'.[14] But the fundamental problem, Nassetta understood, was the company's culture. "There was no culture of innovation," he said. "It was more a culture of do it at a relatively slow pace and do it the way we've always done it." Changing that would be a daunting challenge. But Nassetta was confident he knew what had to be done, recalling, "I knew what was wrong at a high level with Hilton." He also knew that, with strong backing, he'd be empowered to make the dramatic changes required, no matter how much pushback they might provoke from company insiders. He wouldn't have to worry, either, about any jitters that board directors might feel about the changes. He could move with great speed to restructure Hilton's management, which Jon Gray was also intent on doing, and quickly put in place the building blocks for longer-term transformation. Gray would also back Nassetta in making a series of fast operational fixes, streamlining and modernizing the company's hidebound and inefficient corporate processes.

Meanwhile, the capital brought to bear would allow for considerable investment in growth and, particularly, capitalizing on long-overlooked opportunities for expansion overseas—all without the burden of continuously making the case for the transformational moves to Wall Street. What especially appealed to Nassetta as he engaged deeply with Gray in formulating the strategic plan was the combination of Blackstone's intent for rapid improvement, its "real sense of urgency," and its "scrappy, entrepreneurial" approach to value creation. In addition, "they always understood that the core fundamental of what was going to turn this business around was about rebuilding the culture." Nassetta took the leap.

Then, just weeks later, the financial meltdown of 2008 commenced, and the Great Recession that followed clobbered the hospitality industry with powerful force. By the end of 2008, the share prices of leading Hilton competitors Starwood and Marriott were down over 66 percent. Hilton's revenue plummeted, and Blackstone was forced to write down the chain's value by 49 percent at the end of 2008. The deal began to look disastrous: the burden of the debt for the purchase became ominous and prospects for an exit looked dire. Reflecting on the great stress of that period, Chris Nassetta has quipped, "I slept with an eye open." But with the combination of Nassetta's stellar management track record and Blackstone's deal-making prowess, Nassetta and Gray got the lenders who'd backed the deal to restructure the debt. The timeline for repayment was extended, and the lenders accepted a $1.2 billion loss, which would, the expectation was, eventually be recouped through a postponed exit, plus considerable additional earnings. The astute negotiations paid off handsomely.[15]

When the hospitality business rebounded in 2010, Hilton's fortunes soared. By that time, Nassetta had "changed 90 percent of the top one hundred people in the company," he told us, which cleared the way for him to quickly begin implementing a high-performance culture. Robust growth followed. In 2013, the company went public in an IPO that earned Blackstone an eventual windfall of nearly $14 billion and that Bloomberg described as "the most profitable private equity deal" in history.[16] Hilton executives reportedly earned, in total, $465 million in equity compensation, with Nassetta's share being $155 million.[17] Nassetta stayed on as CEO following the IPO, and in the following years, Hilton's share price exploded, rising 288 percent as of mid-2023. During his sixteenth year at the helm, he told us that the achievement he is most proud of is fulfilling his long-term vision of creating a great company culture. In 2023, in fact, Hilton was named by *Fortune* as the number one great place to work in the world.

The Hilton buyout represents many of the hallmarks of successful PE deals. The deal partner, Jon Gray, and Nassetta were in great alignment about the investment thesis for value creation and the anticipated exit from the deal, and they formed a close partnership. Indeed, Nassetta was able to convince Gray to remain as chair of the Hilton board even after Blackstone sold off the last of its shares in the company. Gray's experience helped Nassetta on a number of fronts, including navigating a period of intense scrutiny from market analysts and shareholders. That allowed him to focus on moving rapidly forward with the transformation plan despite the dire economic conditions. And he had great clarity about the growth plan and a strong strategy combined with disciplined execution.

By no means do all PE deals work out so well, however. Innumerable unanticipated challenges may arise, which might not be overcome as they were in the Hilton buyout, and the timing for exit must sometimes be pushed out. We spoke with one portfolio company CEO who started in 2016. By 2019, the planned turnaround had been executed well and they were poised to proceed with an IPO. Then the COVID pandemic hit, and that became untenable. He ended up having to restructure the business during 2020, and as of this writing, there was still no clear timeline for an exit. Deals also regularly go entirely south, with anticipated equity earnings evaporating.

Private equity has been heavily criticized for its failures, some of which are notorious. But what has received less coverage is how much the sector has adopted best practices from public companies in pursuit of executing strong growth strategies.

FROM PLUNDERERS TO PARTNERS— AN ONGOING CONVERGENCE

PE has evolved a good deal since the time when a number of high-profile and highly aggressive deals in the late 1980s and 1990s earned it a reputation as a cutthroat business run by corporate raiders characterized as "mercenary dealmakers who bludgeoned opponents."[18] The most infamous of those deals was the takeover of RJR Nabisco chronicled in the best-selling *Barbarians at the Gate*, and later characterized by coauthor of the book Bryan Burrough as belonging in the "pantheon of financial ignominy."[19] Managed by Kohlberg Kravis Roberts (KKR), the deal left RJR with a crushing burden of debt. KKR proceeded to conduct massive layoffs, and the company was forced to break itself up in 1999, by which time its share price had fallen by half.[20]

Yet heavy press coverage of the debacle overshadowed how powerful the fundamental PE model was in driving strong results. Deals from that same period that were remarkable successes, which garnered little if any mainstream media attention, account for the phenomenal growth of the sector. One of these was the little-known purchase of the Accuride unit of Firestone (now Bridgestone/Firestone) by Bain Capital in 1986. Accuride had been failing for years, and Bain developed a strategic plan to concentrate rigorously on a smaller group of the firm's largest customers. Bain also invested in a new automated and highly efficient manufacturing facility that decreased production costs while improving quality. The changes quickly allowed Accuride to compete more effectively with leading rivals, such as the much larger Goodyear, and within two years, profits rose 66 percent and Accuride's market value doubled. No layoffs were conducted. Bain sold the company after eighteen months to the Phelps Dodge Corporation for a return of twenty-five times its investment in the purchase, and Accuride went on to thrive.[21]

What the stories of individual high-profile deal failures also obscure is that the portfolio model of PE funds has proven a powerful counterbalance to losses from any given deal within the portfolio. Funds generally comprise a well-diversified portfolio of companies from different industries, and strong returns from some exits within the fund usually more than compensate for losses from others. That was true even for the fund that took the huge loss in the RJR Nabisco deal. Strong returns for other portfolio companies, including Duracell Batteries and Stop & Shop, meant that the fund ultimately achieved a respectable 11.3 percent return on investment.[22]

Also flying under the radar of mainstream coverage is the fact that hostile takeovers have mostly given way to companies welcoming or even actively courting deals after PE firms began to focus on enhancing the value of their portfolio companies through strategic and operational transformation. PE firms initially focused on financial engineering, quickly extracting value from companies by selling off units, enacting layoffs, optimizing a company's capital structure, and strengthening balance sheets by debt restructuring, but changing market conditions demanded that they shift to producing returns by boosting a company's growth. Stephen Schwarzman recalled, "In the old days, in the 1980s, the business was mostly about cost cutting. The economy was growing well, and you didn't have to focus as much on growth. It was a simple model." But as stock prices rose beginning in the 1990s, "If you bought a company and all you did was cut costs, you couldn't make any money because you were paying so much for the business. You had to start coming up with growth models and you started investing more money in companies. Fast-forward to the current times and it's not primarily about cost cutting. Some of that is taken for granted if the company is not well managed. But the goal now is about growth, because you can only make big money when a company's growing, and the faster it grows, the better the multiple you get on exit."

This is the motivating force behind many PE firms' intense engagement in driving strategy and operational improvements and in working closely with portfolio company management to develop and execute those plans. PE firms have, in this regard, converged with the public sector, building up staffs of professionals with expertise in strategic development and the best practices of public company operations. Some have set a higher standard for operations. To do so, they've hired top talent from corporations and consultancies to join their staffs, bringing on board experts in all areas of corporate processes, from strategy to supply chain, lean manufacturing, branding, pricing, sales, product development, and recruiting. The best firms now offer a caliber of input that's become the envy of the corporate world. Along the way in the industry's evolution, as financial journalist Jason Kelly remarked, the term *leveraged buyout* was swapped out for the more dignified *private equity*, which emphasizes the value-building firms are doing.[23]

Most companies targeted by PE firms are small to mid-cap in size, so they can't afford anything like the expertise many PE firms now provide. This is why they increasingly court PE buyouts so that the PE firm can guide them through strategic and operational transformations. Even some of the corporate behemoths have sought PE ownership, as was true with the Hilton buyout. The CEO who agreed to the deal, Stephen Bollenbach, approached Blackstone because Hilton had for years been unable to improve shareholder value, which investors were clamoring for, and the heat was on. Blackstone had proved it could work wonders in turning around the fortunes of companies in the industry. So intent was the Hilton board on gaining the advantage of that expertise that the directors decided not to pursue any competitive offers to avoid losing the deal.[24]

It's important to highlight that the expertise in PE firms' corporate best practices is not universally of such high caliber. Some PE firms still inspire heated criticism, particularly in recent years regarding the high numbers of buyouts of health-care companies and nursing homes, with accusations of cost-cutting measures leading to nursing shortages, increases in serious medical errors, and scaling back in low-profit areas of care, among other negative consequences.[25] Alarms have also been raised about how many companies are now operating behind a "veil of secrecy."[26] Calls for more transparency have put the industry under intensified regulatory scrutiny. In 2023, the Securities and Exchange Commission, for example, approved a set of new rules providing some protections for private equity fund investors, such as requiring that quarterly statements be issued to investors and audit reports distributed annually.[27] But the degree of transparency in PE firms is still a great deal less than that required of public companies. In this regard, convergence with the public sector has been quite limited.

Also substantially different are the nature of PE governance and the drive to achieve an exit, and these make the PE CEO journey so distinctive.

A MORE INTENSIVE SERIES OF STAGES

Whether the acquiring PE firm retains the CEO or brings in new leadership, the beginning of ownership is, as Stephen Schwarzman said, a major reset. When we shared our findings about the public CEO Life Cycle stages with Schwarzman, he remarked that they were similar to the stages of life Erik Erikson described. He concurred, "The idea of a life cycle for a CEO is completely correct," and he noted that the PE CEO Life Cycle is more compressed. PE CEOs really have to hit the ground running.

The first stage, Proof of Performance, can range from less than a year in duration to an upper range of two years, depending on the results being achieved. Although the Launch stage for public company CEOs is intense, private equity partners, CEOs of PE portfolio companies who have also been public company CEOs, and directors who've worked with both the public and PE models unanimously agreed that the expectation for fast results is even greater for the PE CEO. Instead of being afforded a honeymoon or the exploratory period of a listening tour, a PE CEO is expected to immediately begin implementing the elements of the detailed investment thesis.

The thesis was developed during an extensive due diligence process generally conducted over several months or longer that involved rigorous evaluation of the company's financial condition and all aspects of operations, from the quality of product offerings to the strength of branding and sales, customer and supplier relations, production and IT capabilities, and company leadership. A series of benchmarks for results to be achieved on a strict timeline was also created. The PE CEO is usually given financial incentives tied to achieving those numbers, and much of the anticipated compensation will not be received if they're not met.

PE firms act quickly if early targets are missed. Indeed, research has found that one-third of PE CEOs are forced out within the first one hundred days of PE ownership. And according to a 2018 survey by AlixPartners, which conducts research on the PE business, 58 percent of PE CEOs had been replaced within two years.[28]

Therefore, although PE CEOs do not have the pressure of quarterly earnings calls, monitoring of their progress is actually more rigorous and more continuous than for public company CEOs. Brandt McKee is CEO of portfolio company Interior Logic Group and was formerly senior managing director of the PE firm Centerbridge Partners. He shared that "in a private setting you actually have greater pressure because you are updating on a more regular basis. I have biweekly calls with my private equity firm and we review the financials on a monthly basis." Some PE deal sponsors told us they meet even more frequently with their portfolio CEOs. There is also no hiding results. Because a PE firm owns the company, or a large portion of it, the financials are entirely transparent to it versus the tightly controlled reporting to market investors done by public companies. McKee underscored that PE "boards and ownership teams have more data points upon which to evaluate the CEO and his or her team faster than a public company."

Limited partners who invest in funds expect to earn returns significantly above that of the public markets. This has been the driving force behind the phenomenal growth of the sector, but it also ups the ante on PE CEOs. According to a calculation by consulting firm Bain, over the last thirty years, PE buyout funds have earned average net returns of 13.1 percent versus 8.1 percent average returns for the public markets.[29] The excess return over public markets is referred to as *alpha*, and it's this extra edge of earnings that has led to investment pouring in from large institutional investors, including pension funds and sovereign wealth funds, as well as wealthy individuals. But alpha has been getting harder to achieve. Between 2009 and 2020, for example, that same Bain study found that the returns of the US public equity markets have been on par with those from PE buyouts, at 15 percent. We should note, however, that the study also found that "an elite group of firms has found a way to buck this trend." For those firms, which the study does not name, returns have "essentially held steady."

During the holding period, limited partners demand to see regular estimations of returns, which are generally reported as the internal rate of return (IRR), a complicated assessment of the likely value of the company by the anticipated time of exit. Prakash Melwani of Blackstone underscored that, with such close scrutiny, "You'd better be constantly driving results. I often say, we're focused on long-term value creation in a hurry."

During the Proof of Performance stage, the CEO must empha-size achieving efficiencies in operations, which may involve layoffs, for which PE firms have been criticized, and sell-offs of some parts of the company. Efficiencies also include all manner of improve-ments in operations, such as implementing better procurement and supply chain practices and IT transformation.

When these low-hanging-fruit improvements have been made, as Stephen Schwarzman highlighted, emphasis shifts from gaining efficiencies to achieving growth. In the Pivoting to Growth stage, the CEO must lean more heavily on the leadership skills of talent management and cultural transformation. Schwarzman noted that some leaders who excelled in the first stage find this second stage more challenging. "You have to coach the person to make that pivot," he shared, which some find extremely difficult. He used the analogy of military generals, some of whom are great at leadership in the frontline combat situation but aren't as capable of leadership over the wider theater of command. "You have to see how the per-son evolves and, hopefully, they're good in each phase," he said. "But if they're not, you explore other options."

For those who perform well, the third and final stage—Executing the Exit, preparing for and managing a successful exit—generally requires learning a new set of skills. Most PE CEOs do not have experience in making the case to potential buyers about a company's enhanced value and future prospects or in leading an IPO. There is, therefore, plenty of learning going on for PE CEOs, as for public CEOs, but on a compressed schedule and with the PE firm providing substantial and ongoing guidance. What there is no time for in the PE CEO's journey, at any point, is complacency.

Those who perform well throughout the holding period and who lead a successful exit then face a critical juncture. If the company goes public, a new board will be appointed, and a strategy will be developed in partnership with those new directors. If the sale is to another PE firm, a new investment thesis will be determined, and if the company is acquired by another company, such as a larger player in its industry, that company's management will execute an integration.

The CEO can opt to be a sprinter and leave the company, taking earnings and moving on to new opportunities. Or they can aim to be a marathoner, staying on to take the company to yet greater heights, as Chris Nassetta did. The new owners may, however, prefer to change leadership. In that event, a successful PE CEO has many other options, such as a subsequent PE CEO gig. Some successful PE CEOs have been hired for second or third or more go-rounds. PE CEOs are also in high demand for board directorships and as advisers to PE CEOs.

THE PE ENGAGEMENT MODEL

A major difference in the PE CEO journey from that of the public CEO is that the leadership model is one of more distributed authority. As opposed to the hourglass model of the public company—in which the CEO controls the flow of information to the board—the PE model is a leadership triad. The PE firm deal lead and board directors have full access to information and are closely involved in the running of the company.

Public boards typically limit their interactions with CEOs and other company leaders to formal scheduled meetings. PE boards eschew that approach in an effort to stay deeply connected with company decisions. Courtney della Cava, global head of portfolio talent and organizational performance at Blackstone, shared, "We encourage our board members to interact regularly with their respective business and functional leads as well as the CEO and other board members." She emphasized that, whereas public company CEOs tend to think of board relations as about managing the board, in the PE model, that approach won't work. A partnership mentality is best in the public context, also, but under PE ownership, it's imperative. PE firm boards aren't interested in slide presentations or any of the theater of public board meetings.

In recent years, to further enhance the support the board can provide, some PE firms have been appointing a select number of independent directors to work directly with senior executives in addition to the CEO. These directors have special expertise that complements that of the PE firm's directors and can assist with specific aspects of the investment thesis, such as digital transformation.

The close engagement of the PE firm can also be seen with its ops teams. The team is led by an operating partner, generally a salaried employee of the PE firm, and the team comprises specialists in the performance areas the company is working on. Members of the ops team travel regularly to consult at the portfolio company offices and production sites, and many work at the offices for some time. They usually work directly with managers leading performance improvements, such as with the chief technology officer implementing a digital transformation or a general manager upgrading a procurement system.

This close engagement means that information flows more freely and the PE CEO, unlike their public company peer, cannot act as a gatekeeper, as a public CEO can. Sociologist Ron Burt made an extensive analysis of corporate structures, the networks within them, and the flow of information through them and has studied the ways public company CEOs have the power to act as gatekeepers. A gatekeeper can control and, if they choose to, restrict the flow of information and resources throughout the domain over which they have authority. For CEOs, specifically, controlling the flow of information between the internal and external worlds is a significant source of power. They can limit the information shared with boards and investors, including keeping them from knowing about problems bubbling up. There may be no more glaring case of gatekeeping than when Volkswagen withheld information about the intentional engineering of ignition switches to produce inaccurate low measures of their cars' greenhouse gas emissions. Court cases in the wake of that scandal made clear that the CEO, Martin Winterkorn, was aware of the deceit and kept that information from the board.

Public CEOs can also restrict which information is shared with staff, including the executive team, about board discussions and plans being put in motion, such as a merger or selling off a division, discontinuing a product line, or a game plan for enacting layoffs. Doug Steenland, a former CEO of Northwest Airlines and member of the Hilton board, shared, "A public company CEO, if he or she wants to, can try to aggregate power in a way that no PE company CEO in a responsible private equity firm ever could."

In the PE model, information flows much more freely to the PE board through multiple channels. Ops teams not only provide support for the CEO but also report directly to the deal lead and PE board about issues they're uncovering. Members of those teams, as well as the deal lead and board members, can reach out directly to company managers at any time. Leaders who are keen to play the role of gatekeeper, particularly those who want to use it as a means of consolidating power, are not a good fit for the PE model.

For those who favor collaborative partnership, the trade-offs for less autonomy can be great benefits from much more intensive guidance than a public CEO can access. A number of CEOs working under PE management, as well as directors who've served on both public and PE boards, highlighted the advantages of the high engagement of the PE firm. Scott O'Neil, the CEO of Merlin Entertainment, the world's second-largest tourist attraction operator, described how helpful it has been for him to have the PE support system at his disposal. "They pressure-test assumptions and provide resources, which are incredible." He highlighted that one of the directors on his board, Jørgen Vig Knudstorp, was the CEO who led the hugely successful turnaround of Lego. "He came in as a thirty-three-year-old CEO and took it from bankrupt to what it is today. And now he's on our board. Talk about an exceptional resource."

A key competitive advantage of Merlin is its global presence in 120 cities across twenty-four countries, which it intends to continue doubling down on with the support and extended global reach of the PE universe. "If we're working on an acquisition, our partnering PE firms have members of their teams that will help lend insights and pressure-test our modeling. When I was going to China, they put me in touch with one of their limited partners who is with a sovereign wealth fund in China. You have an incredible wealth of resources."

PE firms also introduce portfolio CEOs to other portfolio CEOs, who share advice. O'Neil described a phone call with three hundred CEOs in which they discussed their views about whether or not a recession was looming. When polled, only 4 percent of them said they expected a recession soon, at a time when economic pundits were almost unanimously saying one was right around the corner. Firms also hire outside specialists as advisers to help portfolio CEOs with particularly knotty issues, such as government regulatory actions or recruitment. Former portfolio company CEOs and executives may also be appointed as board members, advisers, or coaches. For example, former CFOs of portfolio companies are particularly helpful audit chairs on the board and can provide great support to new CFOs, coaching them about the role.

We heard resounding appreciation from CEOs and directors of how much more involved and knowledgeable about the company and its challenges PE boards are, with unanimous agreement that this PE governance model is superior, facilitating not only much greater transparency but also speed of decision-making. Doug Steenland emphasized, "You have a degree of connectivity to your owner that's unparalleled. You have constant regular contact, feedback, input, direction, and opportunity to have conversations that you don't have in the public space." Also, because the board is so closely involved in decision-making, pivots can be made more quickly.

Because the CEO is shielded from market analysts and need not make public quarterly reports, costly moves devoted to longer-term improvements, such as strategic investments in new manufacturing or IT capabilities, can be made out from under the pressures of public admonition. This was a big benefit for shoe company Crocs when it sought PE investment. CEO Andrew Rees was working as a consultant on the deal Crocs made with Blackstone. He'd founded and led the retail and consumer products practice at LEK Consulting, and he had strong experience in the footwear industry, having served in several executive roles at Reebok. Blackstone hired his firm to conduct due diligence, assess what was going wrong with the brand and what its future value could be, and develop a road map for transformation. He was curious about why Crocs wanted PE investment, given that the company was actually well financed, with strong cash flow. "They knew Crocs needed a strategic change," he recalled, "and they felt that the best way to set the company on a positive new trajectory was to seek a minority investor from the private equity community." Sales of the distinctive colorful clogs had been slumping, and the share price had been pummeled.[30] Some industry arbiters thought the quirky brand had peaked, proving to be a trendy flash in the pan. Rees, by contrast, saw great potential, and he put his name in for the CEO job.

Crocs negotiated with Blackstone to sell it a 13 percent stake for $200 million, rather than an outright buyout, and awarded two board seats as part of the deal. Blackstone was deeply engaged in assisting with the turnaround, digging into data and helping drive change. The firm's involvement also provided "tremendous air cover," Rees said, meaning protection from the market's punishment of the stock. For five years of "what was a very challenging, deep-seated turnaround," he described, Crocs "didn't worry about quarter-to-quarter decision-making; rather we set our focus on long-term, multiyear decision-making, which was initially difficult, as our stock was moving dramatically" due to those moves.

The shift in strategy paid off. Rees shrunk the company to grow it. He shut down unprofitable product lines, refocused on the brand's iconic "classic clog" that brought the company to fame, and closed roughly a third of company-run stores, which were underperforming. He also resuscitated marketing, applying his branding prowess to make Crocs hip again, such as through a collaboration with musical artist Post Malone to produce a line of clogs featuring Malone-inspired graphics. Revenue soared, as did share price, which rose 85 percent from $15 at the time of the deal in 2014 to 2018, when Blackstone exited the deal and sold Crocs back half of the stake it had purchased.[31] Shares continued to soar from there and reached a high of $102.62 in January 2022, before slumping with the general market downturn that year and then recovering strongly.

CEO AS A COO PLUS?

Opinion about the high-engagement PE model is not universally positive. Some criticize the intense involvement of PE firms for turning the CEO into more of a "COO plus." In this view, PE firms are primarily interested in hiring executives great at execution, who will put strong emphasis on operational improvements. They aren't looking for input—or not much—into the strategy for growth, and they curtail CEO power.

The truth is, whether a PE CEO is viewed as a COO plus or as a full partner in strategy and the overall transformation varies by firm. It may also vary with the type of deal being done. Doug Steenland said that he has seen cases in which "the CEO was really a COO, more an implementer than a strategy setter or change maker." This is more often the case in takeovers of smaller companies rather than large firms. Also, the more distressed a company is, the more the PE firm may limit the CEO role to a focus on rapid-fire operational turnaround. In that event, a CEO may well have a narrow mandate. In contrast, the acquisition of a company that's been underperforming but has a strong foundation of revenue and brand equity may allow for a longer runway and more CEO latitude. Generally speaking, the more defined the timeline to exit, the more enticing it is to focus on shorter-term objectives versus setting a long-term vision.

Sometimes there can be a gap between a PE firm's scenario planning toward a successful exit and the practical realities a CEO has to deal with in running a company as well as how quickly improvements can be made. One former CEO who has served on PE boards told us he sometimes had to play the role of intermediary and urge a PE firm to ease up on pressure. "PE firms are much faster on the trigger [than public companies] to make a change at the CEO level," and "sometimes they're too quick. On one or two occasions, I have gone to battle with the deal person, who's wanted to fire the CEO."

With some PE firms, the problem isn't overly intrusive involvement but not being involved enough. Some PE firms are described as practicing "seagull management," swooping in to engage only when problems arise. Bob Segert, who has been CEO of five private equity portfolio companies, most recently at Athena Health, recounted his experience of the degree of involvement as being all over the map. "I've had private equity firms that wanted daily cash reports. Some want a three- or four-pager every month. Others are ad hoc, and we would connect during quarterly board meetings. For some, I'd be on the phone with the partners every two weeks."

The degree of involvement of ops teams and how much operational freedom a CEO is afforded also vary a good deal. Brandt McKee commented, "Every single ops team is different. They are a snowflake, and they are a snowflake reflection of the leadership and values and vision of the individual leaders of that investment firm. Some are incredibly hands-on. Some are incredibly hands-off. I would tell you that ops teams are also like doctors in the United States. There is a population curve. Some are outstanding, some are horrible, and you've got to figure out what you've got." CEOs can also push back on engagement they deem intrusive.

In all cases, an essential truth is that the CEO is still the one primarily in charge of running the company. The PE firm provides an idealized model of the transformation process, and the CEO brings the wisdom of experience in how to actually manage the messier, human process of execution. Courtney della Cava shared, "We have a high-level investment thesis, and we need leaders who are going to come in and bring the operational acumen to validate and refine it." Prakash Melwani noted that PE partners generally don't have hands-on experience in leading a company. "I know I can't run a business," he said. "But what I can do is pick a great CEO who then can run the business well." One CEO of a portfolio company told us emphatically that the private equity partner "doesn't run the company, and they don't want to." They do have strong opinions about the moves to make, and he described a vigorous debate with his backer about a deal to buy a company he wanted to pursue. The partner advised against it because he didn't think the deal was big enough, and the CEO pressed the case but eventually conceded. "You either love that or hate that," he said about the pushback. "For me, it's great because it helps me prioritize."

The CEO is also the one who rallies the troops and builds enthusiasm for the investment thesis with the company staff. Another enormous responsibility is bringing in new talent that can drive the performance enhancements expected. In fact, a PE CEO usually has to replace from 30 percent to 40 percent of those running departments and 50 percent to 65 percent of those in the level below that. This is a huge responsibility left largely to the CEO's discretion.[32]

We wondered whether the PE firm's authority over company direction undercuts the CEO's passion for the company's vision, given a lower sense of ownership of it. Can a PE CEO feel the same degree of engagement in building a legacy achievement that we heard so many public company CEOs speak of, such as Dave Cote, Indra Nooyi, and Mark Hoplamazian? Our conclusion is that they definitely can. One director shared a story about a CEO hired by a PE firm to take over a food company. The company was in the firm's portfolio for eight years, and during that time, "He was a fanatic about the business, he lived it, breathed it. The business was his passion." There is no necessary divide between the vision and ambitions of the CEO and the aims of the PE firm. They can be, and should be, in powerful alignment. There is nothing to stop a CEO from being intensely enthused about a firm's investment thesis, assuming they're in agreement with it, other than a desire to be more exclusively in charge.

Any leader aspiring to the role should be aware, though, that PE CEOs are not generally showered with the accolades the media heaps on public CEOs who pull off great feats. The PE firm tends to receive the lion's share of credit. For example, in a search of articles reporting about the Hilton IPO, including in the *Wall Street Journal*, *Washington Post*, CNBC, and *The Street*, plentiful credit for the turnaround is given to Blackstone, whereas Chris Nassetta is not mentioned. Any references to the role of the company's management refer to Hilton, as in "Hilton Worldwide made its market debut last week,"[33] and "Backed by private equity and real estate firm Blackstone Group, Hilton priced its shares at $20."[34] Yet, if the CEO stays with the firm after exit and puts a powerful stamp on the company's ongoing performance improvement, then accolades may well be theirs. That's certainly been true for Chris Nassetta. As he took Hilton's share price on a strong ascent, he received a steady stream of press, praised, for example, in a long article about the buyout and IPO in the *Washington Post* as "The man who turned around Hilton."[35]

LEADERSHIP ALPHA

Further indication that some PE firms understand that they should not view the CEO as a COO plus comes from the emphasis they place on CEOs having strong people leadership skills. In the past, primary emphasis was placed on financial and operations acumen—still, obviously, important—but today the vanguard of innovators in the sector increasingly appreciate a CEO's people leadership skills for achieving the above-market returns investors expect. Generating alpha has become more challenging for PE firms. As Ted Bililies, managing director of AlixPartners, a consulting firm specializing in the PE sector, has noted, the supply of companies ripe for buyout has shrunk. As the number of PE firms has grown, many of the best prospects for turnaround have been gobbled up. Improving the performance of companies that are performing fairly well is now the predominant objective, and PE firms have learned that a CEO's people leadership abilities are the vital complement to strength in finance and operations for this new frontier of performance improvement.

A study of PE firm hiring, in which managing partners of thirty-two firms were interviewed, including many industry leaders, found that seeking CEOs with leadership skills is a widespread priority. Firms "pay less attention to attributes such as track record and experience, the criteria typically most prized by recruiters, and give more weight to softer skills."[36] Bililies summarized this skill set as being "adept at managing, motivating, and inspiring people," being "authentic, credible," and having "high EQ."

These skills have become all the more important, Bililies said, because Millennials and Generation Z account for approximately 50 percent of the workforce of North American and western Europe as of 2023. The quality of their work life is more important to them, as is believing the company they work for upholds strong values and has a serious commitment to environmental stewardship, diversity, and social justice. Bililies noted that these workers are communicating all the time on social media, rating their companies and the leadership of their CEOs largely on these terms. If portfolio companies are to attract and retain them, they need leaders who understand the values of these workers and can motivate and inspire them.

Some PE firms have invested heavily in conducting in-depth assessments of candidates' people leadership skills, such as with diagnostic tools and working with firms like ours, to discover the leading candidates. But as of yet, they are focused mostly on discovering talent rather than developing it. In this regard, the PE sector can still learn from public companies, many of which have created extensive leadership development programs. As competition among PE firms continues to escalate, talent development is becoming a new frontier in their evolution.

When it comes to investing in leadership development, PE firms have thus far focused on providing executives of portfolio companies a richness of opportunity for networking and peer-to-peer exchanges with other leaders in their portfolio companies and their vast network of advisers. They've worked to create rich ecosystems to facilitate these kinds of opportunities. "We spend a lot of time nurturing our talent network," Courtney della Cava shared. These networks provide entrée to hundreds of other C-suite leaders, board directors, and company stakeholders who can provide input, from customers to suppliers and regulators. "We actively cultivate communities among our various executive cohorts," she explained. This may be done, for example, by hosting regular gatherings where leaders can confer about issues and build relationships. The firm may also take the lead in making introductions across the ecosystem. A CEO of a mid-cap health-care company might, for example, be introduced to her counterpart at a fast-growth tech company who has invaluable expertise in cybersecurity or AI implementation. Or the CEO of a small retailer just learning the ropes of applying AI to customer discovery and ad targeting might reach out to one of the leading innovators in that area who has consulted other portfolio firms. Few leaders in the public sector have such easy access to this wealth of talent across a wide range of industries.

Firms also work to find new opportunities for the alumni of deals after exit. For example, della Cava wanted to keep within the fold Girish Rishi, who successfully led Blue Yonder to exit. Though the firm didn't have another immediate CEO spot that was right for him, he was nominated for the chair position on the board of another portfolio company. "He's been adding great value as board chair and coach to that CEO," she added.

To optimize opportunities for leaders it wants to bring in and retain in its fold, Blackstone has pioneered by actually creating a company for two standout talents. The firm perceived an opportunity to build a company for Thomas Staggs and Kevin Mayer to lead. Both men had been passed over to succeed Bob Iger at Disney. First, the firm bought Reese Witherspoon's company, Hello Sunshine, and then they added children's entertainment Moonbug and Exile Content Studio, creating Candle Media, with Staggs and Mayer as cofounders and co-CEOs.

Yet, when it comes to investing in actual development training like so many public companies do, PE firms face a real challenge. Demonstrating the return on investment of these practices is much more difficult than quantifying the boost from financial and operational improvements. In addition, talent development is a longer-term process than the short timelines for producing results that portfolio companies expect. Both put pressure on PE firms to justify investments in leadership development, with the value add to returns on investment being scrutinized by investors.

Another difference is that public companies' investments in talent development aim to nurture the talents of leaders in levels below the C-suite, to prepare them for higher-level executive roles and provide the backbone for the 76 percent of CEO successors appointed from the inside. The payoffs come after the many years of nurturing the skills and building the experience of leaders, such as by moving them into new roles that stretch them to learn. That kind of deeper-bench development is not yet on the agenda of many PE firms. Companies they bring into their portfolio may have such development processes in place, which they may continue under PE management, but PE firms still have an opportunity to become more involved in implementing them. In most PE portfolio companies, the role of human resources is focused more on the administrative aspects of the work, such as payroll processing and benefits administration, and less on the work of creating a pipeline of talent for the future and succession planning because, again, seeing the payoffs from first upskilling people capabilities and then implementing these processes is generally on a timeline that exceeds the term of the deal.

With so many companies under PE management, however, the possibilities for applying the practices of public company talent development across portfolios are numerous. If PE firms were to take a longer-term view of growing talent from deeper within the companies in their ecosystems, they could institute such practices as mentoring and job rotations, not only within companies but also between portfolio companies. They could develop their ecosystems even more broadly than the talent academies at some large public companies, such as PepsiCo, P&G, and Microsoft, do. As the PE sector diversifies its investment strategies, further development of firm ecosystems and cross-pollination will surely be on the agenda for many.

In the war for talent, thus far, systematic talent development is a terrain where the PE juggernaut still lags behind the public sector.

8

SUCCEEDING WITH
SUCCESSION

"Almost half of companies . . . have
no meaningful CEO succession plan."

In earlier chapters, we discussed how complex the relationship between public company CEOs and boards can be. CEOs need to devote considerable effort to cultivating a close partnership and strong board support. The difficulty of building that partnership results from the public company model, where a board comprises eight to twelve directors who come together for meetings four to eight times a year. By design, public boards are substantially less involved in running the business and oversight of the CEO than are the boards of private equity portfolio companies. And this can lead to challenges throughout a CEO's tenure. Recall that establishing a good relationship with directors was described as one of, if not the most, vexing challenge of the Launch stage. Without a good relationship, when a CEO experiences a sophomore slump, relations may be badly strained. Gaining board support for new strategic initiatives is a heavy lift in the Reinvention stage even for leaders who have racked up impressive results. Then, in the Complacency Trap and Legacy years, CEOs are often given too much deference, which contributes to performance issues.

One way in which we hope our CEO Life Cycle findings will help bend the curve of success for CEOs is by shedding light on these junctures so that CEOs can anticipate and prepare for them and boards can address these problems. In this chapter, we focus on another way the board relationship is often problematic: when a board is not closely involved with a CEO throughout their tenure, they are missing the opportunity to ensure that a strong bench of talented leaders who could be the next CEO are identified and their abilities are developed.

Though selecting a successor is widely considered a board's most important role, whereas some boards are rigorous about it, far too many boards engage in little succession planning. In our experience, even when boards are more engaged in the process, they often fail to develop the necessary depth of understanding about contenders' capabilities. CEOs are sometimes allowed too strong a hand in selecting their successors, and too few prospects are given serious consideration. Among other outcomes, these shortfalls lead to many rocky transitions, and this contributes to the high incidence of CEO failure in the early stages. It also contributes to the great difficulty so many CEOs have in deciding to step down.

In this chapter, we describe an optimal succession-planning process, one in which CEOs and boards work closely in partnership throughout the CEO's tenure. First, we'll delve into the underlying reasons succession planning is often so problematic. Where better to start than with a brief look at the succession travails of the Walt Disney Company under the leadership of CEO Bob Iger.

◄◄◄◄◄ ►►►►►

Thomas Staggs was flying high in early February 2015. He'd just been appointed COO of Disney, and as is true at so many companies, his assumption of the role was considered the last leg of a journey of preparation to succeed the CEO, in this case, the highly regarded Bob Iger. Staggs had prevailed in the two-man competition for the job with CFO Jay Rasulo, who six months later departed Disney.[1] Both had been with the company for over two decades, performing impressively in increasingly prominent roles. Rasulo served as senior vice president of corporate alliances and ran the company's theme parks and resorts business. Staggs had racked up impressive achievements in a twelve-year stint as CFO, having played a key role in several widely praised acquisitions, including those of Pixar and Marvel Entertainment.[2] His financial acumen was so respected on Wall Street that he was repeatedly named the number one CFO by *Institutional Investor* magazine.[3] In 2010, Staggs and Rasulo had traded positions, with Staggs taking over as head of theme parks and resorts and Rasulo becoming CFO. With that, it was clear to company observers, a two-man race for the CEO prize had begun.

As head of theme parks, Staggs led unprecedented growth, and he admirably oversaw the complex construction of the company's massive new $5.5 billion park in Shanghai, a tremendous stretch challenge with which he'd reportedly impressed Iger. Indeed, when Staggs won the number two spot in 2015, press reports—later corroborated by Disney—indicated that he'd been "handpicked" by Iger.[4] Iger, who was sixty-four that year, had announced his intention to step down in 2018, which gave Staggs three years to tackle additional challenges and win the full board's approval. That would prove a tall order. The board reportedly intended to scrutinize his performance and evaluate his talents more closely in that time. Some directors were said to harbor reservations about him becoming CEO, particularly because of his lack of experience in leading the development of creative content.[5] Iger, by contrast, had done that to great success before joining Disney, as president and then board chair of the American Broadcasting Company.

As Staggs' first year as COO progressed, those voices of dissent expressed increasing concern about him succeeding Iger. Then, in March 2016, in a move that stunned observers of the company, Iger informed Staggs that the board and he himself "lacked the full confidence" that Staggs should become CEO.[6] The next month, Staggs announced his resignation from Disney, with no objections from Iger or the board about his departure.

His appointment as COO had been used by corporate governance specialist David Larcker, of Stanford Business School, as "a textbook case of smooth succession."[7] It turned out, instead, to be a textbook case of how complicated and unpredictable the process of succession planning and transitioning to a new CEO can be. This may be true even if a CEO and board have followed what seemed to be rigorous succession-planning processes. Disney was characterized as having done so in this case, by grooming Staggs and Rasulo as top contenders for at least six years. And yet, as we've seen many times, the intensity of evaluation once the actual choice is imminent often throws a wrench in the works. What's more, even a board that has already experienced such a succession setback may find itself grappling with some other unanticipated twist next time around.

Consider how Disney handled its next succession effort. Fast-forward to February 2020. Iger, having postponed his anticipated retirement date repeatedly, suddenly announced that he would step down, effective immediately. That was twenty-two months earlier than his latest announced retirement date of end of 2021. Despite the board having previously checked Iger's intention to handpick his successor, in the face of such an abrupt disruption, this time the board deferred to his choice and immediately appointed Bob Chapek.[8] Chapek had no experience leading creative content development, which had concerned the board about Staggs, and hadn't been widely considered a leading contender. The directors reportedly even waived the opportunity for due diligence in interviewing Chapek. They agreed to the highly unusual, and dubious, condition that "Chapek would serve both as CEO and CEO-in-training," and Iger would retain creative control of the company as executive chair of the board.[9] This was a succession debacle for the history books in the making.

Three years later, due in part to Iger's urging, the board ousted Chapek, who recounted that his tenure was "three years of hell," during which he'd felt "unrelenting fear that Iger wanted his job back."[10] The board did ask Iger to return as CEO, and the saga of his succession was extended for several more years.

The Disney succession drama was particularly protracted and high-profile, but such problems with succession are all too common. Despite the cases of glaring failure that get reams of press, and even after two decades of calls for the adoption of better succession practices, at far too many companies, inertia prevails and more robust procedures are not instituted. A litany of companies have suffered upheaval because of succession failures. Sometimes the succession process goes so far off the rails that a company suffers a series of rapid-fire CEO replacements. Video gaming retailer GameStop churned through five CEOs in the five years from 2018 to 2023. Shares of the company cratered, and, as characterized by *Barron's*, "GameStop has become the poster child of CEO turnover."[11] Tyson Foods replaced four CEOs in the seven years from 2016 to 2023, three of whom served two years or less, and one just eight months. The stock plunged with each departure.

A flurry of corporate scandals in 2001 prompted a vigorous push for change. The most notorious wrongdoing was the financial malfeasance of energy giant Enron, where several executives, including CEO Ken Lay, were convicted of conspiracy and fraud. In response to the scandals, the Sarbanes-Oxley Act of 2002 instituted many reforms in corporate governance, including making boards officially responsible for succession planning. Previously, the naming of a successor had been almost entirely left up to the sitting CEO. Then, boards generally began requiring CEOs to present them with two or three top candidates so the board could formally vote to choose the successor. But too often CEOs still exerted far too much sway over decisions. Many boards remained largely disengaged from the process of developing a good selection of contenders as well. Little to no formal planning was instituted at many companies. Indeed, in a widely noted 2005 *Harvard Business Review* article, Ram Charan, a leading adviser to CEOs, declared, "The CEO succession process is broken. . . . Almost half of companies with revenue greater than $500 million have no meaningful CEO succession plan."[12]

A couple of years later, momentum built to improve succession practices. It was driven by a series of CEO ousters for which the boards were castigated in the media. Particularly harsh criticism was directed at the enormous severance payments for CEOs who were forced out after only a year or two, such as the $7.2 million in cash and $18 million in company stock paid to Leo Apotheker when he was fired as Hewlett-Packard CEO just eleven months after his appointment.[13] Fearing such rebuke, many boards snapped into action, and some have adopted much more effective procedures. But too many have still not even instituted a formal planning process. In a 2019 survey of 222 CEOs of companies around the globe, 76 percent reported that there was not a leader within the company who was ready to take over their role, and 60 percent said that their company lacked a succession plan.[14] A 2021 study by Stanford researchers found additional evidence of the lack of preparedness, revealing that 22 percent of CEO appointments from 2017 to 2021 were interim—effectively placeholders while boards searched for a permanent successor. In another 10 percent of cases in which the departure of the CEO was announced, the board didn't even have a good interim candidate to appoint. The transition was delayed considerably while the board searched for a successor.[15]

Inadequate succession planning comes at great expense. A study of CEO transitions at the world's 2,500 largest public companies determined that the average cost in shareholder value of a poor succession decision—defined as needing to fire the CEO—was $1.8 billion per company.[16] The cumulative value destruction is staggering. Researchers who evaluated the total annual cost of poor CEO transitions by the S&P 1500 estimated it comes to nearly $1 trillion. Insufficient onboarding support for new CEOs alone amounted to missed opportunities of $109 billion in value creation. Those same researchers concluded that improving succession planning could produce as much as a 20 to 25 percent gain in company valuations and investor returns for the large-cap US equity market.[17] One way valuations could be lifted is by boards proactively initiating a succession when CEOs are producing mediocre results. But, as discussed earlier, boards often fail to replace CEOs who have underperformed the S&P 500 for several years running. When you consider that 38 percent of CEOs outperform the S&P 500 by more than 20 percent in their first year of tenure, the loss of shareholder value is underscored.

To make progress in this area, we must first understand why succession planning and transitioning are so fraught with difficulties. Given how prevalent and unpredictable the twists and turns of succession planning are, a much more thorough and rigorous process of developing and selecting candidates is needed, as is significantly more support for new CEOs as they learn to contend with the intense challenges of the job.

THE MESSY HUMAN FACTORS

Although succession planning is often written about in step-by-step terms as a straightforward process, the truth is that any succession is an extraordinarily complex, anxiety-producing, and emotionally intense human process. The stakes are exceptionally high for all parties involved, and that often leads to problematic behavior.

One contributing factor is that the timing for succession is usually left to the CEO, except when the CEO is ousted. Our CEO Life Cycle data shows that after the first three years in the role, the percentage of CEOs forced out drops precipitously. Of those who leave in the first three years, roughly a third of departures are easily identifiable as oustings. In year four, that share drops to 14 percent and continues to decrease thereafter to a mere sliver of about 6 percent or less of total departures for years ten through fifteen. Boards tend to become increasingly deferential to CEOs the longer the CEO serves, especially with the timing of their retirement. This characteristic seems to have been in play at Disney when the board allowed Iger such a strong hand in choosing Bob Chapek as his successor. At that point, Iger had been CEO for fifteen years and was widely considered as one of the most accomplished CEOs of his generation.

One thing that makes leaving succession timing to the CEO's discretion problematic is that for many longtime CEOs, leaving the job is such an excruciating life transition. We discussed this difficulty regarding marathoner CEOs in Chapter 6, but walking away from the job is difficult after any amount of time in the position. Whereas some enthusiastically embrace the process of succession planning, for many others, considering stepping down from the role can provoke fear about what the future may hold. Some CEOs have become accustomed to the extraordinary rigor of their schedules and the authority they wield and the status the position confers. Our colleague Cathy Anterasian has worked with many departing CEOs, and she said, "They're crossing the chasm to a very different life." The process also prompts them to think about their leadership legacy at the company, and that brings its own worries. Will their achievements be furthered, or will a successor drop the ball? What will they be remembered for? Have they left their mark? A successor may well steer the company in a different strategic direction. Or perhaps dismantle or sell off units created, discontinue products launched, or change course in many other ways.

Taking the plunge to initiate a succession can be extremely anxiety provoking even for CEOs who want to make the change. We talked with Keith Barr, who decided to step down as CEO of InterContinental Hotel Groups after six years because he was eager to take on a new challenge. "I felt that my learning had ended," he told us. He also thought the timing was good because he'd finished with a major restructuring, and the company was doing well. Nonetheless, he found going ahead and making the decision "was really hard," he recalled. "Anyone who says that being CEO does not become part of your personality is not giving you the full picture. It is difficult to not let the role become part of your identity. Every day of my life had been scheduled. Every day I represented the organization." He loved the job, and as is true for so many, said it was "a huge part of my life." He'd been with the company for over two decades. On top of all that, "My wife thought I was nuts," he shared, for wanting to step down.

Barr knew major readjustments to his daily life would follow, and some would be quite tricky. For one, he'd have a good deal more time with his family, but "that doesn't mean things need to change for them as drastically as they do for you." He was aware he'd need to be sensitive about expecting them to reorient and devote more time to him. "You need to realize you need to reconnect with your family in different ways," he said.

He also understood that the pace of his life would slow dramatically, which, as he feared, was tough for him. "It feels like going from a hundred miles an hour to twenty miles an hour in an instant. The adrenaline feed goes away, and you find yourself asking, How do I spend my time?" He had both good days and bad. "Sometimes you fill the day with things you love, and other days you crave the busy routines and being in demand." Contributing to the difficulty was the fact that during the COVID pandemic, he'd spent significant time in his last years working out of his home office. That meant he couldn't make the clean cut of leaving his workspace behind him. When he spent time in that room at home, he felt thrown right back into his old role. The biggest thing he looked forward to when we first talked was moving, because it would be so decisive and more fully help him make the transition. "It will help me enter the next chapter of my life," he said.

The good news is that a few months later, Barr wrote to us that he was now greatly enjoying his new life, spending more time with his family and pursuing long-standing interests he hadn't had time for. "It takes about six months to decompress and find new routines that are not based on what others want you to do and you need to do for work," he said.

Many CEOs are reluctant even to discuss the subject of succession, let alone get started actively planning for it. We've worked with companies whose leaders not only won't engage in the process but also actively thwart their boards' efforts to get planning in motion. One CEO, for example, was extraordinarily adept at finding reasons his board should keep him in place, including casting aspersions on every potential candidate they discussed with him. As is often the case with such resistance, the board was stymied and kept him on through several years of unimpressive performance, devoid of a viable alternative.

In another case, a CEO who had been working closely with the board on succession plans and had highly commended two top contenders to them suddenly berated both candidates at the final board meeting before a vote was to be held. His emotions had clearly run away with him. He accused each of exhibiting unethical behaviors he'd never said a word about before, and he spoke in highly charged terms, becoming visibly overwrought. But the board had come to know the two internal candidates so well via a thoughtful succession process, and the CEO's comments contradicted everything he had said about them earlier in the process. The board wisely discounted his last-minute accusations and proceeded with its vote as planned. Later, it was revealed that a high-powered position the CEO had been expecting to move into had fallen through. Without that to throw himself into, stepping down had become an intensely upsetting prospect for him, triggering a glaring subconscious threat response.

At the other extreme, CEOs can suddenly announce their departure, as Bob Iger did. Although it's customary for CEOs to give boards at least a rough idea of when they expect to leave up to a year in advance, nothing in corporate governance law requires them to do so. Many are reluctant to give the board a date until they are certain about their decision. And with the decision so difficult to make, many go back and forth in their thinking about it, often waiting for what seems like an optimal time. Bob Iger said he chose his surprise timing because he thought that having completed Disney's merger with Fox and the launch of the Disney+ streaming service, he'd found a great window.[18]

As for boards, they are often hesitant about raising the issue of a target date with CEOs. In some cases, they worry that the CEO will react badly or misinterpret the inquiry as a suggestion that a change is needed imminently. Equally, boards fail to start discussions because CEO selection is the most high-stakes decision a board makes. They're all too aware that it's fraught with the possibility of failure. Making the process even more daunting is the fact that many board directors have little experience with CEO selection. Although they have tremendous business experience, regarding succession, they're babes in the wood. This is a big difference between public and PE boards, whose members are regularly involved in these choices. The result is that many boards dither, even when, as we've seen with the Complacency Trap, a CEO's performance is lagging.

In general, board engagement in the succession process is limited until the time of the decision, which is usually within a year of the transition. Then, they might rush to judgment based on just one or perhaps two interviews with candidates, people with whom they've often had little or no other interactions. So little hands-on knowledge of candidates fuels the numerous cognitive biases in their decision-making. One bias is the preference for simplifying narratives, or relying on stereotypes about what a CEO should look and sound like to privilege candidates who are super confident or have a powerful physical presence or can claim bold, even brash, achievements.

We confronted this bias when we were advising about a succession and recommended the board take a more serious look at a candidate. They'd dismissed Alex as not having the needed smarts and being just a solid "doubles hitter" rather than the star slugger they were looking for. But our assessments indicated he had the smarts in spades, and as a doubles hitter, he was a real standout. We brought some of his accomplishments that had been underappreciated back to the board's attention. We also coached him to project a stronger image, including sprucing up his attire. The combination did the trick, and the board selected Alex, who went on to achieve a great deal of success in an eight-year tenure.

Once a formal succession process is underway, directors are eager to get to know the internal options better. However, as they meet with candidates, they can be too quick to create simplifying narratives about them, as the board above did with Alex. And once they do, they sometimes prematurely eliminate certain candidates and elevate others. Many times, boards do not allow the time that's required to develop a more thorough understanding of candidates. Sometimes a sense of urgency is understandable. It might be fueled by an accelerated timeline for the sitting CEO's departure or by the CEO's firing. But it is important to push back against the rush to judgment, especially when timing isn't tight.

The process of evaluating prospects is discomforting, not only because the stakes are so high but also because it's so complex. No matter how sophisticated the diagnostics used to assess people's talents, doing so is an imperfect science. There are so many variables to consider, and the demands on a CEO have become so multivariate—they must have not only great business acumen but also strong people leadership skills and sophistication about stakeholder relations, including sensitivity and thoughtfulness about social issues CEOs are increasingly expected to weigh in on. It's human nature to want to free ourselves from such complicated decision-making. This tendency often leads boards to prematurely narrow their field of candidates and opt for a choice in hand, even if they have reservations, rather than widening the field of consideration. Some great options, therefore, often go unconsidered. As the selections of Mary Barra and Chuck Robbins from leapfrog positions demonstrate, stellar candidates may be in roles a level or two below the common levels boards select candidates from.

The sense of urgency boards feel about making a selection can also provoke intense emotion if the decision process is derailed, which may lead to erratic decision-making. In one case, a board believed they were cruising to the finish line. They'd been considering three general managers and a functional leader and were leaning toward one of the three GMs as their pick. They had a well-planned process for the next few months and were keeping their minds open to all options. But then their number one suddenly announced that she'd accepted a CEO job at another firm. The board felt betrayed. In response, rather than thoughtfully reconsidering the other three candidates as good alternatives, which they had previously believed to be true, they became fixated on the inadequacy of their other choices and decided to more thoroughly consider outside prospects. The pendulum had swung from enthusiasm for internal options and limited interest in external options to the opposite. Fortunately, time and a disciplined process countered the emotional reaction. One of the three remaining inside candidates was actually very well qualified. When she was formally interviewed by the board and had a chance to share her vision for the future, the directors rallied around her, seeing more clearly the limitations of their external options in comparison with her talents. It was as though their judgment had been clouded by their irritation with their first choice.

Though their frustration was understandable, boards must be aware that top talent may be lured away at any moment, which is not always a mark against a candidate's character or an intentional snub of the board. This does not mean that boards should move faster to make offers to their top choices; as we've said, a deliberate and carefully considered process is always best. What all these uncertainties and potential human foibles involved in the process do mean is that boards should devote more time, over many more years than they generally do, to developing broader slates of prospects and getting to know contenders much more thoroughly so that they can see past simplified narratives and resist a rush to judgment.

Ideally, succession planning is a continuous process that doesn't begin at some point during a CEO's tenure but rather as part of a company's larger talent development work. This ongoing attention to the effort allows for a robust field of candidates to be given opportunities, over the course of many years, to build strengths in areas where they've had little experience. That helps ensure that when internal candidates are selected, they get off to a strong start and are well prepared for the wide range of headwinds they'll face throughout the CEO Life Cycle. A continuous process that involves the CEO from the start of tenure also helps prepare the CEO for the personal difficulty of leaving the role. Regular discussions and the development of a strong bench facilitate the decision to step down.

SUCCESSION AS AN ONGOING LEADERSHIP DEVELOPMENT PROCESS

Even before Ajay Banga assumed the CEO role at Mastercard, he and board chair Richard Haythornthwaite considered how they would go about appointing his successor. In fact, they discussed succession in their first meeting, before Banga was hired by Mastercard. They wrote about their process in the *Harvard Business Review*, reporting that they had agreed that planning for a smooth transition of power "would be an open and integral part of everyday senior leadership development from day one."[19]

The process began during Banga's first year as CEO, 2010, and continued throughout the ten years of his tenure. "Our early start," they recall, "allowed us to do something that in our opinion is key to a strong and well-received CEO succession: we cast a wide internal net." They initially selected forty-two leaders from a wide range of positions in the company, including a number from two and three levels below the C-suite. Their intent was not only to find a strong CEO appointment but also to develop the talents of this whole cadre of leaders and to retain them at the company by continuing to find them exciting new opportunities to grow. They actively pushed people to take on new challenges, encouraging them to move out of their comfort zones. For example, one of the forty-two was Michael Miebach, who'd joined Mastercard the same year Banga became CEO. He was appointed to run Mastercard's Middle East and Africa operations following his strong career in commercial banking, most recently as a managing director of Barclays. After a few years in that role, when he expressed his desire to next run the larger Asia division, Banga asked him, "How does your going to Asia . . . make you more attractive to me" as a successor? Instead, Miebach agreed to take on the role of chief product officer that was based in the home office in the United States, which required him to stretch by diving deeply into the emerging technologies that were becoming crucial to the bank's future, such as mobile payments, AI, and digital identity capabilities, like voice recognition.

The Mastercard chief human resource officer was integral to establishing and conducting the leadership development process. Leadership development then became part of the larger, company-wide talent development procedures, which included every manager assessing direct reports' development priorities annually. The forty-two leaders selected for succession consideration were enrolled in a new "senior management excellence program," in which Banga was closely involved. Each individual was given training and coaching as well as assignments to present at board meetings. They were able to interact with board directors in "informal coffees or speed-dating sessions" that were made part of quarterly board gatherings. Through this process, a number of particularly strong contenders were identified, and by 2018, Banga and the board were confident they had several prospects who were getting close to being ready to take on the job.

Next, the prospects went through more intensive development, including additional personal coaching, immersive off-site programs, 360-degree reviews, and psychometric testing. That led to a focus on four front-runners who were compared with a set of external leaders for consideration, which was important in benchmarking internal contenders against the wider field of talent.

By late 2019, Banga announced that he would be stepping down the following year, and the board was ready to move into the decision phase. Haythornthwaite then made a round of calls to discuss each director's favored choice with them, followed by a board meeting in which they vigorously discussed the decision for three hours. The directors unanimously voted for Michael Miebach, and in February 2020, his selection was announced. In a yearlong transition into the role, Miebach was first promoted to the position of president and took over leadership of the company's sales, marketing, and technology businesses. In January 2021, he stepped into the CEO job. At that time, Haythornthwaite resigned as board chair, and Banga moved into the role of executive chair, which he held for a year, providing support for Miebach.

Integrating succession planning into a company's larger talent development process in this way combats the emotional tensions and biases that plague so many efforts. No succession will ever be without them, but we've seen in additional prominent cases how effective this approach can be in achieving a smooth transition, even when the departing CEO has had a long and illustrious tenure. Essentially the same process was followed, for example, by Dave Cote and his board in choosing his successor at Honeywell, as he describes in detail in his book *Winning Now, Winning Later.*

As mentioned in Chapter 6, this allowed Darius Adamczyk to make a smooth transition into the role even as analysts and investors expressed concerns about who would replace such a "highly successful and highly visible" CEO, as analyst Steve Winoker said.[20] By working so far in advance in close collaboration with Cote, the Honeywell board had identified Darius Adamczyk as a key prospect for successor years in advance of his appointment so that he could be given more responsibilities, including being promoted to COO the year before his appointment. As COO, a full nine months before he stepped into the CEO job, he gained agreement on a strategic plan for going forward that he could announce when he was appointed. Wall Street expressed confidence in him well in advance of that, with Steve Winoker, for example, sharing his view that, "in Mr. Adamczyk, Honeywell is looking at an accomplished, stable leader with a track record of success across a wide range of businesses."[21]

Succession planning as a continuous process, which the board never sets aside for later, and that every new CEO immediately becomes involved with, has important additional benefits. Vitally, it obviates the awkwardness of raising the issue of succession at some point during a CEO's tenure. In addition, the new CEO is informed right away of the full bench of talent that's been in development and is provided the individuals' evaluation histories. This is extremely helpful with the crucial job of quickly assessing the executive team, including finding replacements if some team members decide to leave following the new appointment, as is almost always the case. What's more, with this ongoing approach to succession, no matter how abruptly a CEO may step down or what cataclysm may require an ouster, a strong slate of candidates is at hand.

A close partnership among the CEO, the chief human resource officer (CHRO), and the board is key to the process running smoothly. Although the amount of influence CHROs have with their CEOs and boards is highly variable, most S&P 500 companies have talented CHROs who play an important role in shaping and executing successions. We've seen some take a firm hand in advising CEOs who weren't attending to succession planning to get a good process going. In one case, a new CHRO recognized that only one executive was being seriously considered as the successor. The CEO had indicated he planned to step down in about five years, and he didn't think more serious consideration of prospects to replace him was needed at present. The CHRO convinced him to initiate a rigorous process of identifying a wider field of prospects, which included a number of leaders from tiers below the C-suite, and some of them were given additional responsibilities to develop their skills. Four years later, the board had a strong field of contenders when the CEO announced his departure date. CHROs are so important to a strong planning process because they are in charge of a company's overall talent development processes. As such, they are much better prepared to identify prospects from all around the firm, including many levels below the top tier of leadership, which the CEO and directors would not be able to do.

One important problem this type of succession planning can address is the lack of diversity in the slates of final candidates for CEO jobs. Building more diverse talent pools for CEO appointments has been many companies' stated mission for years. Yet appallingly little progress has been made. In 2023, just six of the S&P 500 CEOs were African American, which is 1.2 percent, and only 8.8 percent were women. What's more, a 2020 Stanford University study found that, although women held 25 percent of C-suite positions in Fortune 100 companies, only 13 percent of them were in the positions that most commonly lead to CEO appointment—divisional CEO, COO, and CFO.[22] A highly intentional process of building a more diverse leadership pipeline and rigorously assessing whether qualified candidates and those from underrepresented groups have been given appropriate development opportunities and unbiased evaluations will go a long way in correcting for these egregious imbalances. As important as asking, "Who do we have?" is "Who is conspicuously absent?" And this should be done, of course, for the talent pool currently under consideration for the CEO role and as an ongoing part of leadership development at all levels of the company. Top leadership must make a serious commitment to combating biases in hiring and promotion decisions that hold so many highly qualified people back and ultimately from contention for the CEO role.

Susan Story shared that she and her board made this a priority at American Water. She emphasized looking for opportunities to provide women and underrepresented minorities more stretch opportunities at levels below the top two tiers of management so that a better pipeline was created and everyone had broader experience by the time a slate of CEO contenders was picked. "Actively encouraging them to put their hat in the ring for next-level jobs earlier is key," she said. Research shows, for example, that many women underestimate their abilities, whereas many men overestimate their abilities. Women who were ready for a new challenge would tell her, "I think I need two or three more years where I am," even as male candidates who did need more experience would assert, "I can do the job, I have no doubt about that." She provided coaching for talented prospects to help them build the confidence to take on challenges sooner and worked closely with her CHRO to identify a broad slate of candidates.

The CHRO should take the lead, in close consultation with the CEO and often in partnership with an outside firm, in creating development plans for each prospect that list specific capabilities the prospect can work on and ways of measuring their progress. The assessment of individual progress can be part of annual succession reviews that should be shared with the CEO and board. The CHRO can also help the CEO by recommending good stretch positions and prospects who would be the best candidates for them. Prospects can be divided into "tiers" of readiness, with some designated as the top set, closest to fully prepared. Others may be identified as needing more development.

Crucial to the process is creating a profile of the CEO the company needs. This should be revisited regularly and updated as the challenges the company is facing evolve. Ideally, the CEO profile should include a range of timelines for when a new CEO may step in, for example, the transition is in two years, five years, or ten years, because the requirements may be quite different at each time. If the company is in the midst of a major transformation, the skills to carry on with that should be emphasized. That was true for the successor to Carl Bass, CEO of Autodesk. Bass had put in motion the transition from software in a box to the cloud-based subscription model. With Bass stepping down midway through that process, paramount in the selection of his successor was very strong operations expertise for bringing the process to a successful conclusion. When Michelle Gass succeeded Levi Strauss CEO Chip Bergh, in contrast, a change in expertise was prioritized because the work Bergh had been appointed to achieve—restoring the reputation of the brand—had been accomplished, and expertise in direct-to-consumer retail had become more important. "I was the right guy for twelve years ago," Bergh explained, "when the brand was broken. I'm a brand guy. But now, more and more of our business is retail. We have grown our direct-to-consumer business from roughly 20 percent to over 40 percent."[23] Gass had strong retail experience as CEO of the Kohl's chain.

In our experience, the process of succession planning at many companies is too near-term-focused and does not include such consideration of the needed capabilities of a future CEO.

Prospects can be designated as the most likely contenders for various scenarios. So, maybe you have three prospects who are top contenders if you have to make the selection within the next two years. Of those, one is considered to have the advantage if the economy plunges into a financial crisis because they have risk management credentials and an especially strong command of the balance sheet. The second contender might be designated the top pick should the company undertake a major acquisition because they have experience with M&A integrations. Perhaps the third would lead the pack if an emerging technology suddenly gained momentum, as happened with AI and the release of ChatGPT.

To easily keep track of all this, create a succession map for charting the progress of all prospects across multiple time horizons. The map will evolve as people complete assignments and move into new ones, and as new evaluations are conducted. It will also evolve as business conditions and the needs of the company change. A succession map is enormously helpful in surveying the full range of prospects regularly and considering stretch roles or other development work to move people into. The succession map can help pinpoint prospects who emerge as surprise contenders given how well they are coming along.

For example, in one situation a leader was viewed as a great general manager but her operations talents weren't matched by people management or strategic skills. The CEO and CHRO decided to test her management mettle by creating a new set of leadership positions that would report to her and take on more of the load of driving daily operations. They were stunned to see that she immediately began offering high-quality strategic advice to the CEO, revealing that she was adept at taking an enterprise-wide perspective. As it turned out, she wasn't a "stuck in the weeds" type by any means, but just had been forced to spend so much time in operations without that extra set of managers taking on more of the load. She was then elevated as a leading contender.

Another essential component of a talent development plan is creating plentiful opportunities for prospects to interact with directors. Just a presentation to the board here and there isn't sufficient. It's vital that board members gain a much more thorough and nuanced understanding of candidates' talents and weak spots through firsthand experience with them, as Banga and his board arranged. When it came to their final slate of contenders, they required that each director meet with each candidate one-on-one. CEOs can create many kinds of opportunities, from inviting prospects to work on special projects in which the board is engaged to holding board meetings at a regional division headquarters where directors can meet and schedule one-on-one meetings with the general manager and other executives.

The merit of getting to know prospects to choose a good successor was evident in Charles' case. He'd risen to the top of the heap of candidates through a long and rigorous process during which the board had gotten to know him well. They'd been presented with a wealth of information about his accomplishments and leadership talents, and they felt confident he was right for the job. But then he totally whiffed his interview with them by showing up in the manner of a direct report rather than speaking to the directors as a peer. He didn't come across as the authoritative leader they could rely on to be forceful with them or to make the tough calls and bold moves that would take the firm where it needed to go. They were really taken aback, and they began to reconsider an external candidate.

But all that they had learned about Charles over the prior five years ultimately prevailed. Because of the experience they had with him, they agreed when we urged them to give him another chance to present. We gave him feedback and shared what the board had said about his prior performance before them. He took the feedback well and returned very much as the in-command CEO the board wanted to see. This ability to take feedback and adapt gave them even more confidence that he would continue to grow once in the role. Charles was appointed and has had a highly successful tenure.

We'll make a final point about benchmarking external candidates. Over the past ten to twenty years, we have observed boards and CEOs come to see success in succession as the appointment of an internal leader. In fact, we often hear, "If we have to go outside, it is a failure." But as John Lundgren's appointment by the board as Stanley Tools CEO illustrates, an external candidate is sometimes the best option. The imperative is not to promote from within but to make the best possible appointment. Even boards that have strong internal options must consider the best available external talent. This is usually done confidentially, but most internal candidates are made aware that the board is also considering outside options. Strong internal candidates benefit from the board fully considering all the options. If you are chosen from among the best available, you will enjoy more support and confidence from your board once you are CEO and navigating the ups and downs of the role.

THE CRUCIBLE OF THE FINAL DECISION

As the board moves into the process of making a selection, tensions will run higher. The final candidates go through an intensive additional assessment process that generally involves new 360-degree interviews with peers and direct reports and various tests of their skills and capabilities. Candidates are also asked to prepare a strategic vision paper or business plan to present to the board.

The process is a pressure cooker. After all, the candidates have given so much of themselves to get to this place. They've sacrificed so much time in pursuit of this goal that they could have been spending with family. They may have moved to a country they never had the slightest interest in working in and taken on jobs that were far from their true passions. They're also well aware of how few opportunities they might have to be selected for another CEO position, for which they'll have to go through yet another intensive selection process.

Emotions can boil over, and candidates can easily scuttle their chances. In one case, an executive who was in the final running shot himself in the foot in various ways. He became more antagonistic and less of a team player with his peers, whom he viewed as competitors. Meanwhile, he began micromanaging his direct reports and applied undue pressure on them for better results, because he was so intent on impressing the board. But that approach backfired, as it generally does, and the group's results began to lag. In addition, he was blatantly trying to present himself in the mold of the incumbent CEO rather than presenting himself as his own type of leader. People across the ranks began asking where the person they knew so well had gone. Ultimately, his behavior became so problematic that not only was he dropped from the group of final contenders, but he was also forced out of the company.

The CHRO is instrumental in helping candidates manage the stress of this period. A big stress reliever is making sure candidates have a clear understanding at the beginning of how the selection process will be conducted and the anticipated timeline. Also important is ensuring that candidates feel the process is giving them a fair shot. CEOs should distance themselves from this final assessment phase so they do not appear to be biasing the process. They should not, for example, attend the board meetings where candidates present their strategic visions. Their presence would add a great deal of tension, constraining candidates in sharing their honest assessment of the business and equally holding directors back from asking direct questions. Showing no preference was important to Ajay Banga and Richard Haythornthwaite as they moved into the decision phase. "We wanted to keep everyone engaged and active and all serious contenders under consideration for as long as possible to ensure the best decision," they wrote. "So the two of us never even hinted at which way we were leaning. We told the board, 'When you're ready to vote, we'll tell you what we think.'"[24] As for boards, they should act with alacrity in making their selection decision after the candidates' presentations. Drawing the decision out will turn the volume up on the already roiling stress.

It's no wonder that so many top contenders who are not selected leave companies after the new CEO is appointed. In a study of 121 transitions at the one hundred largest companies in the United States, Stanford University researchers found that 74 percent of contenders who were not chosen left the company. Of those, 30 percent moved on to become a CEO at another firm, 41 percent took another position below the CEO level, and 30 percent retired.[25] Yet, boards and the incoming CEO can work to mitigate an exodus. In one succession we worked on, the CEO created a new position for another candidate that made him a very visible number two at the company. As for directors, if they've developed good relationships with runners-up, they can initiate conversations with them to assure them that their value to the company is appreciated.

SUPPORTING A SMOOTH TRANSITION

As soon as the decision is made, the incumbent CEO, the CHRO, and the board should work on a transition plan for the new leader. This detailed game plan optimizes use of the time between when a new CEO is appointed and when they step into the job and then lays a framework for how the new CEO will be supported through the transition and for at least the first full year. We call the time between announcement and start date the *preparation sprint*. Our data shows that for internal appointments, this is on average three months, whereas for external hires, it's a mere six weeks. Optimizing this crunch time is vital.

The agenda, of course, varies for each new CEO, but developing stronger relationships with board members is a top priority. Unfortunately, one of the biggest problems with successions is that, in almost all cases, once the selection is made, the board disengages. They've done their job, they think, and now it's up to the in-house leadership team to make things work. That's a big mistake, and it's a key reason the Launch stage is so difficult for new CEOs. Learning how to build a relationship with the board is, hands down, the hardest part of a CEO's early going. Directors should not leave the relationship building up to the CEO. They have so much knowledge of the company they can impart. They can share their concerns about company issues more candidly now as well as their views about how best to address them.

The transition plan should include a new round of one-on-one meetings of the CEO with directors, which, for internal hires, can begin right after the announcement. One option to consider is actually appointing the CEO-elect to the board. Before Sarbanes-Oxley, it was common practice to groom a CEO designate by giving them a board seat. Boards mostly abandoned the practice as independent directors became the norm. But Sarbanes-Oxley requires that only half of the board be independent directors, so there is no legal prohibition against doing this.

The outgoing CEO should become deeply engaged in mentoring, sharing more about issues the company is facing and their perspectives on board members and company leaders, and should introduce the CEO-elect to any unfamiliar company executives. But caution is in order.

One way that boards have sought to ensure the outgoing CEO provides ongoing guidance is to make them an executive chair, generally for a one- or two-year term. But this can result in the chair having excessive influence and make it harder for the new CEO to establish a good relationship with directors. This is especially the case when a long-tenured CEO becomes executive chair; they are more likely to move into the role. Our CEO Life Cycle data shows that the longer an outgoing CEO has been in the role, the higher the likelihood they'll be appointed chair or executive chair. This happens up to 70 percent of the time. Their presence can make taking firm charge of the company more difficult for the new CEO. One director shared the story of a very difficult situation for a new CEO when the predecessor not only remained on the board for two years but kept an office at the company headquarters. Executives who'd worked with him for years tried to influence him to sway the board against changes the new CEO was putting in place. "It was a very unhealthy situation."

At the least, a well-articulated understanding of the activities the executive chair will engage in is vital, and the incoming CEO and executive chair should have a substantive conversation about exactly how they will divide responsibilities. When Carol Bartz stepped down as CEO of Autodesk, the directors asked her to stay on the board for two years. She worked out an arrangement with her successor, Carl Bass, in which she would take over some responsibilities he preferred not to be saddled with. "He wasn't fond of travel and he asked me to take all of the South Africa and India trips and go meet our development units and do some customer relations. We very clearly delineated what I was going to do and what he was going to do."

In stark contrast—and a cautionary tale for the ages—when Bob Iger was appointed executive chair at Disney for an anticipated period of twenty-two months, he not only retained the authority to "direct the company's creative endeavors" but also kept his office. Within weeks of handing the reins to Chapek, the fact that Iger was not, in truth, relinquishing power was clear enough that the *New York Times* reported Iger had "effectively returned to running the company," an assertion Iger did not dispute.[26] No matter what details of Chapek's tenure may have contributed to the fiasco of the succession, what is entirely clear is that Iger and the Disney board utterly failed to support Chapek in the transition.

The handover to a successor is without doubt one of the most difficult, and delicate, challenges of a CEO's tenure. CEOs who work hard to ensure a strong selection is made and a smooth transition is achieved are richly rewarded in knowing they've done all they can to leave their company on sure footing. There is no finer crowning achievement of a CEO's tenure than leaving the company in strong hands that can navigate the tempestuous crosswinds of the unpredictable future. Mark Brown, who stepped down after a remarkably successful twenty-five-year run as CEO of beverage maker Sazerac, expressed this view powerfully. For eight years, he devoted himself to ensuring a smooth transition, and he told us, "My ultimate success is not in the last twenty-five years but in the next five years. What you really want to happen is that people will be saying, 'Wow, the company is doing much better now than under you.'"

APPENDIX 1

THE CEOS AND DIRECTORS WE LEARNED FROM DURING OUR STUDIES

We would like to express our profound gratitude to the CEOs and directors who shared their insights and experiences so generously with us. We list all of those we spoke with here, along with their affiliations and, for the CEOs, the years of their tenure.

THE CEOS WHOM WE LEARNED FROM DURING OUR STUDIES

Name	Company	Tenure*
José Almeida	Baxter International	2016–present
Andrew Anagnost	Autodesk, Inc.	2017–present
Richard Anderson	Delta Airlines	2007–2016
Ajaypal Banga	Mastercard, Inc.	2010–2021
Keith Barr	InterContinental Hotels Group PLC	2017–2023
Carl Bass	Autodesk, Inc.	2006–2017
Christophe Beck	Ecolab, Inc.	2021–present
Mark Brown	Sazerac Company, Inc.	1997–2023
Robert Bruggeworth	Qorvo, Inc.	2015–present

Name	Company	Tenure*
William Cobb	H&R Block, Inc.	2011–2017
Steven Cooper	TrueBlue, Inc.	2005–2018; 2022–2023
David Cote	Honeywell International	2002–2017
James Craigie	Church & Dwight Company, Inc.	2004–2015
Terrence Curtin	TE Connectivity	2017–present
Patrick Decker	Xylem, Inc.	2014–2023
Joseph DePinto	7-Eleven, Inc.	2005–present
Gregory Ebel	Enbridge, Inc.	2023–present
Michael Egeck	Leslie's, Inc.	2020–present
Richard Fain	Royal Caribbean Group	1988–2022
Matthew Farrell	Church & Dwight Company, Inc.	2016–present
Michael Farrell	ResMed, Inc.	2013–present
Roger Ferguson	Teachers Insurance and Annuity Association of America	2008–2021
Nicholas Fink	Fortune Brands Innovations, Inc.	2020–present
Dan Garton	AMR Eagle	2010–2014
Eric Green	West Pharmaceutical Services, Inc.	2015–present
Evan Greenberg	Chubb Corporation	2004–present
Timothy Guertin	Varian Medial Systems, Inc.	2006–2012
Piyush Gupta	DBS Bank Ltd.	2009–present
James Hackett	Anadarko Petroleum Corporation	2003–2012
Lew Hay III	NextEra Energy, Inc.	2001–2012

Name	Company	Tenure*
Joseph Hogan	Align Technology, Inc.	2015–present
Randy Hogan	Pentair PLC	2001–2018
Mark Hoplamazian	Hyatt Hotels Corporation	2006–present
Hubert Joly	Best Buy Company, Inc.	2012–2019
Patricia Kampling	Alliant Energy Corporation	2012–2019
Leo Kiely III	Molson Coors Brewing Company	2002–2008
Harry Lawton III	Tractor Supply Company	2020–present
Rod Little	Edgewell Personal Care Company	2019–present
Steven Loranger	Xylem, Inc.	2013–2014
Charles Lowrey Jr.	Prudential Financial, Inc.	2018–present
John Lundgren	Stanley Black & Decker, Inc.	2004–2016
Terry Lundgren	Macy's, Inc.	2004–2018
Mahesh Madhavan	Bacardi Ltd.	2017–present
Paul Markovich	Blue Shield of California	2013–present
Brandt McKee	Interior Logic Group Holdings LLC	2022–present
Michael McMullen	Agilent Technologies, Inc.	2015–present
Larry Merlo	CVS Health Corporation	2011–2021
William Meury	Karuna Therapeutics, Inc.	2023–present
John Miller	Denny's Corporation	2011–2022
Shantanu Narayen	Adobe, Inc.	2007–present
Christopher Nassetta	Hilton Worldwide Holdings, Inc.	2007–present
Steven Nielsen	Dycom Industries, Inc.	1999–present
Indra Nooyi	PepsiCo, Inc.	2006–2018

Name	Company	Tenure*
David Novak	Yum! Brands, Inc.	2001–2014
Eric Nyman	Revelyst	2023–present
Christopher O'Connell	Waters Corporation	2015–2020
Scott O'Neil	Merlin Entertainments Ltd.	2022–present
James Owens	Caterpillar, Inc.	2004–2010
Robert Painter	Trimble, Inc.	2020–present
Kevin Parkes	Finning International, Inc.	2022–present
George Paz	Express Scripts Holding Company	2005–2015
Christopher Peterson	Newell Brands, Inc.	2023–present
Douglas Pferdehirt	TechnipFMC USA, Inc.	2016–present
Andrew Rees	Crocs, Inc.	2017–present
Vincent Sadusky	Univision Communications, Inc.	2018–2020
Barry Salzberg	Deloitte Touche Tohmatsu LLC	2011–2015
Ronald Sargent	Staples, Inc.	2002–2016
Kevin Sayer	Dexcom, Inc.	2015–present
George Schaefer Jr.	Fifth Third Bancorp	1991–2007
Daniel Schulman	PayPal Holdings, Inc.	2015–2023
Stephen Schwarzman	Blackstone, Inc.	1985–present
Mark Sheahan	Graco, Inc.	2021–present
Gregory Smith	Teradyne, Inc.	2023–present
Douglas Steenland	Northwest Airlines	2004–2008
William Stein	Digital Realty Trust, Inc.	2014–2022
David Steiner	Waste Management, Inc.	2004–2012
Susan Story	American Water	2014–2020

Name	Company	Tenure*
L. Scott Thomson	Finning International, Inc.	2013–2022
Carol Tomé	United Parcel Service, Inc.	2020–present
Nigel Travis	Dunkin' Brands Group, Inc.	2009–2018
Nish Vartanian	MSA Safety, Inc.	2018–present
John Venhuizen	Ace Hardware Corporation	2013–present
Darren Walker	Ford Foundation	2013–present
Poul Weihrauch	Mars, Inc.	2022–present
Beth Wozniak	nVent Electric PLC	2018–present
* Present is December 31, 2023.		

THE DIRECTORS WHOM WE LEARNED FROM DURING OUR STUDIES

Name	Current and Former Boards
Michael Anglin	Antofagasta PLC; SSR Mining, Inc.; Ember-Clear Corporation; Tulla Resources
Carol Bartz	Autodesk, Inc.; Cisco Systems, Inc.; Yahoo!, Inc.; Intel Corporation; NetApp, Inc.; New York Stock Exchange, Inc.
Peter Browning	EnPro Industries; GMS, Inc.; ScanSource, Inc.; Acuity Brands, Inc.; Lowe's Companies, Inc.; Sykes Enterprises, Inc.; Nucor Corporation
Christopher Coughlin	Centene Corporation; Dun & Bradstreet Holdings, Inc.; Allergan PLC; Alexion; Tyco; Monsanto Company; Interrepublic Group of Companies
Peter Currie	Schlumberger; Palamon Capital Partners, Ltd.; New Relic, Inc.; Sun Microsystems, Inc.; Safeco Corporation; Clearwire Corporation; Twitter

Name	Current and Former Boards
David Dorman	CVS Health Corporation; Dell Technologies, Inc.; PayPal Holdings, Inc.; eBay, Inc.; Chairman of Motorola Solutions, Inc.; Yum! Brands, Inc.
Cheryl Grisé	Dollar Tree; ICF International; PulteGroup, Inc.; MetLife, Inc.; Pall Corporation; Dana Holding Corporation
Ann Fritz Hackett	MasterBrand, Inc.; Fortune Brands; Capital One Financial
William E. Kennard	AT&T, Inc.; MetLife, Inc.; Ford Motor Company; Velocitas Partners, Inc.; Astra Capital Management
Catherine Kinney	MetLife, Inc.; New York Stock Exchange, Inc.
Thomas Pritzker	Hyatt Hotels
Susan Schwab	Boeing Company; Marriott International, Inc.; Caterpillar, Inc.; FedEx Corporation; Petroleum & Resources Corporation
Laurie Siegel	Scoop Technologies; CECO Environmental Corporation; FactSet Research Systems, Inc.; Lumen Technologies; California Resources Corporation; Volt Information Sciences, Inc.
Elizabeth Tallett	Chair of Elevance Health, Inc.; Moderna, Inc.; Qiagen N.V.; Phosplatin Therapeutics; Immunotope; Biotechnology Council of New Jersey
Robin Washington	Alphabet; Salesforce, Inc.; Gilead Sciences; Vertiv Holdings Company; Honeywell
Stephen Wilson	CF Industries Holdings, Inc.; GATX Corporation; Ameren Corporation; Terra Industries

APPENDIX 2

In this appendix, we provide more detailed information about the data discoveries we made in our CEO Life Cycle study. In addition to explaining more about the analyses we performed, we'll introduce some additional nuances in the findings.

The database we built includes a wide range of statistics regarding company performance during the tenure of every CEO who led an S&P 500 company between 2000 and 2022. Some CEOs were already in the role before 2000, and some continued in the role beyond 2022. The total number of CEOs in the study is 2,077. We used this sample to analyze CEO trends over time, such as the appointments of insiders and outsiders, changes in tenure length, and turnover in any given year. In none of our analyses did we include CEOs appointed in an interim capacity because their time in the role is not representative of a permanent appointment's experience, which is our subject of study.

We included in the dataset a wide range of measures of financial performance, including total shareholder return (TSR); revenue; earnings before interest, taxes, depreciation, and amortization (EBITDA); operating income; efficiency ratios; stock volatility; R&D spend; CapEx spend; financial leverage; and M&A activity. This data was sourced from SQ Capital as well as from balance sheets, income statements, cash flow statements, SEC filings, press releases, and company websites. We added in data about CEOs that Spencer Stuart collected, including whether they held a previous CEO role, what role they were in prior to being appointed CEO, their board experience, and whether they were an insider or outsider appointment.

So much data allowed us to discern patterns in CEO performance through the course of their tenure. We also found the answers we've presented throughout the book to questions about CEO success, for example, that there is no significant difference in the overall tenure performance of insider appointments versus outsider appointments. The robustness of the database enabled us to uncover the trends in CEO hiring and performance between 2000 and 2022, such as the decrease in the percentage of appointments whose prior role was as president/COO.

THE DISCOVERY OF THE CEO LIFE CYCLE STAGES

To perform our analysis of TSR performance through a CEO's course of tenure, we pulled a subset of CEOs whose tenure ended before December 31, 2022. In this subsample, we had complete tenure data for all included CEOs. We excluded CEOs who stayed in their role less than two years and those for whom we could not gather enough data points to study year-over-year. This sample included 1,365 CEOs.

We chose TSR for this analysis because it includes both stock price appreciation and dividends received by shareholders over a specified time frame, thereby offering a more complete assessment of performance than just share price. TSR also facilitates comparison across industries. In addition, it is a transparent and objective metric that is not subject to accounting manipulations. Because we intended to compare performance over time, we needed to separate the conditions of the broader economy from a CEO's performance. To do so, we market-adjusted our data to account for any effects that were happening in the market. If a CEO was showing negative TSR in a given year, we wanted to understand how well or how badly they did relative to the index.

Our interest was in determining whether any pattern of performance was specifically associated with the amount of time in the job. Because CEOs started in the role on so many different dates and were in the role for variable amounts of time, investigating their TSR performance as they progressed in their role over time allowed us to further neutralize the effects of market-wide upturns and downturns on any pattern that might emerge.

To understand this, consider the Great Recession of 2008, which officially began in December 2007 and ended in June 2009, a period of eighteen months. For CEOs who started in January 2008, the recession's effects on TSR showed up in the first year and a half of their tenure. For CEOs who started earlier, the effects showed up in later years. So, if a CEO started in January 2007, the recession affected their TSR performance starting at the very tail end of their first year and lasted until midway through their third year. For those who started in 2006, effects started showing up in year three of their tenure. For those who started in 2000, effects showed up in their eighth year. Because the year-by-year variation in new CEOs starting in the role is relatively small—on average, fifty-three CEOs start in a year—the recession's effects on TSR were spread out throughout the CEO Life Cycle stages in the full sample. That wouldn't be true if 2008 was an anomalous year in which many more CEOs started their tenure, let's say, one hundred CEOs. If that were the case, the effects of the recession would have distorted the TSR picture downward for the Launch stage. Likewise, if many more CEOs had started in 2000, eight years before the recession, then our TSR finding would have been distorted downward for the end of the Complacency Trap stage.

But because the number of new starts is relatively consistent year to year and performance was market-adjusted, when we combined the data for all the CEO tenures, the effects of the recession were canceled out and did not contribute to rises and falls we saw in the combined average TSR data for all CEOs.

Similarly, we could control for the effects of industry-wide upturns and downturns because the CEOs worked in a wide range of industries. For example, a downturn in the market for computer chips affected the TSR of a relatively small number of CEOs in those years. In another time frame, a spike in grain prices might have affected the TSR of food companies with particular force. Having data for so many CEOs across so many industries meant that, in total, these effects would not stand out in any underlying pattern associated with a CEO's length of time in the role.

Capturing TSR data from the CEO's start date rather than using calendar-year delineations—in other words, tracking from anniversary to anniversary of starting—highlighted any pattern caused by the point of time in a tenure rather than larger market conditions. If a market downturn happened in the first few months of a year, for example, and a CEO started in May of that year, our anniversary-to-anniversary data for the CEO's performance would not be tainted by results outside of the actual period of tenure. The result is that our analyses chart the ups and downs in performance that were associated with the years of CEO tenure rather than with the larger headwinds and tailwinds of the overall economy or their industry.

The combined TSR data for the complete dataset produced the striking performance pattern below through the course of a CEO's tenure, over fifteen years. We limited the analysis to fifteen years because so few CEOs stay in the role that long—only 7 percent of CEOs stay fifteen years or longer—so any pattern in those years would not be statistically significant.

The CEO Life Cycle

How total shareholder return varies by stage
compared to the average return across all stages

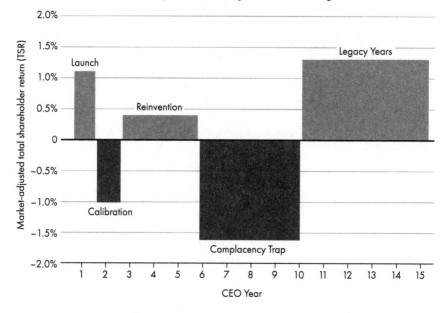

To produce this graph, we centered the data, meaning we calculated the "grand average" of TSR for the full set of years—which is represented by the 0 percent line—and then subtracted that average from the TSR data for each year. In this way, we isolated just the rise above or decline below the average for each year. The *y*-axis represents the degree of increase over the average or decline below the average. Although a rise of 1 percent in the Launch stage may seem quite moderate, it represents 1 percent of the total market capitalization of a company, and for S&P 500 companies, that amounts to a great deal of shareholder value. For example, for Procter & Gamble, with a total market capitalization of $346 billion as of this writing, the 1 percent translates into $3.46 billion. These differences also compound over time.

Of course, for any given CEO, that spike up might have been much greater or smaller. The TSR might also have dropped in the first year. We should emphasize again that the CEO Life Cycle pattern is an average result for the 1,365 CEOs. Just as any given company may experience a contraction during the expansion stage of the macroeconomic business cycle or an expansion during the contraction stage, any given CEO may beat these odds in the stages of their tenure or do more poorly. We hope the pattern helps CEOs and their boards anticipate these common swings and therefore prepare for them—or outperform the average.

Beating the Average

The CEO Life Cycle represents the entire group of CEOs we studied and indicates in which direction performance may be heading. As we described earlier, the CEO Life Cycle is not only a tool to understand the distinct stages of leadership but also a device to help leaders improve their performance and succeed in every stage. It is a verifiable yardstick of when success is more or less likely,

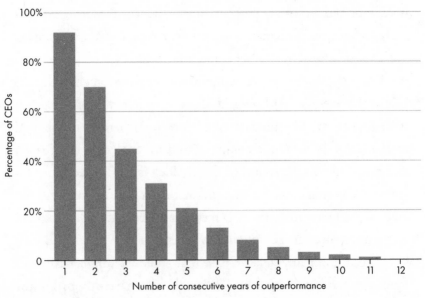

Market Outperformance Streaks by CEOs

How many CEOs outperformed the Life Cycle over a period of their tenure

Percentage of CEOs (y-axis)

Number of consecutive years of outperformance (x-axis)

what high performance in any given year looks like, and how long someone can sustain outperformance. To that effect, we studied the percentage of CEOs who achieved outperformance streaks. We wondered how many CEOs were able to outperform the CEO Life Cycle and for how long relative to those with similar or longer tenure lengths. For example, 24 percent of CEOs in our sample celebrated their eleventh anniversary, and of those, only 1 percent outperformed the CEO Life Cycle throughout their entire eleven years.

We saw significant drop-off in a CEO's ability to continuously outperform the CEO Life Cycle. In fact, just 45 percent of all CEOs with at least three years of tenure outperformed the Life Cycle three years in a row. This percentage drops rapidly as we broadened the time window: 21 percent of CEOs with at least five years in the role outperformed the S&P 500 five years on the trot. Only three CEOs outperformed the Life Cycle for eleven years in a row. Of those, only Occidental Petroleum and Intuit were listed on the S&P 500 for the full duration of the outperformance streak.

Even for CEOs with shorter tenures, it is immensely challenging to beat the market consistently—let alone every year of their tenure. Across the CEOs in our performance sample with fewer than ten years of tenure, just 3 percent beat the CEO Life Cycle in every year of their leadership. These findings underscore the demands of the job, how these challenges evolve over time, and how CEOs—in order to thrive in the role—must evolve as well. In every CEO Life Cycle stage, CEOs must critically reflect on their leadership, abandon some of their ways of leading, and develop new abilities. Each stage holds its own lessons, and we hope that the rich analysis in this book helps future CEOs navigate these challenges, embrace constant change, and lean forward to bend the performance curve in their favor.

ACKNOWLEDGMENTS

Every undertaking like this book stands on the shoulders of giants and this one is no different. Throughout the last five years, we have experienced a tremendous amount of support and received invaluable advice. It was a privilege to see how the spark of an idea travels and sets in motion a wave of support of countless people.

Serving our clients provided us with a front-row seat to understanding what CEOs do and how they feel. We are grateful for the privilege to coach, advise, and learn from so many over the years. Through the creation of this book, we spoke with many CEOs about their individual journey, and countless others are not featured in this book because our conversations had to remain confidential, yet critical learnings emerged. Thanks to them, we began asking ourselves what the different stages of leadership look like and how to codify them.

When we first saw the emerging patterns of the CEO Life Cycle, Jim Citrin saw the potential of the idea, and he has been a staunch supporter every step along the way. Our managing partner, Ben Williams, was equally excited by what he saw and encouraged our efforts. Ram Charan, a leading business thinker, and our agent, Rafe Sagalyn, pushed us to develop our ideas into a book. Eric Leventhal and Ben Machtiger helped us lay the groundwork for the book project and provided us with the support to kick into action years of studying the performance patterns of CEOs.

While we knew we were on to something special, a phenomenal analytics team composed of Madeline Conlin, Karen Wozniak, Rebecca Bendel, Parker Simon, Lamprini Dergianli, Cassandra Thomas, Hannah Ford, Paulina Kenny, and Linus Wössner did so much heavy lifting over the last few years. They were led by Melissa Stone and Roald Schuring and fueled by insatiable curiosity. Together, we have been in the depth of the data, both qualitative and quantitative, to extract the great insights we share in this book—and we continue to learn together every day.

We were fortunate to be surrounded by some of the best leadership advisers on the planet. We tapped into the wisdom of our colleagues Cathy Anterasian, Ellen Kumata, Tony Byers, Julie Daum, Ann Yerger, Sabine Vinck, Colin Graham, Jordan Brugg, and many others to gain additional context of the inner game that CEOs face day in and day out. Many of them connected us to exceptional CEOs we were keen to include in our research. In particular, Tom Neff, Jerry Noonan, Jennifer Bol, Malini Vaidya, Susan Hart, and Joel von Ranson opened many doors for conversations. Jason Baumgarten, Patrick Hynes, Nicolas Albizzatti, Bob DeVries, Kristin Wait, Seonaid Charlesworth, Stephen Patscot, and Deborah Op den Kamp helped us translate many of our learnings into advisory concepts to share with our clients and test in the market. Among many colleagues who specialize in helping pre-CEOs prepare and new CEOs outperform in the role, Janine Ames, Brett Clark-Bolt, Darleen DeRosa, Chris DeRose, Nick Falk, Casandra Frangos, Adam Kling, Filomena Leonardi, David Metcalf, Michael Milad, Kathy Schnure, Levi Segal, Christopher Uhrinek, and Muthiah Venkateswaran have been generous with their time and wisdom.

There were those who constantly cheered us on to try new approaches and bring the ideas of Moneyball for CEOs to its full potential, in particular Tom Daniels, Winthrop Ruml, and George Anderson. Others such as Dayton Ogden, Jim McTaggart, and Claudia Kelly shared with us the wisdom that you can develop only from decades-long advisory work.

This being our first book, we relied on the great expertise of John Mahaney, our editor. In the creation of this book, Emily Loose provided invaluable insight and expertly guided our process to balance comprehensive analytics with engaging storytelling.

Many hours with Marc Rexroth and Jeffrey Lagomarsino debating the impact of our ideas pushed our thinking to new heights. Mark Reigelman was always a great sounding board to make our learnings accessible to many.

Finally, and most importantly, family and friends have been the bedrock of this undertaking. We both continued to support clients and fulfill our responsibilities within the firm, forgoing most evenings, weekends, and vacations, which required understanding and support from loved ones. Ning Yu and Jordan Stark were unwavering in their support and we are lucky to be the recipients of their love, kindness, and wisdom. Jordan is a highly successful CEO coach who has taught Bob so much about the art and science of coaching. As an artist, Ning understood better than any of us at the outset how consuming this project would be and has helped Claudius to strike the balance between the science of data and the art of storytelling.

NOTES

Introduction: Discovering the Life Cycle

1. Scott Davis, Carter Copeland, and Rob Wertheimer, *Lessons from the Titans*, audiobook narrated by Jim Denison (New York: McGraw-Hill, 2021), chap. 5.

2. David Cote, "Successful Leadership, Strategizing, and the Value of Learning with David Cote," interview by Diane Hamilton, July 3, 2020, https://drdianehamilton .com/successful-leadership-strategizing-and-the-value-of-learning-with-david-cote/.

3. David M. Cote, *Winning Now, Winning Later* (New York: HarperCollins Leadership, 2020), 118.

4. Davis et al., *Lessons from the Titans*, chap. 5.

5. Shawn Tully, "How Dave Cote Got Honeywell's Groove Back," *Fortune*, May 14, 2012, https://fortune.com/2012/05/14/how-dave-cote-got-honeywells-groove-back/.

6. Jeffrey Sonnenfeld, "The Hero Complex: A Common, Curable Leadership Malady," *Fortune*, February 2, 2015, https://fortune.com/2015/02/02/hero -complex-leadership/.

7. Sonnenfeld, "The Hero Complex."

8. Peter Senge, *The Dance of Change* (New York: Crown Currency, 2012), 11.

9. J. T. Hamilton and R. Zeckhauser, "Media Coverage of CEOs: Who? What? Where? When? Why?" (unpublished working paper, Stanford Institute of International Studies, 2004).

10. Stephen J. Dubner, "How to Become a C.E.O.," January 24, 2018, in *Freakonomics Radio*, produced by Max Miller, podcast, 44:16, https://freakonomics.com /podcast/how-to-become-a-c-e-o/.

11. "A Guide to Sabermetric Research," Society for American Baseball Research, https://sabr.org/sabermetrics#:~:text=What%20is%20sabermetrics%3F,SABR%20 50%20at%2050%20feature.

12. Ehren Wassermann, Daniel R. Czech, Matthew J. Wilson, and A. Barry Joyner, "An Examination of the Moneyball Theory: A Baseball Statistical Analysis," *Sport Journal*, January 2, 2005, https://thesportjournal.org/article/an -examination-of-the-moneyball-theory-a-baseball-statistical-analysis/.

13. John Schuhmann, "NBA's Three Point Revolution: How 1 Shot Is Changing the Game," NBA, October 14, 2021, www.nba.com/news/3-point-era-nba-75.

14. Karl F. Roeper, "Everett Rogers: A Biography of Diffusion Theory," *Proceedings of the Laurel Highlands Communications Conference*, annual 2010, https://link.gale.com/apps/doc/A247338956/AONE?u=nysl_oweb&sid=googleScholar&xid=65326a49.

15. Indra Nooyi, *My Life in Full* (New York: Portfolio Books, 2021), 191.

16. "Stanley and Black & Decker: The Perfect Deal?" DealBook, *New York Times*, November 3, 2009, https://archive.nytimes.com/dealbook.nytimes.com/2009/11/03/stanley-and-black-decker-the-perfect-deal/; and "Toolmaker Deal Ends a 28-Year Courtship," DealBook, *New York Times*, November 3, 2009, https://archive.nytimes.com/dealbook.nytimes.com/2009/11/03/toolmaker-deal-ends-a-28-year-courtship/.

17. Thomas H. Davenport and Randy Bean, "Portrait of an AI Leader: Piyush Gupta of DBS Bank," *MIT Sloan Management Review*, August 31, 2021, https://sloanreview.mit.edu/article/portrait-of-an-ai-leader-piyush-gupta-of-dbs-bank/.

Chapter One: Ascent

1. The account is based on Josh Lowell and Peter Mortimer, *The Dawn Wall* (Sender Films, Red Bull Media House, The Orchard, 2017) as well as *Outdoor Journal*, "The Dawn Wall Project: Revisited," June 26, 2018, www.outdoorjournal.com/focus-2/dawn-wall-project-revisited/; and "How Many People Have Climbed the Dawn Wall," Climbing Shoe Review website, www.climbingshoereview.com/how-many-people-have-climbed-the-dawn-wall/.

2. Guy Raz, "Mastercard: Ajaypal Singh Banga," February 16, 2022, in *Wisdom from the Top with Guy Raz*, podcast, 40:26, https://open.spotify.com/episode/4oL6FEdaMAPQb7z6blLd5J.

3. Raz, "Mastercard: Ajaypal Singh Banga."

4. Raz, "Mastercard: Ajaypal Singh Banga."

5. Linda A. Hill, Emily Tedards, Jason Wild, and Karl Weber, "What Makes a Great Leader," *Harvard Business Review*, September 19, 2022, https://hbr.org/2022/09/what-makes-a-great-leader.

6. Daniel Roberts and Alexandra Mondalek, "How MasterCard Became a Tech Company," *Fortune*, August 11, 2014, 88–91; quotes were updated by Ajay Banga.

7. Alison Beard, "CEO Series: Mastercard's Ajay Banga on Promoting Financial Inclusion," May 13, 2021, in HBRIdeaCast, episode 794, podcast, 28:37, https://hbr.org/podcast/2021/05/ceo-series-mastercards-ajay-banga-on-promoting-financial-inclusion; and Clifton Leaf, "Why Mastercard Isn't a Credit Card Company, According to Its Outgoing CEO Ajay Banga," *Fortune*, December 3, 2020, https://fortune.com/longform/mastercard-ceo-ajay-banga-credit-card-payment-company/.

8. "Mary Barra Biography & Career," Thomasnet, April 23, 2021, www.thomasnet.com/articles/other/mary-barra-biography/.

9. Hannah L. Miller, "Mary Barra: From Co-Op Student Employee to GM's CEO," Leaders, January 25, 2022, https://leaders.com/articles/women-in-business/mary-barra/#:~:text=Ray%20Makela%20was%20a%20first,term%20relationship%3A%20it%20becomes%20predictable.

10. Michael A. Fletcher, "GM Names Mary Barra as Car Industry's First Woman CEO," *Washington Post*, December 10, 2013, www.washingtonpost.com/business/economy/gm-names-mary-barra-as-car-industrys-first-woman-ceo/2013/12/10/7d7827e8-61b8-11e3-8beb-3f9a9942850f_story.html.

11. Tim Higgins and Bryant Urstadt, "Exclusive: The Inside Story of GM's Comeback and Mary Barra's Rise," Bloomberg, December 12, 2013, www.bloomberg .com/news/articles/2013-12-12/exclusive-the-inside-story-of-gms-comeback-and -mary-barras-rise?leadSource=uverify%20wall.

12. Satya Nadella, *Hit Refresh* (New York: Harper Business, 2017), 55.

13. Eshita Srinivas, "Road to Success: First Jobs of Popular and Successful Indian-Origin CEOs," Lifestyle Asia, October 3, 2022, www.lifestyleasia.com/ind /living/people/road-to-success-first-jobs-of-popular-and-successful-indian-origin -ceos/.

14. Victoria Barret, "Ubiquitous Upside," *Forbes*, June 16, 2008, www.forbes.com /forbes/2008/0616/106.html?sh=1e179e292d98.

15. Barret, "Ubiquitous Upside."

16. Barret, "Ubiquitous Upside" (for amount of the Macromedia deal); and for Flash on 98 percent of computers: Tom McNichol, "Adobe Battles the Flash-Bashing," Bloomberg, June 28, 2010, www.bloomberg.com/news/articles/2010-06-24 /adobe-battles-the-flash-bashing.

17. Eliza Gray, "CVS Wants to Be Your Doctor's Office," *Time*, February 12, 2015, https://time.com/3706697/cvs-wants-to-be-your-doctors-office/.

18. Kenneth R. Gosselin, "For Pharmacist Turned CEO: CVS' Larry Merlo Faces Biggest Challenge in Aetna Acquisition," *Hartford (CT) Courant*, December 31, 2017, updated December 6, 2018, www.courant.com/business/hc-biz-larry-merlo-ceo -cvs-20171228-story.html.

19. Knowledge at Wharton Staff, "MasterCard's Ajay Banga: Why 'Yes, If' Is More Powerful Than Saying No," Knowledge at Wharton, July 24, 2014, https://knowledge .wharton.upenn.edu/article/mastercard-competitive-strategy/.

20. Raffaella Sadun, Joseph Fuller, Stephen Hansen, and P. J. Neal, "The C-Suite Skills That Matter Most," *Harvard Business Review*, July–August 2022, https://hbr .org/2022/07/the-c-suite-skills-that-matter-most.

21. Priyank Shrivastava, "How an Idea—and a Lot of Perseverance—Built Adobe Captivate Prime," Adobe Blog, April 22, 2021, https://blog.adobe.com/en /publish/2021/04/22/how-an-idea-built-adobe-captivate-prime.

22. Pete Bigelow, "Mary Barra's Ascension to GM CEO Draws Praise from Industry Leaders," AutoBlog, December 10, 2013, www.autoblog.com/2013/12/10 /mary-barras-ascension-gm-ceo-draws-praise-industry-leaders-video/.

23. Robert Hackett, "Why Cisco's Board Chose Chuck Robbins to Lead as CEO," *Fortune*, May 6, 2015, https://fortune.com/2015/05/05/cisco-ceo-chuck-robbins/.

24. "GM CEO Dan Akerson on Choosing Mary Barra as His Successor," December 10, 2013, *USA Today*, video, 2:03, www.usatoday.com/videos/money/cars/2013/12 /10/3965835/.

25. Kevin McLaughlin, "Cisco CEO Robbins Carves New Path," *The Information*, September 13, 2017, www.theinformation.com/articles/cisco-ceo-robbins-carves-new-path.

26. Marshall Goldsmith and Howard Morgan, "Leadership Is a Contact Sport," Marshall Goldsmith, https://marshallgoldsmith.com/articles/leadership-contact-sport/.

Chapter Two: Launch

1. Indra Nooyi, *My Life in Full* (New York: Portfolio Books, 2021), 187.

2. Emily Bobrow, "CEO David Novak Learned Leadership by Making Mistakes," *Wall Street Journal*, March 11, 2022, www.wsj.com/articles/ceo-david-novak-learned-leadership-by-making-mistakes-11647019449.

3. Theresa Howard, "Quick-Serve Artist," *Adweek* Eastern Edition, October 11, 1999, Business Source Complete.

4. Joseph M. Hogan, biography, Align, https://investor.aligntech.com/board-directors-management/joseph-hogan#:~:text=Mr.,company%20based%20in%20Zurich%2C%20Switzerland.

5. Carolyn Dewar, Scott Keller, Vikram Malhotra, and Kurt Strovink, "Starting Strong: Making Your CEO Transition a Catalyst for Renewal," *McKinsey Quarterly*, November 17, 2022, www.mckinsey.com/capabilities/strategy-and-corporate-finance/our-insights/starting-strong-making-your-ceo-transition-a-catalyst-for-renewal.

6. Egon Zender, *The CEO: A Personal Reflection* (Zurich: Egon Zehnder International, Spring 2018), https://ceostudy.egonzehnder.com/The-CEO-report-Egon-Zehnder.pdf.

7. Brooks Barnes, "Disney C.E.O. Says Company Is 'Opposed' to Florida's 'Don't Say Gay' Bill," *New York Times*, March 9, 2022, www.nytimes.com/2022/03/09/business/disney-ceo-florida-lgbtq-bill.html.

8. Peter Drucker, "The American CEO," *Wall Street Journal*, December 30, 2004, www.wsj.com/articles/SB110436476581112426.

9. Dave Cote, *Winning Now, Winning Later*, Kindle ed. (New York: HarperCollins Leadership), 22.

10. Big Think, "Daniel Kahneman: The Trouble with Confidence," YouTube video, 2:56, February 11, 2012, www.youtube.com/watch?v=tyDQFmA1SpU.

11. Brooke Sutherland, "In One Earnings Call, UPS CEO Makes Job Her Own," Bloomberg, July 30, 2020, www.bloomberg.com/opinion/articles/2020-07-30/ups-new-ceo-carol-tome-has-impressive-earnings-debut.

12. Carol B. Tomé, "The CEO of UPS on Taking the Reins amid Surging Pandemic Demand," *Harvard Business Review*, September–October 2021, https://hbr.org/2021/09/the-ceo-of-ups-on-taking-the-reins-amid-surging-pandemic-demand.

13. Sutherland, "In One Earnings Call."

14. Sutherland, "In One Earnings Call."

15. David Novak, "Larry Merlo, CVS Health CEO—Craft a Simple and Compelling Vision," September 17, 2020, in *How Leaders Lead*, podcast, 57:00, https://podcasts.apple.com/us/podcast/leading-with-care-ceo-of-cvs-health-larry-merlo/id1223803642?i=1000491535027.

16. Tomé, "The CEO of UPS."

17. David Gelles, "Inside Corporate America's Frantic Response to the Georgia Voting Law," *New York Times*, April 5, 2021, www.nytimes.com/2021/04/05/business/voting-rights-ceos.html.

18. "Laws and Legislation Should Make It Easier to Vote," UPS, April 1, 2021, https://about.ups.com/us/en/newsroom/statements/ups-supports-equitable-poll-access-and-voting.html.

19. Buzz McClain, "How NoVA Native Chris Nassetta Successfully Revamped the Hilton Brand," *Northern Virginia*, August 14, 2019, https://northernvirginiamag

.com/culture/culture-features/2019/08/14/how-nova-native-chris-nassetta-successfully
-revamped-the-hilton-brand/.

20. Navjeet Nanda, "Blackstone and Hilton Hotels: The Beauty of LBOs," Strategy Story, April 10, 2021, https://thestrategystory.com/2021/04/10/blackstone-hilton
-lbo/.

21. Jaime Kammerzell, "Cazalot's Track to Marathon," Rigzone, August 26, 2011, www.rigzone.com/news/oil_gas/a/110540/cazalots_track_to_marathon/.

22. "Shell Writes Off $3.9 bln in Losses from Russia Exit; and $1.6 bln from Sakhalin-2, $1.1 bln from Nord Stream 2," Interfax, May 5, 2022, https://interfax
.com/newsroom/top-stories/78922/.

23. "Hilton Hotel Unveils $1bn Drive Before Reunifying Brands," *Marketing Week*, January 19, 2006, www.marketingweek.com/hilton-hotel-unveils-1bn-drive
-before-reunifying-brands/.

24. Catherine Yang and Diane Brady, "Marriott Hip? Well, It's Trying," *BusinessWeek*, September 26, 2005, Business Source Complete.

25. Michael Craig, "It's Terry Lundgren's Town, We Just Shop in It," *Observer*, November 12, 2014, https://observer.com/2014/11/its-terry-lundgrens
-town-we-just-shop-in-it/.

26. Thomas Gryta, "GE Ousts CEO John Flannery in Surprise Move After Missed Targets," *Wall Street Journal*, October 1, 2018, www.wsj.com/articles/ge-names
-new-ceo-replacing-flannery-1538392715.

27. Michael Sheetz, "Why GE Removed John Flannery as CEO After Little More Than a Year," CNBC, October 1, 2018, www.cnbc.com/2018/10/01/why
-ge-removed-john-flannery-as-ceo.html.

28. Cote, *Winning Now*, xi.

Chapter Three: Calibration

1. Bradley Barnes, "The Sophomore Slump: Myth or Reality?" The Boar, September 30, 2023, https://theboar.org/2023/09/the-sophomore-slump-myth-or
-reality.

2. Sbtrey23, "MLB Victims of the Sophomore Slump," Couch Guy Sports, June 26, 2018, https://couchguysports.com/victims-of-the-sophomore-slump/.

3. Jack Trent Dorfman, "Dodgers 2018 Season Grade: Bellinger Suffers Sophomore Slump," Dodgers Way, January 3, 2019, https://dodgersway.com/2019/01/03
/dodgers-grade-bellinger-sophomore-slump/.

4. Dorfman, "Dodgers 2018 Season Grade."

5. Samantha Stainburn, "The Sophomore Slump," *New York Times*, November 1, 2013, www.nytimes.com/2013/11/03/education/edlife/getting-over-the-sophomore
-slump.html.

6. Stainburn, "The Sophomore Slump."

7. Chloe Clark, "Dodgers News: Cody Bellinger Reacts to Non-Tender in Cubs Introduction," FanNation, December 24, 2022, www.si.com/mlb/dodgers/news
/dodgers-news-cody-bellinger-reacts-to-non-tender-in-cubs-introduction-cc22.

8. Chuck Stogel, "He's Got Game," *Brandweek*, April 5, 1999, Business Source Complete.

9. Harrison Caplan, "Keys to Success: Church and Dwight Have Them," SeekingAlpha, October 31, 2017, https://seekingalpha.com/article/4118758-keys-to-success-church-and-dwight.

10. "Forget Gold; Take a Look at Church & Dwight," *Herald-Tribune* (Sarasota, FL), May 21, 2006, www.heraldtribune.com/story/news/2006/05/21/forget-gold-take-a-look-at-church-dwight/28478901007/.

11. Luis Filipe Silva Moreira, "Colgate-Palmolive: It's Time to Show Its Teeth," SeekingAlpha, August 28, 2018, https://seekingalpha.com/article/4202519-colgate-palmolive-time-to-show-teeth.

12. Robert Reiss, "Former Best Buy CEO Hubert Joly Shares the Secret to Company Turnarounds," *Forbes*, April 20, 2012, www.forbes.com/sites/robertreiss/2021/04/20/former-best-buy-ceo-hubert-joly-shares-the-secret-to-company-turnarounds/?sh=3f52f3706b01.

13. Reiss, "Former Best Buy CEO Hubert Joly Shares."

14. Michael J. de la Merced, "Best Buy's Tough Earnings May Lift Schulze's Hopes a Little," *New York Times*, August 21, 2012, https://archive.nytimes.com/dealbook.nytimes.com/2012/08/21/best-buys-tough-earnings-may-lift-schulzes-hopes-a-little.

15. Hubert Joly, *The Heart of Business*, Kindle ed. (Boston: Harvard Business Review Press, 2021), 30.

16. Figures provided by Hubert Joly.

17. Trefis Team, "Factors That Led to a 40% Decline in Best Buy's Stock Price in 2014," *Forbes*, April 25, 2014, www.forbes.com/sites/greatspeculations/2014/04/25/factors-that-led-to-a-40-decline-in-best-buys-stock-price-in-2014/?sh=32fffc26771f.

18. James B. Stewart, "Underdog Against Amazon, Best Buy Charges Ahead," *New York Times*, December 14, 2013, www.nytimes.com/2013/12/14/business/fast-rise-of-best-buy-in-the-face-of-amazon.html.

19. Team, "Factors That Led to a 40% Decline."

20. Jesse Solomon, "Best Buy Tells Amazon: Take That!" CNN Business, November 20, 2014, https://money.cnn.com/2014/11/20/investing/best-buy-earnings.

21. Indra Nooyi, *My Life in Full* (New York: Portfolio Books, 2021), 229.

22. Claire Atkinson, "Why Have More Than 1,300 CEOs Left Their Post in the Past Year?" NBC News, November 6, 2019, www.nbcnews.com/business/business-news/why-have-more-1-000-ceos-left-their-post-past-n1076201.

23. Nooyi, *My Life in Full*, 226.

24. David Dye, Chiara Corso, Claradith Landry, Jennifer Rompre, Kyle Sandell, and William Tanner, "Leadership Intuition Meets the Future of Work," in *How Well Do Executives Trust Their Intuition?*, ed. Jay Liebowitz, Yolande Chan, Tracy Jenkin, Dylan Spicker, Joanna Paliszkiewicz, and Fabio Babiloni (Boca Raton, FL: CRC Press, 2018), www2.deloitte.com/us/en/pages/public-sector/articles/leadership-intuition-meets-the-future-of-work.html.

25. Chitra Narayanan, "If There's Change, Be Clear About the Metrics: Adobe's Shantanu Narayen," *Business Today*, May 10, 2015, www.businesstoday.in/magazine/leadership-spotlight/story/adobe-systems-shantanu-narayen-on-future-strategy-products-50476-2015-05-01.

26. Dave Cote, *Winning Now, Winning Later*, Kindle ed. (New York: HarperCollins Leadership), 114.

27. Chip Heath and Dan Heath, *Decisive: How to Make Better Choices in Life and Work* (New York: Crown Currency, 2013), 23.

28. Geoff Brumfiel, "U.S. Navy Brings Back Navigation by the Stars for Officers," NPR News, February 22, 2016, www.npr.org/2016/02/22/467210492 /u-s-navy-brings-back-navigation-by-the-stars-for-officers.

29. Stephen J. Dubner, "What Does a C.E.O. Actually Do?" January 17, 2018, in *Freakonomics Radio*, podcast, episode 27, 38:31, https://freakonomics.com/podcast /what-does-a-c-e-o-actually-do/.

30. Dubner, "What Does a C.E.O. Actually Do?"

31. Cote, *Winning Now*, 23.

32. Cote, *Winning Now*, 86.

33. Cote, *Winning Now*, 91.

34. Elisa Lipsky-Karasz, "How Darren Walker and the Ford Foundation Reinvented Philanthropy for the Pandemic," *Wall Street Journal Magazine*, November 17, 2020, www.wsj.com/articles/darren-walker-interview-ford-foundation -philanthropy-pandemic-11604679844.

35. Carmine Gallo, "In This Candid Conversation, Legendary CEO John Chambers Reveals the Critical Skill Leaders Need Now," *Forbes*, December 4, 2018, www.forbes.com/sites/carminegallo/2018/12/04/in-this-candid-conversation -legendary-ceo-john-chambers-reveals-the-critical-skill-leaders-need-now/?sh=213d d0e86cb0.

36. Philip van Doorn, "Why Cisco CEO John Chambers Had to Go," MarketWatch, May 4, 2015, www.marketwatch.com/story/why-cisco-ceo -john-chambers-had-to-go-2015-05-04.

37. Mike Robuck, "Cisco's Robbins: No, We're Not a Subscription Software Company," Fierce Telecom, June 12, 2018, www.fiercetelecom.com/telecom /cisco-s-robbins-no-we-re-not-a-subscription-software-company.

38. Russ Britt, "Cisco Systems Making Noise As New CEO Takes Reins," *Investors Business Daily*, August 13, 2015, www.investors.com/news/technology /cisco-stock-rises-on-q4-earnings/.

39. Maria Monteros, "Target Shaped Private Labels into Powerhouse Brands. Now Others Want to Do the Same," RetailDive, November 10, 2021, www.retaildive.com /news/target-shaped-private-labels-into-powerhouse-brands-now-others-want -to-do/609762/.

40. Lila MacLellan, "Bed Bath and Beyond Tried Decluttering and Shoppers Rebelled," Quartz, January 31, 2022, https://qz.com/2119168/decluttering -was-a-mistake-for-bed-bath-and-beyond.

41. Ron Lieber, "An Oral History of the World's Biggest Coupon," *New York Times*, December 19, 2020, www.nytimes.com/2020/12/19/business/bed-bath-and-beyond -coupon.html.

42. SA Transcripts, "Best Buy Co., Inc. (BBY) CEO Corie Barry on Q2 2021 Results—Earnings Call Transcript," SeekingAlpha, August 25, 2020, https:// seekingalpha.com/article/4370651-best-buy-co-inc-bby-ceo-corie-barry-on-q2-2021 -results-earnings-call-transcript. The term was used by Mark Tritton in the September 30, 2021, Best Buy earnings call.

43. Lieber, "An Oral History of the World's Biggest Coupon."

44. SA Transcripts, "Best Buy Co., Inc. (BBY) CEO."

45. Suzanne Kapner, "Bed Bath and Beyond Followed a Winning Playbook—and Lost," *Wall Street Journal*, July 23, 2022, www.wsj.com/articles/bed-bath-beyond-ceo-private-label-brands-11658547084?mod=Searchresults_pos3&page=1.

46. SA Transcripts, "Best Buy Co., Inc. (BBY) CEO."

47. Peter Cohen, "How BBBY Got into So Much Trouble," *Forbes*, September 29, 2022, Business Source Complete.

48. Cohen, "How BBBY Got into So Much Trouble."

Chapter Four: Reinvention

1. Maxwell Murphy, "CVS Profit at High End of Expectations," *Wall Street Journal*, August 4, 2011, www.wsj.com/articles/SB10001424053111903366504576487933407132782.

2. Robert Cyran and Richard Beales, "Pharmacy Tie-Up Without Benefits," *New York Times*, May 5, 2011, www.nytimes.com/2011/05/06/business/06views.html?searchResultPosition=26.

3. Murphy, "CVS Profit at High End."

4. Joseph Rago, "The Revolution at the Corner Drugstore," *Wall Street Journal*, January 23, 2015, www.wsj.com/articles/the-weekend-interview-the-revolution-at-the-corner-drugstore-1422056524.

5. Katie Gilbert, "The Alchemist: How Larry Merlo Is Transforming CVS," *Institutional Investor*, August 25, 2015, www.institutionalinvestor.com/article/2bsvdo3iiteanzse69hq8/portfolio/the-alchemist-how-larry-merlo-is-transforming-cvs.

6. Kenneth Gosselin, "For Pharmacist Turned CEO: CVS' Larry Merlo Faces Biggest Challenge in Aetna Acquisition," *Hartford (CT) Courant*, December 31, 2017, www.courant.com/business/hc-biz-larry-merlo-ceo-cvs-20171228-story.html.

7. Indra Nooyi, *My Life in Full* (New York: Portfolio Books, 2021), 225.

8. Michael Wayland, "GM Trails Far Behind Tesla in EV Sales—CEO Mary Barra Bet the Company that Will Change," CNBC, July 24, 2022, www.cnbc.com/2022/07/24/why-ceo-mary-barra-is-confident-gm-can-beat-tesla-in-electric-vehicles.html.

9. Sharon Edelson, "Lundgren at Top of Retail Heap," *Women's Wear Daily*, March 1, 2005, https://wwd.com/feature/lundgren-at-top-of-retail-heap-581920-1955301/.

10. Carla K. Johnson, "Shoppers Protest Name Change of Chicago Store," Chron, September 9, 2006, www.chron.com/business/article/Shoppers-protest-name-change-of-Chicago-store-1881277.php.

11. Ellen Byron, "A Clothes Horse Sets Out to Remake Department Stores," *Wall Street Journal*, July 17, 2006, www.wsj.com/articles/SB115309445961308208.

12. Byron, "A Clothes Horse Sets Out."

13. Byron, "A Clothes Horse Sets Out."

14. Darrell Rigby, "The Future of Shopping," *Harvard Business Review*, December 2011, https://hbr.org/2011/12/the-future-of-shopping.

15. "How Macy's Implemented a Successful Omnichannel Approach," Centric Digital, March 30, 2016, www.centricdigital.com/blog/how-macys-implemented-a-successful-omnichannel-approach.

16. Dan Moskowitz, "Macy's, J.C. Penney, and Sears: A Clear Winner Stands Among Them," Motley Fool, January 29, 2014, www.fool.com/investing/general/2014/01/29/macys-jc-penney-and-sears-a-clear-winner-stands-am.aspx.

17. E. Tory Higgins, "Promotion and Prevention: Regulatory Focus as a Motivational Principle," *Advances in Experimental Social Psychology* 30 (1998): 1–46.

18. Linda Tischler, "Dynamic Duos: PepsiCo's Indra Nooyi and Mauro Porcini on Design-Led Innovation," *Fast Company*, September 23, 2013, www.fastcompany.com/3016310/pepsico-indra-nooyi-and-mauro-porcini.

19. Indra K. Nooyi and Vijay Govindarajan, "Becoming a Better Corporate Citizen," *Harvard Business Review*, March–April 2020, https://hbr.org/2020/03/becoming-a-better-corporate-citizen.

20. Jennifer Reingold, "PepsiCo's CEO Was Right. Now What?" *Fortune*, June 5, 2015, https://fortune.com/2015/06/05/pepsico-ceo-indra-nooyi/.

21. Hubert Joly, *The Heart of Business*, Kindle ed. (Boston: Harvard Business Review Press, 2021), 47.

22. Rose Gailey, Ian Johnston, and Andrew LeSueur, "Aligning Culture with the Bottom Line: How Companies Can Accelerate Progress," Hedrick & Struggles, www.heidrick.com/en/insights/culture-shaping/aligning-culture-with-the-bottom-line-how-companies-can-accelerate-progress#RefN2.

Chapter Five: Complacency Trap

1. John Clarke, "A Twenty-First-Century Shipwreck," *New Yorker*, December 10, 2014, www.newyorker.com/sports/sporting-scene/twenty-first-century-shipwreck.

2. Darrell Nicholson, "Operator Error Strands Vestas Wind," *Practical Sailor*, June 17, 2015, www.practical-sailor.com/safety-seamanship/operator-error-strands-vestas-wind.

3. Nicholson, "Operator Error Strands Vestas Wind."

4. Elaine Bunting, "Comment: How the Team Vestas Wind Crash Really Happened, and the Crucial Things We Can Learn from It," *Yachting World*, March 9, 2015, www.yachtingworld.com/blogs/elaine-bunting/comment-how-the-team-vestas-wind-crash-really-happened-and-the-surprisingly-simple-things-we-can-learn-from-it-62634.

5. "GM Agrees $900m Settlement for Faulty Ignition Switches," BBC News, September 17, 2015, www.bbc.com/news/business-34276419; and Bill Vlasic, "G.M. Begins Prevailing in Lawsuits over Faulty Ignition Switches," *New York Times*, April 10, 2016, www.nytimes.com/2016/04/11/business/gm-begins-prevailing-in-lawsuits-over-faulty-ignition-switches.html.

6. Andrew Grove, *Only the Paranoid Survive*, Kindle ed. (New York: Crown Currency, 2010), 3.

7. Kendra Cherry, "How the Status Quo Bias Affects Our Decisions," VeryWellMind, December 13, 2003, www.verywellmind.com/status-quo-bias-psychological-definition-4065385.

8. Nigel Travis, *The Challenge Culture*, Kindle ed. (New York: PublicAffairs, 2018), 34.

9. Stephanie Anderson Forest, Gail DeGeorge, and Kathleen Morris, "The Script Doctor Is in at Blockbuster—Again," *BusinessWeek*, July 28, 1997, Business Source Complete.

10. Richard Siklos and Stephanie Anderson Forest, "Blockbuster Finally Gets It Right," *BusinessWeek*, March 8, 1999, Business Source Complete.

11. Travis, *The Challenge Culture*, 52.

12. John Antioco, "How I Did It: Blockbuster's Former CEO on Sparring with an Activist Shareholder," *Harvard Business Review*, April 2011, https://hbr.org/2011/04 /how-i-did-it-blockbusters-former-ceo-on-sparring-with-an-activist-shareholder.

13. Antioco, "How I Did It."

14. Roger Martin, "Underestimating the Risk of the Status Quo," *Rotman Magazine*, Spring 2007, https://rogerlmartin.com/docs/default-source/Articles/strategy /rotman_spring07_riskofstatusquo.

15. Michael E. Porter and Nitin Nohria, "How CEOs Manage Time," *Harvard Business Review*, July–August 2018, https://hbr.org/2018/07/how-ceos-manage-time.

16. Travis, *The Challenge Culture*, 190–191.

17. Dave Cote, *Winning Now, Winning Later*, Kindle ed. (New York: HarperCollins Leadership), 61.

18. Reed Hastings, *No Rules Rules*, Kindle ed. (New York: Penguin, 2020), 293–295.

19. Travis, *The Challenge Culture*, 173.

20. Katrina Brooker and Julie Schlosser, "The Un-CEO A. G. Lafley Doesn't Overpromise. He Doesn't Believe in the Vision Thing," *Fortune*, September 16, 2002, accessed at CNN Money, https://money.cnn.com/magazines/fortune/fortune _archive/2002/09/16/328576/index.htm.

21. Brooker and Schlosser, "The Un-CEO A. G. Lafley."

22. A. G. Lafley, biography, Reference for Business, www.referenceforbusiness.com /biography/F-L/Lafley-A-G-1947.html#ixzz85UukGsGr.

23. Brooker and Schlosser, "The Un-CEO A. G. Lafley."

24. A. G. Lafley, biography, Reference for Business.

25. Chris Isidore, "P&G to Buy Gillette for $57B," CNN Money, January 28, 2005, https://money.cnn.com/2005/01/28/news/fortune500/pg_gillette/.

26. *P&G 2007 Global Sustainability Report* (Cincinnati, OH: Procter & Gamble, 2007), https://assets.ctfassets.net/oggad6svuzkv/5789JsCyMoC8iw4ao WI0WU/1214aebf3ddedea66bebca75508da523/2007_Full_Sustainability_Report .pdf.

27. Brooker and Schlosser, "The Un-CEO A. G. Lafley."

28. Bruce Brown and Scott D. Anthony, "How P&G Tripled Its Innovation Success Rate," *Harvard Business Review*, June 2011, https://hbr.org/2011/06/how -pg-tripled-its-innovation-success-rate.

29. "The Purpose of Strategy Is to Win: An Interview with A. G. Lafley," Korn Ferry: www.kornferry.com/insights/briefings-magazine/issue-14/575-the-purpose -of-strategy-is-to-win-an-interview-with-a-g-lafley.

30. Ben Reynolds, "The Outlook for Procter & Gamble," GuruFocus.com, June 18, 2016, accessed via Yahoo News, www.yahoo.com/news/outlook-procter

-gamble-002941168.html; an additional source making the point is Carol Hymowitz and Lauren Coleman-Lochner, "P&G Stops Making Sense," *Bloomberg Businessweek*, April 20, 2015, Business Source Complete.

31. Jeff Gell et al., *Creating Superior Value in Challenging Times* (Boston: Boston Consulting Group, 2012), https://boston-consulting-group-brightspot.s3.amazonaws.com/img-src/Creating_Superior_Value_Challenging_Times_tcm9-101258.pdf.

32. Chris Allsop, "A Modern Day da Vinci," *Profile*, December 14, 2012, https://profilemagazine.com/2012/church-dwight/.

33. Michael Eknoian and Bryan A. Harpine, "Category Leading TSR Through Innovation at Church & Dwight," kHUB, October 1, 2020, webcast, 57:00, https://community.pdma.org/knowledgehub/bok/culture-teams-and-leadership/category-leading-tsr-through-innovation-at-church-and-dwight.

34. Graham Kenny, "Don't Make This Common M&A Mistake," *Harvard Business Review*, March 16, 2020, https://hbr.org/2020/03/dont-make-this-common-ma-mistake.

35. Matthew T. Billett and Yiming Qian, "Are Overconfident CEOs Born or Made? Evidence of Self-Attribution Bias from Frequent Acquirers," *Management Science* 54, no. 6 (June 2008), https://doi.org/10.2139/ssrn.687534.

36. Chris Bradley, Martin Hirt, and Sven Smit, *Strategy Beyond the Hockey Stick*, Kindle ed. (New York: Wiley, 2018), 6.

37. Bill Gates, *The Road Ahead* (New York: Viking, 1996).

38. Khatera Sahibzada, "How to Resist the Lure of Overconfidence," blog, *Scientific American*, August 2, 2019, https://blogs.scientificamerican.com/observations/how-to-resist-the-lure-of-overconfidence/.

39. Guy Raz, "Autodesk: Carl Bass," September 19, 2023, in *Wisdom from the Top with Guy Raz*, produced by Built-It Productions, podcast, 66:00, https://podcasts.apple.com/us/podcast/autodesk-carl-bass/id1460154838?i=1000564894480.

40. Adam Grant, *Think Again* (New York: Viking, 2021), 48.

41. "DBS Launches Digibank, an Entire Bank in the Phone, in Indonesia," DBS, August 29, 2017, www.dbs.com/newsroom/DBS_launches_digibank_an_entire_bank_in_the_phone_in_Indonesia.

Chapter Six: Legacy

1. Greg Stuart, "Top 10: Moments of Michael Schumacher Brilliance," Formula 1, January 7, 2019, www.formula1.com/en/latest/article.top-10-moments-of-michael-schumacher-brilliance.1r4cJET4PaUsysIG8oqgS0.html.

2. Damien Smith, "How Schumacher and Todt Transformed Ferrari," Motorsport, March 31, 2020, https://us.motorsport.com/f1/news/ferrari-special-how-schumacher-and-todt-transformed-the-scuderia/3167912/.

3. Wikipedia, s.v. "List of Formula One World Drivers' Champions," last modified March 2, 2024, https://en.wikipedia.org/wiki/List_of_Formula_One_World_Drivers%27_Champions.

4. Adi Ignatius, "The Truth About CEO Tenure," *Harvard Business Review*, November–December 2019, https://hbr.org/2019/11/the-truth-about-ceo-tenure.

5. Jena McGregor, "How Long Is Too Long to Be CEO?" *Washington Post*, April 16, 2014, www.washingtonpost.com/news/on-leadership/wp/2014/04/16/how-long-is-too-long-to-be-ceo/.

6. Dave Cote, *Winning Now, Winning Later*, Kindle ed. (New York: HarperCollins Leadership), x.

7. David Cote, "Honeywell's CEO on How He Avoided Layoffs," *Harvard Business Review*, June 2013, https://hbr.org/2013/06/honeywells-ceo-on-how-he-avoided-layoffs.

8. Shawn Tully, "How Dave Cote Got Honeywell's Groove Back," *Fortune*, May 14, 2012, https://fortune.com/2012/05/14/how-dave-cote-got-honeywells-groove-back/.

9. Roslyn Courtney, "A Shoutout to Dave Cote," *Wharton Magazine*, July 12, 2013, https://magazine.wharton.upenn.edu/digital/a-shoutout-to-dave-cote/.

10. Tully, "How Dave Cote Got Honeywell's."

11. Cote, *Winning Now*, 50.

12. Cote, *Winning Now*, 95.

13. Brian Sozzi, "Honeywell CEO: Here Are the Three Things I Want to Be Remembered for Most," *The Street*, April 22, 2016, www.thestreet.com/opinion/honeywell-ceo-here-s-what-i-want-my-legacy-to-be-13533183.

14. Kalyani Khodke, "Michael Schumacher—Driving Analysis," World2talkabout, August 30, 2011, https://world2talkabout.wordpress.com/2011/08/30/michael-schumacher-driving-analysis/.

15. Bill Synder, "The Surface Fiasco Fallout: Ballmer, You're Fired," *InfoWorld*, August 1, 2013, www.infoworld.com/article/2611511/the-surface-fiasco-fallout--ballmer--you-re-fired.html.

16. Guy Raz, "Autodesk: Carl Bass," September 19, 2023, in *Wisdom from the Top with Guy Raz*, produced by Built-It Productions, podcast, 66:00, https://podcasts.apple.com/us/podcast/autodesk-carl-bass/id1460154838?i=1000564894480.

17. Bill George, "The Truth About Authentic Leaders," *HBS Working Knowledge Research Collection*, July 6, 2021, 10–13, https://hbswk.hbs.edu/Shared%20Documents/Working_Knowledge_Leadership.pdf.

18. Cote, *Winning Now*, 26.

19. Hubert Joly, "Best Buy CEO on Leadership: A Comment I Made Was Misconstrued," *Star Tribune* (Minneapolis, MN), March 17, 2013, www.startribune.com/best-buy-ceo-on-leadership-a-comment-i-made-was-misconstrued/198546011/?refer=y.

20. Madeline Miles, "What's Generativity vs. Stagnation? It's a Step Closer to Your Goals," BetterUp, July 18, 2022, www.betterup.com/blog/generativity-vs-stagnation.

21. Aparna Joshi, Donald C. Hambrick, and Jiyeon Kang, "The Generativity Mindsets of Chief Executive Officers: A New Perspective on Succession Outcomes," *Academy of Management Review* 48, no. 2 (2021): 385–405.

22. "NextEra Plots $5.8B Renewables Spree," *Power Finance & Risk* 14, no. 29 (July 25, 2011): 34.

23. Morey Stettner, "Traveling 'Right to Left' Guides Pentair's Top Exec," *Investors Business Daily*, January 27, 2014, Business Source Complete.

24. Liz Fedor, "Beth Wozniak Chosen as TCB's 2023 Person of the Year," *Twin Cities Business*, September 20, 2023, https://tcbmag.com/beth-wozniak-chosen-as-tcbs-2023-person-of-the-year/.

25. David F. Larcker and Brian Tayan, "CEO Succession: Data Spotlight," Corporate Governance Research Initiative, Stanford Graduate School of Business, www.gsb.stanford.edu/sites/default/files/publication/pdfs/cgri-quick-guide-15-ceo-succession-data.pdf.

26. Brad D. Smith, "How to Discover Your Why: What I Learned from My Transition from CEO," LinkedIn, October 21, 2019, www.linkedin.com/pulse/how-discover-your-why-what-i-learned-from-my-transition-brad-smith/.

27. Mark Haranas, "Vertiv Going Public After Merger, Former Honeywell CEO David Cote to Be Chairman," CRN, December 11, 2019, www.crn.com/news/data-center/vertiv-going-public-after-merger-former-honeywell-ceo-david-cote-to-be-chairman.

28. World Bank, "Mission to Rewrite World Bank Group Playbook Advances with Banga's Global Tour," press release, June 8, 2023, www.worldbank.org/en/news/press-release/2023/06/08/mission-to-rewrite-world-bank-group-playbook-advances-with-banga-s-global-tour.

Chapter Seven: The Private Equity Sprint

1. Ernst & Young, *Economic Contribution of the US Private Equity Sector in 2022* (American Investment Council, April 2023), www.investmentcouncil.org/wp-content/uploads/2023/04/EY-AIC-PE-economic-contribution-report-FINAL-04-20-2023.pdf.

2. Rebecca Baldridge and Benjamin Curry, "Top 10 U.S. Private Equity Firms of January 2024," *Forbes*, December 1, 2023, www.forbes.com/advisor/investing/best-private-equity-firms/.

3. Rogé Karma, "The Secretive Industry Devouring the U.S. Economy," *The Atlantic*, October 30, 2023, www.theatlantic.com/ideas/archive/2023/10/private-equity-publicly-traded-companies/675788/.

4. Jim Childs, "The Megatrend Shift to Private Equity," Citizens Bank, www.citizensbank.com/corporate-finance/insights/shift-from-public-equity-to-private-equity.aspx.

5. Ernst & Young, *Economic Contribution of the US Private Equity Sector.*

6. Dylan Thomas and Annie Sabater, "Private Equity Dry Powder Swells to Record High amid Sluggish Dealmaking," S&P Global Market Intelligence, July 20, 2023, www.spglobal.com/marketintelligence/en/news-insights/latest-news-headlines/private-equity-dry-powder-swells-to-record-high-amid-sluggish-dealmaking-76609335.

7. Paul A. Gompers, Steven N. Kaplan, and Vladimir Mukharlyamov, "The Market for CEOs: Evidence from Private Equity" (working paper no. 2023-13, Becker Friedman Institute, University of Chicago, Chicago, January 2023), https://bfi.uchicago.edu/wp-content/uploads/2023/01/BFI_WP_2023-13.pdf.

8. "Annual Private Equity Survey: Replacing a Portfolio Company CEO Comes at a High Cost," AlixPartners, May 2017, www.alixpartners.com/media/14430/ap_annual_private_equity_survey_may_2017.pdf.

9. Wendi S. Lazar and Katherine Blostein, "Understanding Executive Arrangements in Private Equity," Reuters, July 14, 2021, www.reuters.com/legal/legalindustry/understanding-executive-arrangements-private-equity-2021-07-14/.

10. Thomas Heath, "Christopher Nassetta: The Man Who Turned Around Hilton," *Washington Post*, July 6, 2014, www.washingtonpost.com/business/capitalbusiness/christopher-nassetta-the-man-who-turned-around-hilton/2014/07/03/43071478-fd5a-11e3-932c-0a55b81f48ce_story.html.

11. Buzz McClain, "How NoVA Native Chris Nassetta Successfully Revamped the Hilton Brand," *Northern Virginia*, August 14, 2019, https://northernvirginiamag.com/culture/culture-features/2019/08/14/how-nova-native-chris-nassetta-successfully-revamped-the-hilton-brand/.

12. Heath, "Christopher Nassetta."

13. David Eisen, "Blackstone Made a Fortune on Hilton. Is It the Last of the Mega-Deals?" Hospitality Investor, June 26, 2022, www.hospitalityinvestor.com/investment/how-private-equity-giant-blackstone-became-real-estate-monolith.

14. Neroli Austin and Ludovic Phalippou, "Decomposing Value Gains—the Case of the Best Leveraged Buy-Out Ever," *Journal of Corporate Finance* 81 (August 2023), https://doi.org/10.1016/j.jcorpfin.2022.102317.

15. Heath, "Christopher Nassetta."

16. Bill Cohan, "The Best Leveraged Buyout Ever," Bloomberg, September 11, 2014, www.bloomberg.com/news/articles/2014-09-11/blackstones-hilton-deal-best-leveraged-buyout-ever.

17. Gail Kalinoski, "Hilton IPO Sets Record," Commercial Property Executive, February 2014, www.commercialsearch.com/news/hilton-ipo-sets-record/.

18. Antoine Gara, "The Private Equity Club: How Corporate Raiders Became Teams of Rivals," *Financial Times*, August 9, 2022, www.ft.com/content/aec70aab-7215-4fa7-9ee3-1224d967dc28.

19. Bryan Burrough, "RJR Nabisco, an Epilogue," *New York Times*, March 12, 1999, www.nytimes.com/1999/03/12/opinion/rjr-nabisco-an-epilogue.html.

20. Floyd Norris, "The Sad Story of RJR Nabisco," *Tampa Bay (FL) Times*, March 11, 1999, www.tampabay.com/archive/1999/03/11/the-sad-story-of-rjr-nabisco/.

21. Paul Rogers, Tom Holland, and Dan Haas, "Lessons from Private-Equity Masters," *Harvard Business Review*, June 2002, https://hbr.org/2002/06/lessons-from-private-equity-masters.

22. Chuck Stinnett, "Bain's Accuride Days Not Likely to Be Campaign Fodder," *Courier & Press* (Evansville, IN), August 12, 2012, https://archive.courierpress.com/news/bains-accuride-days-not-likely-to-be-campaign-fodder-ep-444157485-324895961.html/.

23. Jason Kelly, *The New Tycoons*, Kindle ed. (New York: Bloomberg Press, 2012), 17.

24. Austin and Phalippou, "Decomposing Value Gains."

25. Reed Abelson and Margot Sanger-Katz, "Serious Medical Errors Rose After Private Equity Firms Bought Hospitals," *New York Times*, December 26, 2023, www.nytimes.com/2023/12/26/upshot/hospitals-medical-errors.html; and Marcelo Cerullo, "What Happens When Private Equity Firms Buy Hospitals?" *Harvard Business Review*, March 20, 2023, https://hbr.org/2023/03/research-what-happens-when-private-equity-firms-buy-hospitals.

26. Karma, "The Secretive Industry Devouring."

27. "SEC Enhances Regulation of Private Fund Advisers," JDSupra, September 11, 2023, www.jdsupra.com/legalnews/sec-enhances-regulation-of-private-fund-2626832/.

28. Dan Dunn, "The Private Equity Sector Sees the Return of CEO Turnover," Slayton Search Partners, August 2021, www.slaytonsearch.com/2021/08/ceo-turnover-private-equity-sector-2/.

29. Hugh MacArthur, Rebecca Burack, Christophe De Vusser, Kiki Yang, and Johanne Dessard, "The Private Equity Market in 2020: Escape from the Abyss," Bain & Company, March 1, 2021, www.bain.com/insights/the-private-equity-market-in-2020/.

30. Marilyn Much, "How CEO Andrew Rees Led the Powerful Resurgence of Crocs," *Investors Business Daily*, May 21, 2020, www.investors.com/news/management/leaders-and-success/ceo-andrew-rees-led-the-powerful-resurgence-of-crocs/.

31. Much, "How CEO Andrew Rees Led."

32. Claudy Jules, Vik Krishnan, Vivek Pandit, and Jason Phillips, "A Playbook for Newly Minted Private Equity Company CEOs," McKinsey & Company, September 24, 2021, www.mckinsey.com/industries/private-equity-and-principal-investors/our-insights/a-playbook-for-newly-minted-private-equity-portfolio-company-ceos.

33. Abha Bhattarai, "Checking In on Hilton IPO: 5 Things to Watch," *Washington Post*, December 15, 2013, www.washingtonpost.com/business/capitalbusiness/checking-in-on-hilton-ipo-5-things-to-watch/2013/12/13/e489902c-61e8-11e3-bf45-61f69f54fc5f_story.html.

34. "Hilton Worldwide Prices IPO at $20," CNBC, December 11, 2013, www.cnbc.com/2013/12/11/hilton-worldwide-prices-ipo-at-20.html.

35. Heath, "Christopher Nassetta."

36. "How Private Equity Firms Hire CEOs," *Harvard Business Review*, June 2016, https://hbr.org/2016/06/how-private-equity-firms-hire-ceos.

Chapter Eight: Succeeding with Succession

1. James Rainey, "Disney CFO Jay Rasulo Stepping Down at Month's End," *Variety*, June 1, 2015, https://variety.com/2015/film/news/disney-cfo-jay-rasulo-stepping-down-at-months-end-1201509331/.

2. Kalhan Rosenblatt, "Is Sheryl Sandberg Being Lined Up as Walt Disney Company's First Female CEO?" *Daily Mail*, April 4, 2016, www.dailymail.co.uk/news/article-3523662/Walt-Disney-Company-s-line-CEO-announces-departure-entertainment-giant-throwing-line-succession-disarray.html.

3. Walt Disney Company, "Thomas O. Staggs Named Chief Operating Officer of the Walt Disney Company," news release, February 5, 2015, https://thewaltdisney company.com/thomas-o-staggs-named-chief-operating-officer-of-the-walt-disney-company/.

4. James B. Stewart, "Behind the Scenes at Disney As It Purged a Favorite Son," *New York Times*, April 7, 2016, www.nytimes.com/2016/04/08/business/media/behind-the-scenes-at-disney-as-it-purged-a-favorite-son.html.

5. Brooks Barnes, "Thomas Staggs, Disney's Heir Apparent, Is Stepping Down," *New York Times*, April 4, 2016, www.nytimes.com/2016/04/05/business/media/thomas-staggs-walt-disney-company.html.

6. Barnes, "Thomas Staggs, Disney's Heir Apparent."

7. Stewart, "Behind the Scenes at Disney."

8. Alex Sherman, "Disney's Wildest Ride: Iger, Chapek and the Making of an Epic Succession Mess," CNBC, September 6, 2023, updated October 19, 2023, www .cnbc.com/2023/09/06/disney-succession-mess-iger-chapek.html.

9. Sherman, "Disney's Wildest Ride."

10. Sherman, "Disney's Wildest Ride."

11. Sherman, "Disney's Wildest Ride."

12. Ram Charan, "Ending the CEO Succession Crisis," *Harvard Business Review*, February 2005, https://hbr.org/2005/02/ending-the-ceo-succession-crisis.

13. Paige Cerulli, "Golden Goodbyes: CEOs Who Scored Massive Payouts Despite Being Fired," Cheapism, May 9, 2023, https://blog.cheapism.com/fired-ceos/.

14. "Ready . . . Set . . . Who?: Majority of C-Suite Executives Say There Is Not a 'Ready Now' Successor for Their Role, According to Korn Ferry Survey," *Business Wire*, May 6, 2019, https://tinyurl.com/57jhh2bm.

15. David F. Larcker and Brian Tayan, "CEO Succession: Data," Stanford Business School, Corporate Governance Research Initiative, www.gsb.stanford.edu /faculty-research/publications/ceo-succession-data.

16. Eben Harrell, "Succession Planning: What the Research Says," *Harvard Business Review*, December 2016, https://hbr.org/2016/12/succession-planning -what-the-research-says.

17. Claudio Fernández-Aráoz, Gregory Nagel, and Carrie Green, "The High Cost of Poor Succession Planning," *Harvard Business Review*, May–June 2021, https://hbr .org/2021/05/the-high-cost-of-poor-succession-planning.

18. Lauren Feiner, "Bob Iger to Step Down as Disney CEO, Effective Immediately," CNBC, February 25, 2020, www.cnbc.com/2020/02/25/disney-names-bob-chapek -next-ceo.html.

19. Richard Haythornthwaite and Ajay Banga, "The Former and Current Chairs of Mastercard on Executing a Strategic CEO Succession," *Harvard Business Review*, March–April, 2021, https://hbr.org/2021/03/the-former-and-current -chairs-of-mastercard-on-executing-a-strategic-ceo-succession.

20. Thomas Black and Julie Johnsson, "Honeywell Appoints First COO Since Cote Became Chief in 2002," Bloomberg, April 4, 2016, www.bloomberg.com/news /articles/2016-04-04/honeywell-appoints-first-coo-since-cote-became-chief-in-2002.

21. Black and Johnsson, "Honeywell Appoints First COO."

22. John C. Harpole, Cathy Anterasian, Robert Stark, Kathy Schnure, and Hannah Ford, "Diversity Matters in CEO Transitions," Spencer Stuart, July 2022, www .spencerstuart.com/research-and-insight/diversity-matters-in-ceo-transitions.

23. Alan Murray and Nicholas Gordon, "Levi's Next CEO Accepted a Demotion to Prepare for Her Role Leading the Jeans Maker: 'We Had to Check Our Egos at the Door,'" *Fortune*, December 22, 2023, https://fortune.com/2023/12/22 /levi-next-ceo-michelle-gass-chip-bergh-insider-vs-outsider/.

24. Haythornthwaite and Banga, "The Former and Current Chairs of Mastercard."

25. David F. Larcker and Brian Tayan, "CEO Succession: Data Spotlight," Corporate Governance Research Initiative, Stanford Graduate School of Business, www.gsb.stanford .edu/sites/default/files/publication/pdfs/cgri-quick-guide-15-ceo-succession-data.pdf.

26. Sherman, "Disney's Wildest Ride."

INDEX

Chan Chao

Claudius A. Hildebrand, PhD, advises CEOs on how to accelerate performance and maximize leadership effectiveness as they navigate their organizations through pivotal moments. He is a member of Spencer Stuart's CEO practice and leads the firm's CEO Performance Analytics. Claudius is a regular contributor to *Harvard Business Review* and his work is frequently cited in the *Wall Street Journal, Fortune,* and *Forbes.* His work on mindsets and social networks was awarded "Best Article" by the *Academy of Management.* Claudius holds a PhD in management from Columbia Business School.

Jennifer Graham

Robert J. Stark is a trusted advisor and coach to CEOs, CEO aspirants, and boards. He helps CEOs outperform and thrive, prepares senior leaders for the unique challenges of the CEO role, and guides boards to achieve value-creating CEO transitions. He is a sought-after thought leader on CEO succession planning, CEO performance, and leadership development. His insights appear frequently in business publications, including *Harvard Business Review.*

PublicAffairs is a publishing house founded in 1997. It is a tribute to the standards, values, and flair of three persons who have served as mentors to countless reporters, writers, editors, and book people of all kinds, including me.

I. F. STONE, proprietor of *I. F. Stone's Weekly*, combined a commitment to the First Amendment with entrepreneurial zeal and reporting skill and became one of the great independent journalists in American history. At the age of eighty, Izzy published *The Trial of Socrates*, which was a national bestseller. He wrote the book after he taught himself ancient Greek.

BENJAMIN C. BRADLEE was for nearly thirty years the charismatic editorial leader of *The Washington Post*. It was Ben who gave the *Post* the range and courage to pursue such historic issues as Watergate. He supported his reporters with a tenacity that made them fearless and it is no accident that so many became authors of influential, best-selling books.

ROBERT L. BERNSTEIN, the chief executive of Random House for more than a quarter century, guided one of the nation's premier publishing houses. Bob was personally responsible for many books of political dissent and argument that challenged tyranny around the globe. He is also the founder and longtime chair of Human Rights Watch, one of the most respected human rights organizations in the world.

·   ·   ·

For fifty years, the banner of Public Affairs Press was carried by its owner Morris B. Schnapper, who published Gandhi, Nasser, Toynbee, Truman, and about 1,500 other authors. In 1983, Schnapper was described by *The Washington Post* as "a redoubtable gadfly." His legacy will endure in the books to come.

Peter Osnos, *Founder*